Samuel MacNaughton

Doctrine and Doubt

Or, Christ the Centre of Christianity

Samuel MacNaughton

Doctrine and Doubt
Or, Christ the Centre of Christianity

ISBN/EAN: 9783337167400

Printed in Europe, USA, Canada, Australia, Japan

Cover: Foto ©Lupo / pixelio.de

More available books at **www.hansebooks.com**

DOCTRINE AND DOUBT;

OR,

CHRIST THE CENTRE OF CHRISTIANITY.

BY THE

REV. SAMUEL MACNAUGHTON, M.A.,

AUTHOR OF "JOY IN JESUS," "MEMORIALS OF BELLA DARLING," "THE
GOSPEL IN GREAT BRITAIN," "OUR CHILDREN FOR CHRIST,"
"THE WINES OF SCRIPTURE," ETC.

"*Walk about Zion, and go round about her.*"
"*In Him was Life, and the Life was the Light of men.*"

London:

HODDER AND STOUGHTON,
27, PATERNOSTER ROW.

MDCCCLXXXVI

PREFACE.

THESE Studies, or Sermon-Lectures, do not aim at anything profound or subtle in argument, but are intended for thoughtful men who are troubled with honest doubt and perplexed by Christian doctrines "hard to be understood." The work does not profess to be complete as a theological treatise, or exhaustive in the treatment of the different subjects; but rather to indicate lines of argument and methods of investigation. It is a great matter to have thoughtful seekers after truth set upon the right track. The author does not claim to have discovered a panacea for all intellectual troubles, but wishes simply to give some pictures and representations of the path which he himself has travelled, and in which he found clearer light and had all intellectual difficulties removed. Several topics of considerable interest are intentionally treated with great brevity, and often incidentally, but still, it is hoped, with some degree of clearness and simplicity.

If we seek to know God by means of the Intellect, then a System of Theology must commence by establishing the Existence of God and the possibility of a Revelation of His Will. However, in our practical experience we first find ourselves feeling after God with the heart. What is certain to us at that stage of our spiritual experience is, that we are out of harmony with God, and we want to be reconciled to Him. We recognize the fact of sin, and we want to know God's provision for it. We want to know how God can forgive deliberate sin without seeming to make light of it. Hence the anxious, troubled soul must at once be brought face to face with God in Christ, that God's great love to man may be clearly seen in the light of the cross. This is the first step. In Christ Jesus we have a meeting-place for God and man. Christ must be seen as the true revelation of the Father, as well as the centre of Christianity. It is only by seeing the love, and tenderness, and sympathy of Jesus that the human heart can be assured that "God is love," and that He can love those who have transgressed His law. Until the love of God towards the human race is clearly apprehended it is impossible for troubled souls to approach Him. Apart from Christ the thought of a holy God is absolutely crushing. To seek to know God through a study of what is somewhat vaguely styled "the Attributes of God," will only plunge the earnest seeker after light into deeper darkness, if not into despair. Such a study cannot be profitably undertaken until God is first known and seen "in the face of Jesus Christ," as Father and Friend. It is a study for the systematic theologian, rather than for the anxious soul seeking intellectual rest.

A mind that is perplexed by doubt can deal only with facts. The fact of sin is known, and is not disputed. Theories respecting the origin of sin and its transmission will only introduce uncertainty, and should not be undertaken at this stage of mental and spiritual experience. The historical Christ is a fact. His life, and death, and resurrection can be established as historical facts, apart altogether from the question of Inspiration. Here is sure standing ground. His sympathy, profound teaching, and mighty works prove Him to be a worthy Mediator between God and man. His life of self-denial and self-sacrifice proves Him to be the Friend of man. His sinless life, the power of His teaching, His miracles of healing,—all acknowledged by His enemies,—and the prophecy of His own death and resurrection, are more than sufficient to stamp HIS WORDS with the seal of absolute truth. But He claimed to have come from God, and that He was one with God. If these claims were not true, then His God-given power would necessarily have been withdrawn by a holy God. His own testimony, therefore, proves His divinity. There is no alternative between accepting His real divinity and proclaiming Him an impostor.

The gift of the Holy Spirit at Pentecost, clothing the disciples with marvellous power, is also a fact. It was Christ coming to them again by His Spirit, according to His promise. Here is further confirmation of His Divine power and wisdom. The miraculous gifts which they received could come only from God. This fact that God can come to men and dwell in them, as a new life and a new power, in answer to patient persevering prayer, is the one plea to encourage the troubled heart that wonders whether or not God can condescend to listen to the cry of His creature man. "God heard and answered their prayer, therefore He can hear me and bless me," is an effectual reply to all rising doubts in the heart as to the value and power of prayer. The anxious, troubled heart can now pray; and in answer to prayer the ever-loving God bestows His Spirit, and the peace of God is shed abroad in the heart. From that moment all doubt is banished.

This method will be found to be the true road—I think the only true road—to soul-rest. Whatever questions may afterwards arise in the mind with regard to certain doctrines and interpretations of theologians, this heart-hold of Christ, this personal experience of the power of the Gospel, will for ever make settled doubt impossible. Therefore, throughout this volume, metaphysical arguments have been intentionally omitted in favour of the arguments from fact and personal experience.

The author has sought to give prominence to the grand cardinal doctrines of the Gospel, as held by all evangelical Churches, and by illustration and analogy, and by avoiding technical theological terms, to make them intelligible even to those who have but little acquaintance with theological lore. He has also endeavoured to show the completeness of the Gospel plan of salvation, and how at every point it meets the deepest longings of the human heart. In this consists the strength of Christianity, and this is its defence.

May this unpretentious volume become a messenger of comfort to many earnest souls compelled to wrestle with honest doubt.

S. M. N.

ADDISON ROAD, PRESTON.

CONTENTS.

CHAP.		PAGE
I.	THE CRITICAL SPIRIT OF THE AGE	1
II.	THE EXISTENCE AND REVELATION OF GOD	10
III.	THE STRENGTH OF CHRISTIANITY: SIN AND SALVATION	20
IV.	CHRIST THE CENTRE AND CITADEL OF CHRISTIANITY	33
V.	CHRISTIAN HEROES THE STRENGTH OF CHRISTIANITY	43
VI.	THE LORD'S SUPPER A MONUMENT TO CHRISTIANITY	55
VII.	DEALING WITH DOUBT	65
VIII.	PENTECOSTAL PRAYING AND PREACHING	76
IX.	THE MYSTERY OF GOD	87
X.	GOD IN THE LIGHT: THE TRINITY	100
XI.	CHRIST IN THE FLESH: THE INCARNATION	112
XII.	CHRIST IN THE WILDERNESS: THE TEMPTATION	122
XIII.	CHRIST IN THE GARDEN: THE AGONY	135

CONTENTS.

CHAP.		PAGE
XIV.	CHRIST ON THE MOUNT: THE TRANSFIGURATION	146
XV.	CHRIST ON THE CROSS: SIN AND ATONEMENT	156
XVI.	CHRIST IN THE HEART: SANCTIFICATION	168
XVII.	THE MYSTERY OF SPIRITUAL LIFE	180
XVIII.	THE MYSTERY OF REGENERATION	191
XIX.	THE LAWS OF THE SPIRITUAL LIFE	202
XX.	THE HIGHER LIFE OF HOLINESS	213
XXI.	CHRISTIAN COURAGE AND CONSECRATION	226
XXII.	THE JOY OF SELF-SACRIFICE	236
XXIII.	DIVINE ELECTION AND HUMAN FREEDOM	247
XXIV.	INSPIRATION AND REVELATION	258
XXV.	THE SPIRITUAL FACULTY IN MAN	269
XXVI.	THE MODEL PRAYER: SONSHIP	281
XXVII.	THE MODEL PRAYER: DEPENDENCE	292
XXVIII.	THE MODEL MAN: TRUE MANLINESS	303
XXIX.	THE UNPARDONABLE SIN	314
XXX.	RESURRECTION AND THE RESURRECTION-BODY	322
XXXI.	LIFE IN HEAVEN: THE BLESSED DEAD	333
XXXII.	EXCURSUS ON SHEOL, HADES, AND HELL	346
XXXIII.	THE ORIGIN OF HUMAN EVIL: AN ESSAY	353
XXXIV.	GENESIS AND GEOLOGY	365
XXXV.	JOSHUA AND THE SUN	373
XXXVI.	JONAH AND THE WHALE	375
XXXVII.	THE DEATH AND BURIAL OF MOSES	377

I.

THE CRITICAL SPIRIT OF THE AGE.

"A man was famous according as he had lifted up axes upon the thick trees; but now they break down the carved work thereof at once with axes and hammers."—PSALM lxxiv. 5, 6.

WE are living in a critical age; and Christianity, like everything else, has to stand the test of a most rigid criticism. As Christians, we ought not to regret this, but rather recognize in it the hand of God. We ought to have faith enough to believe that He will overrule for good the critical spirit of the age. Even the enemies of Christ may help on Christianity, if by their opposition they stir up Christian men to do battle for the truth, and compel superficial believers to make sure of the ground they are standing upon. The one thing that is saddening in connection with the destructive criticism of the present day is that there is unquestionably a wide-spread sympathy with those who strive to break down the bulwarks of the Christian faith.

In ancient times a man was famous, and was honoured by the populace, who would go into the forest and provide materials for building and repairing the temple of the Lord. But now it is the man who employs axe and hammer, not in making anything new, not in producing anything useful, but in hacking and breaking down the carved work of the sanctuary, that is cheered on by an applauding multitude. This fact places the defenders of the faith at a great disadvantage.

The critical faculty, however, has done good service in the past, and may do good service still, in exposing errors, and reforming abuses, and breaking down superstition, and in compelling men to seek an intelligent belief, instead of being satisfied with mere blind faith.

It was the absence of the critical faculty in Christendom centuries ago that made it possible for popish superstitions and unmeaning ceremonies to creep into the Church. The people blindly followed their teachers without taking the trouble of thinking for themselves, or of comparing their teaching with the Word of God; and thus corruption and error were widely disseminated. · It was the absence of the critical faculty during the Middle Ages that made the Reformation a necessity. We are not, therefore, to argue against fair criticism and honest investigation; for they help on the cause of truth, and do not hinder it. All criticism and investigation that aim at reformation in doctrine, and a clearer presentation of spiritual truth, are not only allowable, but desirable, in the interests of truth itself. It is a great thing to have the teachers of the Church stirred up to see the necessity of presenting Scriptural truth in such a manner that men of intellect and culture can accept it intelligently, and not merely assent to it because it is the teaching of their Church. The Reformation has settled for ever the right of private judgment; and thoughtful men should not be asked to rest satisfied with a blind faith, where an intelligent belief is possible.

To have a strong faith we must have a clear knowledge of the things believed; and a clear knowledge can be had only by inquiry and thorough investigation. The citadel of truth is not so much in danger to-day from the enemy without, as from the feebleness within the Church, and a lack of clearness and thoroughness on the part of the teachers of the Church. By all means let us have inquiry and criticism. The truth of God has nothing to fear from investigation. Every doctrine that has upon it the imprimatur of God will stand the severest test; and every opinion that fails to stand the strain of honest criticism, whether taught in the Church, or outside of it, is not worth contending for.

Having said thus much in regard to the position that the defenders of the faith and the teachers of the Church ought to assume towards fair criticism and honest inquiry, let us proceed to inquire how far the critical spirit of our day is fair and honest. Is its aim reformatory, or destructive? Does it seek to build up, or to break down? Are the axes used to fell the trees of the forest with the aim of making it a fruitful field, or are they used in cutting down our plantations and ornamental trees that have for ages been the comfort of many? Are the hammers used in preparing stones for the erection of a useful structure, or for breaking down the carved work of some venerated building? In putting criticism into the balances to find out whether it is fair and honest, or not, we must look at its aim and object. Constructive criticism, whose aim is to build up and strengthen, and destructive criticism, whose aim is to break down and destroy, are as wide as the poles asunder. We cordially welcome the one; we offer strenuous opposition to the other.

A man of very small mind and little learning may find fault with a theory or a system, and call attention to some of its weak points; but let him try to put a better theory or system in its place, and he finds himself perfectly helpless. His little critical brain cannot originate a single thought that will bear the light. It is an easy matter to pull down; but, if a man would establish his claim to attention and respect, he must prove his wisdom and skill by building up. You would not think of admiring the skill of a child for pulling to pieces a beautiful flower. If he would prove his ability let him paint the flower. Any fool can daub and destroy a beautiful painting, but it requires an artist to produce it. Ability is not shown by pulling down but by building up. It is clear, therefore, that mere destructive criticism is no proof of ability. A man to command respect must do more than pull down, he must build up; he must do more than criticise, he must construct. A man who pulls down a small house and builds in its place a larger and more commodious one, does good service; but, if he simply pulls down the house and leaves the rubbish there as a desolate waste, his activity is injurious, and not beneficial to the community. And so it is with destructive criticism.

Suppose the Reformers of the sixteenth century had contented themselves with exposing the abuses of the Roman Catholic Church, and throwing discredit upon its teachers, without constructing a new system of doctrine and government, what would their labours have been worth? In turning the people away from the Church they would simply have turned them over to infidelity and heathenism. The Reformers of Reformation times had too much wisdom and ability to do anything so foolish. Luther prepared his theses—his system of doctrine—and nailed them to the church at Wittenberg, showing to the world the reforms that were needed; and gave the Church the opportunity of reforming her teaching and practice, before he publicly assailed the corruptions and errors that drove him and others from her pale. Such criticism as that was fair and honest, and ought always to be welcomed by the teachers of the Church. Its object was to purify and strengthen the Church. Every Church should hold itself free to listen to all fair inquiry, whether in Science or Theology, and to remodel its creed, if need be, and improve its teaching in order to bring itself into harmony with recently-discovered truth, whether in Science or in the Word of God. God's truth is unchanging and unchangeable, but our knowledge and understanding of revealed truth ought to go on improving year by year. And the creeds of the Church, and the teaching of the Church, ought to keep pace with all true discovery in the realm of truth. In this way, and in this way alone, can hostile criticism be disarmed. Looking at the critical spirit of the age in this light, the duty of the Christian Church is not to condemn it, and frown upon it ; but rather to direct it, and turn it to a useful purpose. All honest investigation and fair criticism ought to be made productive of good and not of evil.

The very fact, however, that we have to limit the criticism which we approve to fair criticism, implies that there may be a criticism that is not fair. And no observant person can fail to note that a great deal of the criticism of our time is mere carping fault-finding with time-honoured beliefs and institutions.

A certain class of persons, who are unwilling to conform their lives to the requirements of religion and of God's law, set themselves to find fault with religion and the teaching of the Bible, and to discover flaws in the characters and lives of the professors of religion. Or they have listened to some illiterate preacher, and have taken his wild ravings as a sample of the Christian teaching in the Churches. Or they take the teaching of the Roman Catholic Church, or of some other Church, and measure all teachers and all Churches by what they have heard or seen on one or two occasions. They sit down and write an article, or a book, showing the absurdity of what they heard, and then with a great flourish of trumpets they proclaim to the world that religion is a myth, and that all its professors are either hypocrites, or simple, misguided men and superstitious old women. Such was the method of Tom Paine and many modern unbelievers. Men of that stamp may safely be left to themselves. They can make no permanent impression upon any thoughtful mind.

But there are others—earnest, thoughtful men—who seem to have real difficulties on all matters of religion; and they present them with clearness and candour. They have a fair knowledge of Scripture, and some acquaintance with the results of Science; and they have difficulty in reconciling the Book of Nature with the Book of God. They know something of the fact of sin and its terrible consequences in destroying happiness and producing misery, and they cannot reconcile the existence of sin in the universe with the control and superintendence of an all-wise, all-loving, all-powerful God; and naturally enough they criticise the teaching of the Church on such matters. And just because there is inquiry and independence of thought, weak-minded alarmists in the Church, instead of meeting these difficulties, denounce them, as if religion and the faith were in danger of being utterly destroyed.

Now we hold that the faith is not in danger. Man is so constituted that he must have a religion. His spiritual nature demands to be fed. His spiritual longings are real and indestructible. He has within him a conviction of immortality—that this life is not all of life—that death does not end all. He has within him the voice of conscience approving the right and sternly disapproving the wrong, showing that he holds himself responsible for all his actions to a Supreme Ruler. He cannot help feeling, as a transgressor of law, that he wants to be brought into harmony with the righteous Lawgiver. He feels that he must have peace with God, peace with conscience, and peace with his past record.

Sceptics and infidels may scoff and sneer at these great verities during a portion of their earthly life; but when they come to die they have a profound conviction that death is not the end of life—that memory will live—that conscience will live—that they must meet the holy Judge, and stand before the great white throne. In that supreme moment of life, which is also the moment of death, they want to meet God in peace.

Man is so made that his soul hungers and thirsts

after God. There is no fact in the universe better established than the hunger of the heart and spirit after God. Man is greater than he knows. For a time he may think that he can live on negations, and he may try to appease the hunger of his spirit by keeping the intellect employed with questionings and criticism; but he will soon find out that the longings and cravings of his inner nature demand something real and positive. He will find that he cannot get clear of the fact of sin, or its consequences, by questioning the wisdom or the goodness of the God who permitted it. He will come to realize that sin is a fact—a fact personal to himself; and the question then will be, not that sin should never have been allowed to enter into the world, but how to get rid of its terrible consequences and controlling power.

But, further, when a man comes to realize his true relation to God, and when conscience within, as well as the holy law without, condemns him, he will no longer rest satisfied with discussing the Creation and trying to find discrepancies between Genesis and Geology. He will want to get further back than Genesis and the Creation and the Origin of Evil, and get to the Creator; and he will want to know how to meet God in peace. There are in man's spiritual nature, whether he knows it or not, indestructible elements that will outlive doubt, and criticism, and speculation; and he is a wise man who will recognize this, and lay out to make provision for the hunger of the heart. But, during the inquiring and critical period of his life, let us not denounce him as a sceptic, because he is determined to have clear knowledge on those great questions that concern us all both for time and for eternity. But rather let us point him to the Word of God with its marvellous stores of grace and truth, and its wonderful lessons of Divine love, and tenderness, and sympathy. Let us tell him of the Christ of God, who is the true bread to satisfy the hunger of the soul, and the only medicine to heal the disease of sin. Let us persuade him to study the positive truths of the Bible regarding Sin and Salvation; and when he has found peace with God through faith in the sinner's Saviour, and sees God in all His Fatherly love and sympathy for men, then he may study with profit and comfort the mystery of the origin of sin and the wonders of creation. Nature will appear to him in a new light, when he can look upon its laws, and forces, and agencies, and say, " My Father made them all."

II.

THE EXISTENCE AND REVELATION OF GOD.

"Behold, God is great, and we know Him not; neither can the number of His years be searched out."—JOB xxxvi. 26.

THE greatest problem of all time for inquiring minds is the question, WHAT IS GOD? *What is God? How may He be known?* And *How may we meet Him in peace?* This problem greatly perplexed the minds of the ancients. They eagerly inquired of one another, "Hast thou heard the secret of God?" "Can man by searching find out God? Can he search out the Almighty to perfection?" "Oh that I knew where I might find Him, that I might come even unto His seat!" Such earnest longings as these, added to the sum of human experience, clearly show that, apart from Revelation, man cannot know God. The world around us, and the worlds above us, point to an all-wise and powerful Creator. Man himself, possessed of wondrous powers of intelligence, of acquiring, of reasoning and calculating, of loving and sympathizing, demands a Maker, possessing all these faculties in higher perfection than his own; for the Maker must be greater than the thing made, the Creator must be greater than the creature. We follow back the chain of being until we come to the first man. That first man demands an intelligent and powerful Creator, capable of producing the wonderful mechanism of the human body, besides endowing it with life, and intelligence, and conscience, and the instinct of self-preservation. We cannot think otherwise than that man must have had a Maker. Therefore the intellect of man is a witness to the existence of God.

Every thoughtful mind re-echoes the words of the Psalmist, "The fool hath said in his heart, There is no God." No man capable of clear thought can be an Atheist in the full meaning of the term. He cannot affirm that there is no God. To make this affirmation a man would require to be able to investigate all causes, and forces, and powers in the universe. He would require to visit all worlds, known and unknown to man. For if any single cause, or force, was not investigated, *that* might be God; and if any spot in the universe was not visited, God might be there. And, moreover, he would require to be in all places at the same time, for the God whom he sought might be in one world while he was looking for Him in another. Thus it is evident that a man would require to possess all knowledge, and be capable of being present in all places at the same time—in other words, he would himself require to be God—before he could positively affirm that "there is no God." An age of clear thought has made Atheism impossible, compelling Atheists to lower their colours and proclaim themselves Agnostics. Having discovered that they cannot proclaim the non-existence of God, they take the lower ground, and say, "We do not know that God exists; and, even if there is a God, He cannot be apprehended by the human mind." This is modern Agnosticism. But it is nothing new. It is as old at least as the time of Job: "Can man by searching find out God? Can he search out the Almighty to perfection?" Modern Agnosticism only proves that man needs a revelation of God, showing conclusively that God, in giving a revelation of Himself in His Word and in His Son, thereby met one of humanity's greatest needs. Seeing that man cannot possibly find out God by his own unaided powers, it is in the highest degree probable that a good and benevolent God, interested in the happiness of His creatures, should give a revelation of Himself.

Conscience in man is also a witness to the existence of God. Man is conscious of a feeling of dependence upon One greater than himself, and of responsibility to Him. Conscience within, approving the right and disapproving the wrong, points to a righteous Lawgiver and Judge, who takes note of all our actions, and holds us responsible for them. Hence the thoughtful mind craves for certain knowledge respecting this great Creator and Lawgiver. Has He a heart of compassion? Can He be moved with pity? Can He forgive deliberate sin? Can He draw near to erring mortals as a Father and a Friend? Outside of God's revelation of Himself such questions as these find no answer. Man could never have known God as "longsuffering and gracious, slow to wrath, abundant in goodness, in mercy, and in truth, forgiving iniquity, transgression, and sin," except God had so revealed Himself.

To the ancient heathen sages and philosophers God

was inscrutable. They could not find out the mind and heart of God. To them He was a God afar off. There was nothing in Nature, nothing in Science, nothing in Philosophy, nothing in the human heart, that could reveal to them a God of love—God as Father and Friend—a God ready to forgive—a God of sympathy, who delighteth in mercy. The only God that Science, apart from Revelation, has discovered is FORCE, POWER, A FIRST CAUSE: Force, but no feeling; Power, but no pity; Law, but no love. It is only by Revelation, in the Word and in the Christ, that we can see a God who is wise, and powerful, and just, and yet has a Father's heart of love and sympathy.

It is impossible that man, in his present state, with finite capacities and powers, should be able to attain to a full knowledge of the infinite God. Just as water cannot rise above its own level, so no man, by his own unaided powers, can rise higher than himself. No man by searching can find out God. If God is to be known, He can be known only through Revelation.

Our conceptions of God, apart from Revelation, and apart from Christ as the Revealer of the Father, must necessarily be limited to the operations of natural law. But the operations of natural law are regular and constant. And if our ideas of God be taken from natural law, we will find no place in the heart of God for love, and sympathy, and forgiveness, and watchful care. Every violation of natural law, whether inadvertent or wilful, meets with dire punishment. If you inadvertently slip and fall over a precipice, you are mangled and crushed; natural law stretches out no arm to save you. How is it, then, that we hear of men worshipping God in Nature in preference to worshipping God in Christ? Deists, who deny all revelation of God, whether in the Word or in Christ, evidently overlook the fact that any true conceptions which they have of God have been obtained, in the first instance, not from Nature, but from Revelation.

It is true, indeed, that a man of poetic temperament is mentally refreshed in studying Nature. But the enjoyment of Nature is far more intense, and far more satisfying, to him who can say, as he looks upon fields, and forests, and flowers, and streams, and hills, and dales, "My Father made them all." No man can find the highest enjoyment which natural scenery is capable of affording, until he has learned to know God as his Father and his Friend. Then he will find "sermons in stones, books in the running brooks, and God in everything."

The poet-laureate accurately describes a great truth, known only in experience, when he represents the glad heart going forth under the first impulse of God's forgiving love, and, looking upon Nature, exclaims, "You could not see the grass for flowers." Now that God is reconciled, every blade of grass seems more beautiful than a flower seemed before. Nature has new charms for us the moment we can regard the God of Nature as our dearest Friend. Then as we look out upon Nature's beauties we can "rise through Nature up to Nature's God." But to those who do not know God as revealed in Christ there are no such soul-satisfying joys: "No man knoweth the Father save the Son, and he to whomsoever the Son shall reveal Him" (Matt. xi. 27).

The fact that the Atheist denies the existence of God; that the Pantheist can find no personal God, but takes the whole universe as his God; that the Agnostic declares that even if there be a God He cannot be known by mortals, proves most conclusively the need of a clearer revelation of God than can be obtained from Nature, or from unaided human reason. Man, by his own powers, cannot "search out the Almighty to perfection." But when we look upon God, not simply as the Creator and Governor of the material universe, but as seen in Christ, we have not only a God whom we can understand, but One also whom we can love, and trust, and worship. In Christ, we see God loving, God weeping, God sympathizing, God suffering for us. Such a God, when seen and known as He is, we cannot help loving. You cannot love and worship where there is no heart, no love, and no sympathy. But in Christ we see a God with a loving heart, yearning over men, "not willing that any should perish, but that all should come to repentance." Such a God is just what humanity needs; and the God that can meet all human needs must be the true God.

It is wonderful what different views men have of God. What an interesting collection it would be, if we could only bring together the different conceptions of God held by a single congregation of worshippers! We would probably have as many views or thoughts of God as there were worshippers. So, too, in the different periods of the same life, what different views we have of God! We can easily recall the experience of childhood, when we had our own strange thoughts of God, so full of wonder and mystery, and yet without the shadow of a doubt. Further on, we got a clearer view of His holiness and our sins—a sense of His displeasure when we did wrong. Then perhaps we passed through a period of darkness, and doubt, and dread almost bordering on despair. And many and varied were our experiences and our thoughts of God before we entered into life, and liberty, and joy. But never until we saw God in Christ were we able to get near to God, and to be at peace in His presence. No man can have peace in God's presence until he has become acquainted with God through His Word, and His Son, and the personal dealings of His Spirit. " For through Him we have access by One Spirit unto the Father" (Eph. ii. 18).

We may have seen and learned much of God, and yet He has further revelations of Himself for all who are able to receive them. In order to be able to receive these further revelations we may be called upon to pass through other experiences. Few, perhaps none, are able to see the deep things of God, until they have passed through severe trial of some kind, or experienced deep sorrow. There is one aspect of God that cannot be revealed to those who have never suffered. God cannot reveal Himself as Comforter and Consoler to those who do not need consolation. The Comforter did not come to the disciples until the Master was taken away, and they were left desolate and alone. They had to be led along the pathway of sorrow in order to receive this fuller revelation of God, which filled them with such joy, and clothed them with such marvellous power. They could not comprehend Christ's promise of larger blessing through this fuller revelation of God by His Spirit, until they had passed through the agony of bereavement. While the Master was with them they felt no need of the Comforter. Their profound sorrow qualified them to receive a profounder revelation of God. While Jesus was with them they had learned that God, in His infinite condescension, could dwell *with* men, as their Counsellor and Friend; but when sorrow and loss had prepared them for a higher revelation, they found in their own experience that God could dwell *in* men, as a new life, making them holy and unselfish, and giving them power over sin, and power in service.

I have no doubt that we have here a clue to the mystery of evil, and an explanation of why sin was permitted to enter into the world. Had there been no sin, with its consequent sorrow and suffering, there would have been no Saviour and no Comforter. Man would not have needed redemption and consolation; and we would have been denied the revelation we have of God in the life and work of Christ, and in the indwelling and power of the Holy Spirit. No sooner had sin entered into the world, than God, by the promise of a Redeemer, revealed a new power in His nature—power to love the unlovely, to forgive the erring, and to console the disconsolate.

Jesus possessed in all its perfectness the power of fully revealing God in His relation to men. His life was lived for us. He died His death for us. He drew men near to Him. He entered into their joys and sorrows. He joined the festive throng at the marriage feast at Cana; and He wept with the weeping sisters of Bethany. He thus taught us that we may take God with us in our joys and in our sorrows. See, too, how tenderly He removed the doubts of Thomas, who was sceptical about the fact of His resurrection. He drew him near to Himself, and gave him the very evidence he demanded: "Reach hither thy hand, and thrust it into My side, and be not faithless, but believing." This incident teaches us how tenderly God regards those who are sorely tried by honest doubt. He does not thrust them aside as unworthy of His attention, but draws them near to Him, so near that they feel His touch; and with the touch comes the thrill of a new life and an unquestioning faith.

It was so also in the matter of forgiveness. He freely forgave all who drew near to Him in simple, child-like faith. While He faithfully reproved the woman of Samaria who had had five husbands, He did it so tenderly that her heart was touched, and she recognized in Him the Christ of God, and immediately carried the message of salvation to her people. See, too, how faithfully He revealed God's stern disapproval of hypocrisy and insincerity! What scathing rebukes He administered to those mere formal professors of religion, the Scribes and Pharisees! "Ye whited sepulchres, ye make long prayers, and ye devour widows' houses; how shall ye escape the damnation of hell!" He could read the secret thoughts of every heart. Only One, who Himself was God, could fully reveal the infinitude of God. Therefore, the great problem, which has baffled the wisdom of man in all ages, How may God be known? is solved in Christ.

Tha other puzzling problem also finds its answer

in Him, How can man meet God in peace ? He Him
self lifts the veil and solves the mystery : "Come unto
Me, all ye that labour and are heavy laden, and I will
give you rest" (Matt. xi. 28). Anxious, burdened,
despairing one, crushed and overwhelmed by a sense
of your own unworthiness, you may confidently come
to Him, for He has invited you. And because you
may come to Him, you may come to God the Father,
for He has revealed the Father's heart ; and, coming
to Him, you shall find rest to your soul.

It was much that Jesus should live for us a holy
life, thus becoming our obedience. It was much that
He should die for us, bearing the penalty of our sins
in His own body on the tree. But oh, how comforting,
how soul-satisfying, that He should draw aside the
veil that had hidden God from mortal eyes, and reveal
Him to us in all His love and Fatherhood, so that
now we can meet Him in peace !

III.

THE STRENGTH OF CHRISTIANITY: SIN AND SALVATION.

"Walk about Zion, and go round about her; tell the towers thereof; mark ye well her bulwarks; consider her palaces."—PSALM xlviii. 12, 13.

IN our day the Church of God requires not only to be strong, but also to appear strong. And it is the duty of the watchman on Zion's towers at times to call attention to the Strength of Christianity, and show that the Christian Church and Christian doctrine can be successfully defended from every attack of the enemy. It is worthy of note that the Bible stands firm to-day, uncontradicted by the most recent revelations of Science. The very stones, brought to light in recent years, confirm, even in the minutest details, the very events recorded in this wonderful Book, which have so often been made the object of attack. There is no statement in the Bible that is contrary to Reason, or contrary to Science, while there is much in it that is beyond the ken of either Reason or Science, proving that it is given by inspiration of God.

Its profoundest truths, however, are confirmed in another way. They appeal to man's personal needs, and to his personal experience. They reveal to us the true cause of our feebleness, and waywardness, and sin; and they point us to the true method of recovery. We make trial of the method proposed, and it is found to succeed—to succeed, too, far beyond our highest expectations, and where every other remedy has failed. Man himself thus becomes a witness to the truth of the Bible. Written centuries before he was born, it accurately and minutely describes his inner experience—his trials and temptations, his doubts and fears, his alienation from God and his struggles after reconciliation, his remorse and anxious dread on account of sin, and his joy, and peace, and confidence when he realizes the favour of God and accepts the assurance that his sins are forgiven for Jesus' sake. Christianity transforms the life, gives power over temptation and sin, and fills the heart with love to men and a longing desire to do them good. It teaches men to be contented with their lot; it gives comfort in sorrow; and helps us to meet the King of terrors in peace. This, after all, is the highest and truest test of Christianity. It truly describes our inner experience, and fully meets our needs. These are facts, as fully known and attested by human experience in myriads of instances as any facts of history or Science; and they must be accounted for. Common Sense, as well as Science, refuses to ignore well-authenticated facts. The strength of Christianity is found in the fact that it deals with the needs and longings of our spiritual nature—needs that cannot be supplied from any other source; and, what is more remarkable, it deals with these needs and makes provision for them before they arise. This surely is the perfection of wisdom and benevolence. This is evidence of the highest nature in favour of Christianity.

True this form of evidence is beyond the reach of the rationalist and unbeliever; for until men cordially accept of Christianity, they can never know its power. However, the fault is theirs, and not that of Christianity, since they persist in shutting their eyes to the light. If the eye of the body is persistently closed, of what avail is the light of the sun? And not only so, but if the eye is not used at all it will soon lose entirely the power of vision. The mole that persists in burrowing under ground, never coming to the light, has lost the power of vision. It is so also with the Crustacea—a small species of fish that has inhabited for ages the dark lakes in the Mammoth Cave of Kentucky. Apparently they have eyes. Outwardly the eye is perfectly formed; but inwardly it is a mass of ruins. The optic nerve has entirely lost its power. The eye is a mere mockery. They have eyes, but they see not. Such is the penalty natural law inflicts upon those animals that love darkness rather than light. In time they lose the power of vision.

The same is true of man's spiritual vision. If men persist in shutting their eyes to Divine light,—to the teaching of Christ and the light of His Spirit,—not only must they remain in entire ignorance of God and His gracious relation to man, but the time will come when they will lose the power of seeing God and the beauty of Divine truth. Therefore this inward evidence of the power of Christianity cannot be found in unbelievers, who deliberately close the windows of the soul and exclude the light.

Neither can it be found in all and sundry who profess to be Christians. There are many, it must be confessed, who profess adherence to the doctrines of Christianity, who do not show in their intercourse with their fellow-men that they are actuated by higher and nobler motives than others. Here, again, the fault is in the men, and not in Christianity. If they are selfish, and ungenerous, and grasping, and envious, and unbrotherly, it does not prove that Christianity is weak, but that such persons have never felt its power. It is to be greatly deplored that the Christian religion is often sadly misrepresented by those who call themselves Christians. However, in judging of Christianity, we must take its true representatives. We must study it in those lives which are modelled after the teaching of the Bible ; and especially in the life of Christ, which is the pattern life for all His followers. It is in the life, and teaching, and finished work of the Lord Jesus that we have the strength and defence of Christianity: "The name of the Lord is a strong tower ; the righteous runneth into it, and is safe." It must never be forgotten that the strength of Christianity is seen in its doctrines and in the life and sacrifice of Christ. Christianity must never be judged apart from the personal Christ and His marvellous love to our race.

Take the Christian doctrine of Sin as set forth in the Word of God. Christianity stands alone among all religions in taking due account of the exceeding sinfulness of sin. The Bible stands unrivalled in inculcating purity of heart and life ; in teaching unselfishness and brotherly love ; in fostering a missionary spirit which seeks the highest good of all men in the wide world. Where will you find such high-toned Ethics as in the Sermon on the Mount? The teaching of Confucius, and Zoroaster, and Mohammed are mere puerilities compared with the teaching of Christ. They make no account of the deadly nature of sin, and its withering effect upon human life and human happiness. Other religions either connive at vice, or elevate it to a virtue. The Christian religion unmasks the hideous monster, and cautions men even against cherishing the thought of impurity on the penalty of losing present fellowship with God: " Blessed are the pure in heart, for they shall see God." We are here clearly taught that unholy thoughts even, so blunt the spiritual faculty that we lose the vision of God. Whereas if we walk in the light as He is in the light we have fellowship with Him. (1 John i. 7.)

The great question of the ages has been, How shall man find God, and live in His presence and be at peace? The religion of the Bible answers this longing of the human heart by teaching us that it was sin in man—wilful disobedience to God's good law—that so degraded man, so robbed him of his true manhood and dignity, that he could not stand in the presence of God without shame and confusion of face. The Bible traces back this alienation of man from his God to its true source and finds it in man, and not in God; whereas heathen religions make God hide His face in an arbitrary manner without any cause. In the story of the Fall the man deliberately disobeys God, refusing to believe God's words of warning respecting the consequences of sin. However, he immediately finds out in his own experience, that God's words of warning were words of love, instructing him how to live in order to attain to the highest possible degree of happiness. God's Word, if he had followed it, would have been a perfect chart to guide him throughout the whole voyage of life. But, now that he has disobeyed, God does not hide His face from him, but follows him to his hiding-place with the offer of mercy and reconciliation: "Adam, where art thou?" I have seen thy transgression; I know your fearfulness and shame; but in the counsels of eternity I have made provision for this terrible calamity. The seed of the woman shall bruise the head of the serpent. He shall be bruised for your transgressions; and by His stripes shall ye be healed. Your sin indeed has far-reaching consequences. It will bring sorrow and suffering in its train. On account of it labour will become toil instead of a pleasant recreation. Thorns and thistles shall the earth bring forth; and instead of having merely to till it, you shall have to weed it also.

What an immense power this view of sin gives Christianity over the hearts of men! It enables man to see that God is not unfavourably disposed towards him; while at the same time He cannot be regarded as looking upon sin as a trivial thing. So soon as a man, anxious about his sins and desirous to turn to God, discovers that God has not forsaken him; but that he, by his own folly and waywardness, has shut out the light of heaven from his soul, hope will dawn in his heart. He will see that he alone is responsible for the feeling of alienation and shame that has kept him away from God; and that his first duty is to turn from sin, and to do the will of God, and to accept the provision which God has made for bringing about reconciliation and peace. What an instructive lesson, therefore, is taught us in the fact that the doctrine of sin, with all its terrible consequences, is put in the very fore-front of Bible teaching.

Even in our own day we have blatant unbelievers denouncing the Bible as "an immoral Book" on account of the doctrine of the Atonement, as if, on account of redemption by the cross, God made light of sin. However, the whole teaching of the Bible is in the opposite direction. God does not make light of sin. On account of it man was banished from the Garden of Eden. On account of it, and to show His displeasure against it, God destroyed the old world with a flood, and rained fire and brimstone upon Sodom and Gomorrah. On account of a single falsehood Ananias and Sapphira fell down dead in the presence of the Apostles.

God does not make light of sin. He has shown us in the history of nations and in the history of individuals that persistent sin cannot go unpunished. And although He has devised a way by which the penitent sinner may be pardoned, yet pardon and reconciliation are never bestowed apart from reformation of life. God's plan of salvation provides for a renewed heart and a holy life, as well as for forgiveness of the past. These are the strong towers of the Christian faith. Man's two great needs—pardon for the past and power to lead a new life—are provided for in the finished work of Christ, and in the regenerating power of the Holy Spirit. He who believes in Christ and accepts Him as Saviour, is saved from present sin, as well as from the punishment of sin. It is a false impeachment of the Christian religion to say that in providing for free forgiveness it thereby makes sin easy. Its object is to make sin impossible—to make an end of sin: "He that believeth that Jesus is the Christ is born of God; and whatsoever is born of God doth not commit sin; for His seed—that is, the Divine Spirit—remaineth in him, and he cannot sin, because he is born of God."

The Bible nowhere encourages any one who is living in sin to believe that his past sins are forgiven. In becoming servants of God we are made free from sin: "Being now made free from sin and become servants unto God, ye have your fruit unto holiness, and the end everlasting life" (Rom. vi. 22). And so it is everywhere throughout the Bible. The several stages are inseparably connected. In becoming servants of God we not only receive pardon, we are purified—we are made free from sin; and we will bear new fruit,—no longer the fruit of sin, but fruit unto holiness; and then, but not till then, have we the desired end, namely, everlasting life.

These, then, are the bulwarks of our holy religion. Let us mark them well. They are indispensable to the strength and defence of the Christian Church. If you take away the Bible doctrine of Sin, or condone it, or treat it simply as an indiscretion, and say "peace, peace," to those who are living in sin, when there is no peace, you are removing one of the principal bulwarks of the Church of Christ, and you cannot defend it against the charge of making it easy to sin by proclaiming a free pardon to every penitent. Such teaching is not founded upon the model teaching of Christ. His teaching went to the secret thoughts of the heart; and He denounced mere formalists, who to men appeared holy and separate from sin, as "hypocrites" and "whited sepulchres," because sin and envy still reigned in their unregenerated hearts. This, then, is one of the grand proofs that Christianity is from God, and this constitutes its grand claim upon humanity, that, while it provides pardon for the past, it insists upon a holy, pure, upright life, lived in fellowship with God, and manifesting itself in love to all men, and an earnest desire to do them good.

In inculcating this high-toned morality the Bible stands alone; and in this elevated and ennobling teaching we see the wisdom and the love of God. Other systems of religion accommodate their requirements to the feebleness, and even to the passions of men; and thus seek to maintain a hold upon them. But the religion of the Bible strikes at the root of the evil; and tells man plainly that he stands condemned by sin, and that sin, in all its forms, must be given up and loathed. Thus only can he enjoy peace with God.

But the religion of Jesus does not leave man in this helpless condition; for a will that has taken on a wrong bent has an ever-increasing tendency to go on in the wrong direction. With forgiveness of past sin man requires power to lead a new life. Commands to do right, and penalties attached to disobedience, and Rules of Life set down for guidance, are not enough to meet man's needs. Besides all these, and above all these, he wants *power*—power to enable him to do God's will and to love it.

When a man becomes conscious of his alienation from God, and earnestly desires "to break off his sins by righteousness," he feels more than anything else his inability to do as he would desire. Like Paul, he is constrained to say, " When I would do good, evil is present with me." He 'knows the right, and strives to do it ; but the power. of sinful desire within, and the power of seductive temptation without, prove too strong for him. It is a terrible struggle, a struggle in which many have fallen, and in which no one has come off victorious. Now the religion of Christ recognizes this difficulty, and provides for it. Man's helpless state is recognized. He is not required to struggle on alone against unconquerable foes. · All the powers of Godhead come to his assistance. Here we see infinite wisdom and infinite love. And this in itself is conclusive proof that the Gospel plan of salvation is from God.

Human wisdom and philosophy in all the ages have sought to devise a scheme by which man could become superior to his surroundings, and mount up to God in holy aspiration and fellowship. But his highest reaches after holiness and forgiveness ended only in failure and bitter disappointment. Socrates, the wisest and best of the ancient heathen sages, could devise no method whereby God could forgive deliberate sin : " O Plato, Plato, perhaps God can forgive deliberate sin ; but I cannot see how." Neither could human wisdom suggest any means to enable a man to live a sinless life, and thus merit the approbation of God. Nevertheless, all felt the imperative need of holiness and forgiveness before man could meet a holy God in peace. And every earnest soul to-day feels the same.

No human philosophy has ever been able to supply the motive power necessary to produce holiness of heart and life, and thus make men fit for fellowship with God. Here human wisdom and human effort have ever failed. Here unaided human effort must ever fail. Man cannot save himself; he can only struggle. Forgiveness of past sin would be a mere mockery without power to lead a new life. What would it profit a man to know that he had secured forgiveness for the past, so long as he is conscious of committing fresh sins day by day? He could have no peace in the presence of a holy and just God. He would be compelled to carry about with him the sentence of condemnation. Christianity recognizes this truth, and provides for it. Man requires Divine help, and he may have it. We may be 'endued with power from on high." We may, like Paul, have the power of Christ resting upon us. We may be "strengthened with might by His Spirit in the inner man." God Himself, in His great mercy, supplies the power necessary to enable us to lead a new life. He has not only made provision for the forgiveness of past sin, He has also made provision against sinning. He comes, by His Spirit, to those who seek Him, and dwells in them as a new life and a new power, thus enabling us "to put off the old man with his deeds, and to put on the new man which, after God, is created in righteousness and true holiness."

Herein we see the beauty and completeness of the Bible plan of salvation. It saves, not only from the punishment of sin, but also from the power and practice of sin. It provides for holiness of heart and life here, and thus fits us for present fellowship with God. It recognizes the mighty forces of evil with which we have to contend, and does not inspire false confidence by telling us that we are well able to overcome in our strength. We are faithfully warned that we wrestle, not against flesh and blood merely,—that is, mere human agencies,—but against the rulers of the darkness of this world, against wicked spirits in heavenly places; and that we must put on the whole armour of God in order to be able to withstand the wiles of the devil, and quench all the fiery darts of the wicked one.

Christianity is honest with men, and tells us that our foes are more powerful than we; that they beset us on every hand, so that we need an omnipotent and ever-present Helper. And then we are pointed to the Strong One for help, and are assured that He "will bruise even Satan under our feet shortly."

Now, I think every earnest, thoughtful soul must feel that this is just the religion that meets man's needs. We have all struggled against sin and temptation in our own strength, and have failed in the struggle. We have found out in our own experience that the tempter is more powerful than we; and thus our experience proves to us that the Bible is true.

So far, therefore, as our personal experience goes, it runs parallel with Bible teaching. We have, therefore, a good warrant for confidently trusting the promises that go further than our present experience. God, by His Spirit, is ready to help us. Jesus is ready to be our refuge. "The name of the Lord is a strong tower."

The very completeness of the Gospel plan of salvation stamps it with the impress of divinity. Human wisdom in all the ages had failed to devise a scheme whereby past sin could be freely forgiven, and by which the love and practice of sin could be overcome. When such a scheme is presented, and proves to be the true remedy for sin by meeting man's needs, it is surely a marvel past comprehension that men should doubt that this plan and provision were devised by infinite wisdom and infinite love.

IV.

CHRIST THE CENTRE AND CITADEL OF CHRISTIANITY.

"The name of the Lord is a strong tower; the righteous run into it and are safe."—PROV. xviii. 10.

HAVING shown that the Strength of Christianity is seen in its doctrines,—the doctrines of Sin and Salvation,—we now proceed to show that its strength is seen also in its lives—the holy, happy, beneficent, triumphant lives of Christ, and those whom He has inspired. This is a kind of evidence that all can study for themselves. It is not critical and argumentative, requiring stores of learning to examine it intelligently. It is practical and experimental, and comes within the reach of every careful observer.

We shall commence with THE LIFE OF CHRIST. The personal Christ is the soul, and centre, and citadel of the Christian faith. The Christian Church, like the Christian's hope, rests not merely on a certain number of cardinal doctrines, but upon the living, loving, personal Christ. "Other foundation can no man lay than that is laid, which is Jesus Christ." Christ is the Foundation as well as the Founder of Christianity.

It is fashionable in our day for destructive critics to keep nibbling at the Bible, as if the Bible were the foundation of Christianity, in the hope of showing that it cannot, in all its parts, stand the test of human reason and modern criticism. But suppose the Bible were all destroyed, or suppose it had never been written, it would still remain true that " he that hath the Son hath life, and he that hath not the Son of God hath not life." Still we are told with an air of triumph that the Bible teaches that God is a holy and just God. It also teaches that Christ was without sin, and, therefore, perfectly innocent. It teaches, further, that this innocent Man was made to suffer for the transgressions of sinful men. This, it is affirmed, is not consistent with the justice of a holy God. It is not fair and just, it is said, that the innocent should be made to suffer for the guilty. And as they cannot conceive of God doing an injustice, the inference is, either that Christ was not entirely sinless, or else that He did not suffer for others.

Now, these statements are all true, but they are not all of the truth; and the inferences do not necessarily follow, as it is assumed. It is true that God is just. It is true that Christ lived a sinless life. It is true, also, that He suffered for others. But that is not all. The complete teaching of the Bible adds another stone to the temple of truth, which makes all the rest fit together in perfect harmony and beauty. It is this: *Christ willingly gave Himself.* The Father did not compel the Son to die. Long before He came to the cross Jesus said: "I lay down My life for the sheep. Therefore doth My Father love Me, because I lay down My life that I may take it again. No one taketh it from Me, but I lay it down of Myself. I have power to lay it down, and I have power to take it again. This commandment have I received of My Father" (John x. 15, 17, 18).

There was no conflict here between the Father and the Son. There was no compulsion in the matter. Had the sinless Christ been compelled to die against His will, that would have been an injustice, and unworthy of a holy and just God. But He died willingly, gladly, on account of His marvellous love to men: "He died the just for the unjust, *that He might bring us to God.*" For the joy set before Him in bringing many sons to glory, He endured the cross. The cross, therefore, instead of being an act of injustice, was the crowning act of the beneficent, self-sacrificing life of the Son of God. In this way we can easily defend the teaching of the Bible in reference to the fact that the innocent died for the guilty, just as we can defend the teaching of the Bible on every point it touches.

The Bible is indeed one of the strong towers of Christianity; and, when rightly interpreted, is a source of great strength. It has never been successfully assailed. It has resisted the attack of infidel and atheist, of rationalist and secularist. Human experience declares that it meets man's needs, as no other teaching has ever done, and proves to be the true medicine of the soul. The Bible, therefore, is one of the strong towers of the Christian Church. It is its armoury, where our weapons of defence are stored. The promises of the Bible are given for strength and for defence. Christ used them in warding off the assaults of the tempter. Three times He said, " It is written," and quoted from the sacred page as authoritative. We find men in modern times expressing doubts about the inspiration of the Bible. The Lord Jesus had no doubts on the matter. He quoted it to the devil as the ultimate source of appeal. The devil also quoted it to Christ as authoritative: " He shall give His angels charge concerning Thee, and in their hands they shall bear Thee up, lest at any time Thou shouldest dash Thy foot against a stone.' The Bible is a tower of strength, which neither man nor devil can successfully assail. But although the Bible is a strong tower for defence, and a grand armoury, it must be borne in mind that it is not the foundation of the Christian Church. Our spiritual Zion, like Zion of old, stands securely built upon a Rock—the Rock of Ages. The Lord Jesus, the personal Christ, must ever be the centre of our hopes, and the citadel of our faith, as He is the Head and Foundation of His Church.

Let us, then, inspect this tower of the Christian Church. " The name of the Lord is a strong tower." "I have set My King upon My holy hill Zion." It is a matter of supreme importance in building a house, or a temple, or a city, to secure a firm, immovable foundation. So a Church that is to stand the test of ages, must, like Mount Zion, be founded upon a Rock. This Rock is Christ—His life, His teaching, His moral character, His death and resurrection. The moral character and teaching of Christ have stood the test and criticism of centuries; and to-day His challenge stands unanswered, " Which of you convinceth Me of sin ? " He claimed to have lived a sinless life; and the bitterest opponents of Christianity, even in this sceptical age, are compelled to admit that they can find no fault or flaw in His character. They are compelled to re-echo the judgment of Pilate who tried Him: "I find no fault in this Man."

Look at His life on earth! What a marvellously unique life it was! Even His conception marks Him out as one whose life is to be far superior to other lives. He does not come into the world by ordinary methods of generation. He was conceived by the power of the Holy Ghost, as probably all would have been generated, had it not been for sin. He thus starts life free from any physical hereditary taint. Moreover, His advent to the world brought a special messenger from heaven to announce the glad tidings to the sons of men: " Behold, I bring you good tidings of great joy, which shall be to you and to all people; for unto you is born this day in the city of David a Saviour, who is Christ the Lord."

Then, again, see holy Simeon, a prophet of the Lord, to whom it had been revealed that he should not see death until he had seen the Lord's Christ, taking the Child Jesus in his arms in the temple, and blessing God, and saying, " Lord, now let Thy servant depart in peace, according to Thy word; for mine eyes have seen Thy Salvation, which Thou hast prepared before the face of all people,—a Light to lighten the Gentiles, and the glory of Thy people Israel." That can be no ordinary life that has such a beginning.

Again, we see Him in tender youth disputing with the doctors, obedient to His earthly parents, and yet conscious of possessing a Divine commission. " How is it that ye sought Me? Wist ye not that I must be about My Father's business?" A few years pass, and we see Him grown to manhood, wiser than learned Rabbis. Eager multitudes are hanging upon his lips, exclaiming in wonderment, "Never man spake like this Man." He is kinder than ministering angels. He draws near to the perishing. He stoops to save. He possesses marvellous power; and yet He never uses it for ministering to His own comfort, or for gratifying personal ambition, or for paving a way to a throne. He lives for others. He is always going about doing good. He heals the sick, comforts the sorrowing, gives eyes to the blind, and restores the dead to life; and He accepts no reward except the love and gratitude of overflowing hearts. The admiring populace seek to make Him a King; but He who of all men was best fitted for the office persistently declines the honour. He will be a King of hearts, and accept a seat on *that* throne; but earthly honours have no charm for Him. His chief joy all through life is to speak words of sympathy, and comfort, and pardon, to weary, sin-sick souls: "Daughter, be of good comfort; thy sins are forgiven thee." "Son, be of good cheer; thy faith hath made thee whole." Ah, yes, He forgave sins! And earnest, anxious souls, who felt the marvellous power of His life and teaching, freely conceded His right to do so; and took comfort from His gracious words of sympathy and pardon. He showed His mighty power over evil by casting out devils, and by resisting every form of temptation. "He was tempted in all points"—in every department of His nature—"like as we are, yet without sin." Surely such a life as that is a strong tower—a source of strength and defence to the organization which bears His name.

And now come with me to the close of His earthly career. He is betrayed into the hands of sinners. Sublimely heroic throughout life in the presence of disease and danger, never fearing the leper's deadly touch or the malice of the raging mob, He now appears in all His greatness and heroism. He fears not the arrest. He fears not the judgment-hall. He fears not the jealousy of Scribes and Pharisees. He fears not the cross to which He knew He was tending. Possessing all power to destroy, as well as to save, He spares His persecutors, when He might have called to His aid a legion of angels. He will not let the impulsive Peter defend Him with his rusty sword; and He heals with a touch the ear which Peter had cut off.

He is brought before Pilate for judgment, but His noble bearing proves that the greater is being judged by the less. Pilate is conscious of His superiority, and seeks to have Him released. Everywhere it is the same. In the humble cot among the godly poor; in the streets among the outcasts from society; on the mountain-side feeding the multitudes; in the city crowd healing the sick; on the Sea of Galilee stilling the tempest; in the judgment-hall reasoning with the judge, He is greater than all; He is a King among men. No one had lived such a spotless life. No one had shown such self-denial for the good of others. No one had spoken such words of wisdom and comfort. No one had performed such mighty works. No one had shown such true heroism in defending the right. Such a unique life cannot be accounted for in any other way than that He lived in close and constant fellowship with God.

But again : What tragic scene is that I see enacted on Calvary ? Ah, that is innocence dying ! See the hands, the feet, the brow ! How the life-blood slowly oozes from every wound of nail and thorn ! Although of all deaths that of the cross is the most agonizing, still there is no murmur or complaint. There are no maledictions heaped upon the heads of His cruel persecutors and murderers. What majestic self-composure, what sublime heroism, what forgetfulness of self are seen on that cross! He makes provision for His mother in her distress. He opens the gates of Paradise to the dying thief beside Him. He even intercedes for His murderers : "Father, forgive them ; for they know not what they do." Who ever lived such a life; and who ever died such a death ? No wonder the Roman centurion was constrained to exclaim, "'Truly this was the Son of God."

But why does He die ? Is He really innocent ? Hear His bitterest enemies ! Judas !—"I have betrayed the innocent blood." Pilate !—"I find no fault in this Man." Then, why did He die ? Death is the penalty of sin. Where there is no sin there can be no death; and, having no sins of His own, He could not have died on His own account. Then, why did He die ? "He died for our sins." You cannot account for His death in any other way. For you, for me, He agonized, He bled, He died. "He bare our sins in His own body on the tree." "The Lord laid on Him the iniquity of us all." There is no other possible explanation of His death.

But once more. What do I see and hear? Why do the rocks rend, and why does the earth quake? Why is the veil of the temple rent from the top to the bottom? Why do the heavens gather blackness, and why does the sun withdraw himself? Ah! they have crucified the Lord of glory. The Light of the world has gone out in darkness. Yet it is but for a brief moment; for, see, the Crucified One is risen! Risen indeed; for Mary recognizes the familiar voice —"*Mary!*" Risen indeed; for Thomas, the doubter, is cured of his scepticism. See, he is permitted to put his fingers into the prints of the nails, and to thrust his hand into the pierced side! Risen indeed! He was seen of Peter; then of the eleven; then of five hundred brethren at once. There could be no mistake about the reality of His resurrection; for He remained with them for forty days, speaking to them of the things pertaining to the kingdom of God. Yes, He is risen; and that fact proves at once His innocence and His Divine power. He rises triumphant from death and the grave; and from Olivet's summit He ascends most gloriously—no hand to lift Him up—no angel-wing with which to soar—no chariot of fire with winged steeds to bear Him aloft; but upward He glides by His own power, thus rising superior to the law of gravitation, commanding the homage of earth and natural law. Heaven, too, adds its homage, and clothes Him in a cloud of light and glory. The everlasting doors lift up their heads; the King of Glory enters in. But who is this King of Glory? "The Lord of Hosts, and none but He, the King of Glory is."

We are now entitled to ask, Can any other religion

claim such a Founder as this,—such a wondrous birth, such a holy, beneficent life, such a sublime death, such a triumphant resurrection, such a glorious ascension? Can any other institution claim such an origin and such a Head as the Christian Church? The origin of Christianity, associated as it is with the name of the Lord Jesus, is indeed a strong tower for which every true Christian has good reason to bless God. Surely the greatest marvel of modern times is that any could be found who could for one moment doubt that such a life was Divine.

Of the marvellous history of Christianity—lasting throughout the centuries, while other religions have crumbled to the dust, elevating, and ennobling, and blessing mankind, wherever its influence has been felt—we cannot now speak. But we would call upon all to praise God with one heart and voice for the wondrous birth, and spotless life, and holy teaching, and glorious death, and triumphant resurrection of the Lord Jesus Christ, the Saviour and the Friend of man.

V.

CHRISTIAN HEROES THE STRENGTH OF CHRISTIANITY.

"Thou shalt be His witness unto all men of what thou hast seen and heard."—ACTS xxii. 15.

SO far we have found the city of God securely built. The Christian doctrine of Sin and the Gospel plan of Salvation are towers which have stood the test of ages. They are now hoary with age, and yet they reveal no signs of decay. They appeal to human experience, and meet man's needs to-day as really and as fully as they did centuries ago. The persistent assaults of infidelity have only proved the immense strength and stability of these towers. The battering-rams of Rationalism have not revealed a single seam or flaw in the walls. Modern criticism has been unable to detect any fault in the plan and construction of these towers. They have the proper position assigned to them, being placed at the very entrance of the city. They are there both for strength and defence; and are admirably adapted to that end. The whole city, moreover, is built upon a Rock that has never been shaken. The Christian Church, built upon the immovable Rock, Christ Jesus; fortified by His marvellous life, and teaching, and sacrificial death; guarded and inspired by the personal presence of His Spirit; exhibited to the world in the holy self-sacrificing lives and triumphant peaceful deaths of myriads of mankind, stands out to-day, after the lapse of eighteen centuries, stronger, more blessed, more beneficent, more loved, and more influential than ever it was before. Zion of old, being the work of man, crumbled away before the wasting tooth of time; but this Zion, whose Builder and Maker is God, will stand as long as the sun and the moon endure.

We have seen that Christianity stands alone in taking due account of the deadly nature of sin; in making provision for pardon and reformation of life; in insisting upon holiness of heart as well as purity of life; in helping weary, struggling souls to mount up to God, not only by teaching them the better way, but by giving them a new life, new loves, new aims and aspirations, and power to translate into life the highest and holiest longings of the soul.

But Christianity goes further than the personal safety and the personal comfort of the individual who embraces it. In my quiet walks about Zion I have observed a grand old tower with broad massive base, each angle pointing towards the four corners of the earth. For several centuries this tower was largely covered up with rubbish and overgrown with shrubbery, so that many who have visited Zion, and to whom her very stones were dear, have failed to recognize it as a tower at all; and others, especially in the dark Middle Ages, seem to have regarded it as a mere uninteresting old ruin. But during the early centuries it stood out most prominently, and during the present century the rubbish and shrubbery have been cleared away; and the tower cannot fail to be seen by any interested observer. I see its name deeply cut in indelible letters, read as easily as in the days of Paul—THE BROTHERHOOD OF MAN: and underneath the text, "Go ye into all the world, and preach the Gospel to every creature."

The Religion of the Bible stands alone in teaching unselfishness and brotherly love—in fostering a missionary spirit that seeks the highest good of all men in the wide world. All uncharitableness, and envy, and malice, and evil-speaking are classed in the category of sin, as well as the grosser vices. All injury to our fellow-men is forbidden, whether it be in respect of his person, or his property, or his reputation, or his feelings. Christianity teaches THE UNIVERSAL BROTHERHOOD OF MAN. We are to regard all men as brethren, and be ready to do them good, as we have opportunity: "All things whatsoever ye would that men should do to you, do ye even so to them." Surely such teaching as that is a tower of strength to Christianity. And if it were only lived out in the daily life of all citizens, what a tower of strength it would be to society, and what a palace of comfort, too!

The Brotherhood of Man is pre-eminently a Christian idea. The Golden Rule, which insists that we shall so stamp out selfishness and self-seeking as to be ready to do for others what we would like to receive from them, is not found in any other literature. Who but the Lord Jesus would have thought of teaching, "It is more blessed to give than to receive"? "We that are strong ought to bear the infirmities of the weak, and not to please ourselves." " Bear ye one another's burdens, and so fulfil the law of Christ."

What would the world and society be to-day if these maxims regulated and controlled the actions and conduct of all men ? If all envy, and jealousy, and rivalry, and self-seeking, and greed of gain, and caste, and class distinction, and oppression, and brutality were to perish in a night, and to-morrow we should see the law of Christian love bearing sway in every community, in every home, and in every heart, we would regard it as the greatest miracle that the world has ever seen. Earth would be transformed into a very heaven.

But the teaching of Christianity goes further than merely refraining from injuring others. It teaches that we must cultivate a missionary spirit. We are to go to those whose hearts are failing them in the struggle after a higher and a holier life, and extend to them a helping hand. We are to go to the poor, the lame, the halt, and the blind, and give them heart by our kindness, and sympathy, and counsel.

In this respect Christ has left us an example that we should follow in His steps. He not only taught the universal brotherhood of man, but He also lived it out in His life as no one else ever did. He showed us that the careless and the outcast may be reached and touched by kindness and sympathy. He carried the message of mercy to those who were sunk in iniquity, and new light dawned upon them; and, with it, hope and a new life. He passed no one by on account of his low condition or his past life; but saw under the roughest exterior a human heart needing sympathy—a human soul needing salvation; and that was enough. He saw in every man the image of God, defaced indeed by sin, but still capable of being restored; and He was not ashamed to call them brethren. He saw that the hardest heart could be touched by kindness, that the lowest could be restored to the paths of virtue, and that those who were forgiven most were those who would love Him most, and be most zealous in spreading the good news of the kingdom. So He recognized the brotherhood of man in its fullest extent, and sought to benefit and bless all alike. He came with blessings, not for a select class, but for the world. No one had wandered too far away to be beyond His sympathy. It was enough that men *needed* His sympathy and help. If they were weary of life and laden with sin, no matter what their condition and circumstances were, He said to all alike, "Come unto Me, all ye that labour and are heavy-laden, and I will give you rest." Surely, then, His Gospel is the Gospel for humanity if the world only knew it.

We hear a great deal in our day about the Gospel losing its power—about Christianity losing its hold upon men. But it is not true that the Gospel is losing its power. It is too sadly true that there are large numbers, even in Christian lands, who stand aloof from the religion of Jesus, and are living in vice and practical heathenism. But this is not the fault of the Gospel. Their vice and immorality only prove that they have never accepted the Gospel, or experienced its power. We must estimate the power of the Gospel, not simply by the numbers it has reached, but by its power to elevate those who embrace it—its power to subdue evil passions—its power to create sympathy, and kindness, and brotherly love—its power to promote a true missionary spirit—its power to bind all men together in seeking the good and highest happiness of each and all.

The Gospel is not responsible for not having reached the multitudes who still refuse to accept it. You may force a particular form of religion upon a State, but you cannot force the religion of Christ upon any individual. It is of the very essence of the Gospel that its acceptance is entirely optional. It has respect for man's free will and his right of choice. The Gospel offer is, "Whosoever will, let him take the water of life freely." There is in the Gospel enough for all; it is free for all; it is suited to all; it is offered to all; it has power to elevate and bless all who embrace it; but God leaves every man free either to accept or reject it. The sad fact, therefore, that millions are standing aloof to-day from the Gospel is no evidence that it is lacking in power. You might as well say that Astronomy cannot be a useful science, else we would have many more astronomers, as to say that the Gospel is not adapted to the wants of humanity because all are not blessed and benefited by it. The claim of the Gospel is that it will bless those, and those only, who accept it: "I am not ashamed of the Gospel of Christ, because it is the power of God *to save every one that believeth*." The Gospel, to be a blessing, must first be embraced. We are bound, therefore, in all fairness, to estimate the power of the Gospel in those only who cordially embrace it and live up to its requirements. We must judge of the religion of Jesus, not only by what it does, but by what it is capable of doing. If it blesses, and ennobles, and elevates all those who embrace it, then it has proved its beneficent power. If I were to announce a remedy that would at once arrest hæmorrhage of the lungs, and it proved successful in every instance in which it was applied, it would be no evidence against its potency and power that many were still dying of hæmorrhage who had never tried the remedy. So if the religion of Christ succeeds in meeting man's needs, and in healing his spiritual diseases, wherever it is applied, be the cases many or few, it has assuredly proved its power and established its claim.

Moreover, to know its full capabilities, we must take the best possible examples which the history of the Christian Church furnishes. We must, to commence with, take the life of Christ, as the pattern after which all lives should be modelled. We must judge of Christianity by His life and teaching. The aim of Christianity is to produce lives after that pattern. It is not the fault of the Gospel of Christ, but our fault, if such lives are not produced.

Or, take the life of the noblest hero whom the world ever saw—the grand, heroic, dauntless Apostle Paul. Read the story of his conversion and his entrance upon the new life. Ponder well his previous character, and training, and prejudices. What a power there must have been in the Gospel to set Saul of Tarsus, the blasphemer and persecutor, upon a new track! What humiliation for a man of his proud spirit to be compelled to acknowledge that his former life of fanatical zeal was all a soul-destroying blunder! What a heart-rending struggle it would be for him, as a loyal and zealous Churchman, to break for ever with the established Church of his time, and to abandon for ever the hope of ecclesiastical promotion, which would surely fall to the lot of so learned and so capable a man! But the power of the Gospel was so mighty upon him that he "conferred not with flesh and blood," but banished from his mind every selfish consideration, cordially accepted the Gospel of Christ, and became the grandest exponent of the missionary idea that the world has ever seen.

God by special revelation taught him what never occurred to him before—THE UNIVERSAL BROTHERHOOD OF MAN. From that day his field was the world. The middle wall of partition between Jew and Gentile was broken down; for in Christ Jesus there was neither Jew nor Gentile, bond nor free, rich nor poor; but Christ was all in all. They were all one in Christ Jesus. Like the other Apostles, he was equipped for his work by a special baptism from on high. There was no weakness and no failure in the lives of the Apostles after they received the baptism of the Holy Spirit on the day of Pentecost; and there was no failure in Paul's life after Christ met him on the way to Damascus, and bestowed upon him the gift of the Holy Ghost. They were weak as other men before, but now life is one continuous march of victory. They loved their Master dearly before, but there was weakness, and selfishness, and failure all along the line. But now the power of Christ is resting upon them. They are living new lives, experiencing new joys, speaking with new tongues, and having a marvellous power over men. Temptation has now lost its power over them. They profess to be still weak in themselves, but they are strong in the Lord. Hence Paul breaks forth in notes of triumph, " I can do all things through Christ which strengtheneth me. I know how to be abased, and I know how to abound; everywhere, and in all things,·I am instructed both to be full and to be hungry, both to abound and to suffer need; for I have learned in whatsoever state I am therewith to be content."

This is the triumphant testimony of Paul the aged. How he has grown since he wrote the seventh of Romans, and was constrained to exclaim, "O wretched man that I am, who shall deliver me! from this body of death?" There is no wretchedness now, no weakness, no failure, no fear. They may throw him into prison and make his feet fast in the stocks, but still he will sing praise to God. They may take away his liberty, but they cannot take away his peace. They may deprive him of the privilege of preaching, but they cannot deprive him of the privilege of prayer and praise. He cares not for beating, and stoning, and scourging; he cares not for shipwreck or for storm; he cares not for bonds, and imprisonment, and death. Hear his heroic language, "The Holy Ghost witnesseth in every city saying that bonds and afflictions abide me; but none of these things move me, neither count I my life dear unto myself, so that I might finish my course with joy, and the ministry which I have received of the Lord Jesus to testify the gospel of the grace of God" (Acts xx. 24).

Which is the nobler hero—young Saul of Tarsus, playing the coward's part, keeping the clothes of the men who stoned Stephen, the first martyr, to death; or Paul the aged, changed in nature, as in name, defying all the powers of earth and hell to do him harm? And what is the secret of this marvellous change? In the one case it is Paul fighting *against* the power of God; in the other it is Paul fighting *by* the power of God. And that makes all the difference. This, then, is the strength and defence of Christianity. The Religion that can exhibit in the lives of its heroes such coolness in danger, such composure in adversity, such confidence in the face of death, such self-denial and self-sacrifice for the good of others, needs no other defence. There is a power in the religion of Jesus which no other religion or philosophy can offer, or even understand—the power of Christ resting upon holy, humble men and women, who are willing to be nothing that Christ may be all. Religion is a thing of the heart and the life. Its power cannot be ascertained merely by the study of doctrine and dogma. It must be felt in our personal experience, and seen in the life. When brought before rulers and magistrates and asked to account for his conduct in zealously seeking to spread the glad tidings of salvation, Paul invariably goes back upon his own experience, and tells what great things the Lord has done for him. This he considers sufficient to account for what otherwise would have been regarded as mere fanaticism. His argument always was, God has done great things for me in bringing me out of darkness into light, and I am determined to spend and be spent in leading my brother-man into the same glorious liberty and joy. Paul clearly recognized the law of Christian love and the brotherhood of man. That which gave such blessedness to him he wanted all men to enjoy. This high ideal he was able to live out in a wonderfully devoted and self-sacrificing life. The ideal, therefore, is not too high for the attainment of others.

We have many splendid illustrations of it in our own day. Christian men and women, like John Williams, and John Geddie, and the Gordons, and their wives, landing upon the savage isles of the Pacific, impelled by the law of Christian love to carry the good news of salvation to their brother-man; Henry Martyn exposing himself to all the dangers of uncivilized life to tell to the American Indians "the old, old story of Jesus and His love"; Judson, and Carey, and William Burns, and Alexander Duff, lighting a torch in Africa, and China, and India, which will go on shining more and more unto the perfect day, —these are but samples of the marvellous power of Christianity to enable men to do and to dare for the well-being and happiness of others. And there are tens of thousands in all Christian lands whose names may never appear on the public roll of fame, who, nevertheless, are doing similar work for God and humanity in our Churches and Sunday Schools, in mission work and among the poor, talking the Gospel, singing the Gospel, living the Gospel, and thus blessing larger numbers of the human race than time will ever reveal.

What has Atheism, and Infidelity, and that barbarous freak of modern times—Socialism—to place beside the splendid records of Christianity? Do you suppose it ever entered into the mind of Tom Paine, or Voltaire, or Rousseau, or any living infidel, to go and spend his life on a lonely isle of the sea, and acquire a strange language in order to preach the gospel of no God, and no Christ, and no Bible, and no hereafter, to those uncivilized and benighted savages ? It is a very easy thing to sit down and dash off a witty, clever pamphlet against the religion of Christ, with the absolute certainty that as a financial speculation it will be a success. It is a very easy thing to harangue a crowd on the streets or in the parks, when every vulgar witticism is applauded to the echo, and every base insinuation is received with a cheer. Such is the service Infidelity renders to humanity, but it does not cost much ; and it does not exhibit any of that heroism, and self-denial, and genuine love of man that we see in the lives of the good and great men who have made the history of the Christian Church famous. Where can the annals of Infidelity produce a man like the Apostle Paul, or a man who has done for his country what John Knox did for Scotland, or what Martin Luther did for Germany, or what Wycliffe did for England, or what John Huss did for Bohemia, or Savonarola did for Italy ? Here, then, is the mission of Christianity—to bind men together, first, in love to God and all that is good, and pure, and beautiful, and then in love to each other ; so that all the world over the golden rule will hold sway, and men will do to others as they would that others should do to them. May the Lord hasten it in His time.

VI.

THE LORD'S SUPPER A MONUMENT TO CHRISTIANITY.

"With gladness and rejoicing shall they be brought. They shall enter into the King's palace."—PSALM xlv. 15.

WE have already shown that the Strength of Christianity is seen in its doctrines—in the doctrine of Sin; in the Divine plan of Salvation, including the redemptive work of Christ, and the regenerating and sanctifying power of the Holy Spirit; in the sinless life and sacrifice of Christ; in the brave, heroic lives of those whom Christianity inspired; and in the baptism of the Holy Ghost, clothing holy, humble men with Divine power. The grand central doctrines of Christianity have stood the test of centuries. They have reformed and strengthened the life of nations and of individuals. They have lifted up the fallen and restored the prodigal to the paths of virtue. They have removed the burden of conscious guilt from anxious, troubled souls, struggling after light and liberty. They have sustained the suffering and sorrowing in the hour of trial, when all other sources of comfort failed them. They have enabled the dying saint to meet the King of terrors in peace and triumph, and have dispelled the gloom of the valley of the shadow of death. The precious teaching of the Bible has even transformed death and taken away his terrors, enabling the dying saint to see him no longer as an enemy, but as a heavenly messenger, sent to break the bonds that bind him to earth, and to set the ransomed spirit free.

There are still several strong towers on the walls of our beloved Zion, which we have yet to visit, but we are now to enter the palace of the King. A palace is a place for comfort as well as for protection. Those who are admitted to the palace meet with the King. They are permitted to "see the King in His beauty."

But the King's palace on Mount Zion was fortified. Therefore, it was a bulwark for defence as well as a palace for comfort. In these respects it is beautifully emblematic of the Lord's Supper. As an ordinance in the Christian Church, the Lord's Supper is a tower of strength as well as a feast of love and fellowship. Let us consider it for a little in these two aspects.

The Lord's Supper is a tower of strength to the Christian Church. The very existence of such an ordinance is the surest possible guarantee of the fact which it commemorates. We trace it back in the history of the Church to the time of its institution. There is no break in the chain of history. In every age, whatever else was neglected, this precious ordinance was observed by devout Christians. It never had to be resuscitated in the Church, because it had never ceased to be observed. You can find no beginning for it, and no cause for it, and no meaning in it, until you go back to the events enacted at Calvary. It could not possibly have originated, much less have been perpetuated, apart from the event which it was designed to commemorate. Like every other monument erected to the memory of some distinguished person, it proclaims and proves the historical fact on which it is founded. You look at the monument erected at Haddington to commemorate the noble work of the illustrious Scottish Reformer, John Knox. It never enters the mind to question the fact of his having lived, and wrought, and died more than three hundred years ago. Even if you knew nothing of his life and work, and even if the history of his time had never been written, that monument is conclusive evidence to every rational mind that he lived, and laboured, and won the esteem and admiration of his countrymen. You know that that monument would have been impossible except for his life and labours. And that monumental evidence will be as convincing eighteen hundred years hence as it is to-day. Every sane man knows that that monument could never have been erected in honour of a man who never lived and laboured for the good of his country. The monument establishes the fact which it commemorates.

If you find an old coin with the face of Julius Cæsar, or Augustus, or any other Roman Emperor, upon it, everybody is satisfied with it as proof positive that these men lived and reigned at the time the coin was struck. We conclude at once that these coins could never have originated on any other supposition.

Now, the Lord's Supper is such a monument to the great central truths of Christianity—the life, the death, and the resurrection of Christ. It is utterly inconceivable that the disciples and early Christians should have observed and perpetuated the ordinance of the Supper except it had been instituted by Christ in the manner and for the purpose set forth by them in their writings. See, then, what a strong tower this precious ordinance is to the Christian Church. Were the Bible and all history to perish, so that no written record of the life and work of Christ remained to future generations, this monument in the Church would preserve it all.

In this way the history of God's people was preserved in the olden time, in the memorial stones at Jordan, and in the Feast of the Passover. "Take ye twelve stones out of the midst of Jordan, out of the place where the priests' feet stood firm, and set them up for a memorial, that this may be a sign among you, that when your children ask their fathers in time to come, saying, What mean ye by these stones? then ye shall answer them that the waters of Jordan were cut off before the ark of the covenant of the Lord; and these stones shall be a memorial unto the children of Israel for ever" (Joshua iv. 6, 7). The memorial stones were intended to teach future generations what great things God had done for His people. Such a memorial is the Lord's Supper. It is a commemorative ordinance for the comfort of God's people, and for the instruction of the young. What a splendid opportunity each returning communion Sabbath affords parents for instructing their children in regard to the life and death of Christ. They naturally inquire, "What do you mean by passing round the bread and wine, and each partaking of it?" You then tell them how Jesus lived for us, and loved us, and died for us. His body was broken for us. His blood was shed for us. He took our place, and died for our sins. He set up this memorial ordinance in His Church, and enjoined upon His followers to observe it faithfully until He comes again. Thus this precious ordinance is to be used for instruction. It points to and commemorates, and sets forth, under most expressive symbols, the great central facts of Christianity.

The ordinance of the Lord's Supper not only authenticates the fact of Christ's death, but also gives most explicit testimony as to the object of His death. "This is My body given for you"—"broken for you." Here we have Christ speaking of Himself as our Substitute. What He did and suffered was for us. In dying He "bore our sins in His own body on the tree." And in virtue of His death for us, God can forgive our sins, and still be seen by men to be a holy and just God: "Whom God hath set forth to be a propitiation, through faith in His blood, to declare His righteousness for the remission of sins that are past ... that God might be just and the Justifier of him that believeth in Jesus" (Rom. iii. 25). Apart from the remission of sins, the ordinance has no meaning and no value. "This is My blood of the new covenant, which is shed for many for the remission of sins" (Matt. xxvi. 28). Redemption is not by teaching, nor by moral influence, but by bloodshedding; for "without shedding of blood there is no remission" (Heb. ix. 22).

Christ's own words in instituting the Supper are a promise and a pledge on His part that those who truly receive Him shall have their sins forgiven. The Lord's Supper, therefore, is not only a sign and symbol, but a seal. It seals Christ's promise and pledge to us. The moment we do our part, and lovingly and trustfully accept Him as our Saviour, we have His sure word of promise that our past sins are all forgiven. Hence this ordinance, reverently and intelligently observed, helps in a great degree to confirm and strengthen the faith of all sincere communicants. For, in a very real sense, Christ, by His Spirit, is present in the Supper, as He is present in the Word—present not in any fleshly manner, but by His Spirit comforting, refreshing, inspiring, purifying the hearts of all worthy recipients. By the Spirit of Christ dwelling in us we become one with Him : " He that is joined to the Lord is one spirit" (1 Cor. vi. 17). It is in this sense that we receive Christ in the Sacrament of the Supper. We eat His flesh and drink His blood, not in any carnal sense, but when by faith and love we feed upon Him as the food and strength of our souls. Just as bread, when eaten and assimilated, nourishes and sustains the bodily organism; so Christ, when received and appropriated by faith, nourishes and strengthens the spirit. Food, when eaten and digested and converted into blood, becomes one with the life of the body ; so Christ, received by faith, dwells in us by His Spirit, and thus becomes one with our spiritual life, nourishing and sustaining it. How beautifully, therefore, do these emblems, bread and the fruit of the vine, set forth the spiritual nourishment received by all true believers who feed upon Christ by faith. The body requires its daily supplies of food, else it soon languishes and dies ; so the spirit, in like manner, requires constant supplies. This supply is kept up by union to Christ. And let it be remembered that we are united to Christ only by faith and love and the indwelling of His Spirit. His Spirit dwells in us as a new life, just as our own spirit is in us as our natural life. The one is as real as the other, and no more mysterious. If the spirit leaves the body, the body is dead to all natural things. It hears nothing, sees nothing, feels nothing, enjoys nothing. So also if we have not the Spirit of Christ dwelling in us, we are dead to all spiritual things. We hear not the comforting voice of God. We see no beauty in Divine things. We feel no joy in the consciousness of having Christ's presence with us. We are spiritually dead.

The new life which all the regenerate possess is communicated in the New Birth by the direct agency of the Holy Spirit; and the new life is kept up in the new creature by the continual indwelling of the Spirit of Christ. The new life is the life of Christ in the heart. The Apostle Paul makes this clear: " When Christ, *who is our life*, shall appear"; and again, " Christ liveth in me." This Christ-life in him was preserved by a constant, ever-acting faith; for he adds, " The life which I now live in the flesh, I live by the faith of the Son of God, who loved me and gave Himself for me" (Gal. ii. 20). It is abundantly evident, therefore, from the teaching of Scripture, that Christ is not received in any bodily or carnal manner, but as Spirit and life. Hence the Word of God is in perfect accord with reason and common sense.

The necessary conditions for profitable communion, or the qualifications for the proper observance of the Lord's Supper, may be summed up in three words—

Knowledge, Faith, Love. Knowledge, to discern the Lord's body; Faith, to feed upon Christ, by realizing the touch and life-giving power of His Spirit; Love, as the bond of union to bind the heart to Christ, to His Word, to His ordinances, and to His people. The Lord's Supper has no meaning to us except in it we discern the Lord's body—that is, see the crucified Saviour vividly set forth as our Saviour and Sin-bearer. It also implies personal faith in Him as our Saviour from the love and power of sin; and love and loyalty to Him, shown in the purpose and determination to do His will in all things.

In the institution of the Lord's Supper we have also a touching token of the tenderness of Christ's love. Friends at parting like to give some memorial or keepsake by which they may be remembered. Such a memorial is the Lord's Supper. It is Christ's parting gift to His people, by which they are to bring to remembrance all His love—all He did for them by His life and death in delivering them from the power, and bondage, and punishment of sin. Parting pledges are always mutual, if they have any meaning. In asking to be remembered we pledge ourselves not to forget. This is what the Lord Jesus has done. He assures us that His love to us will never fail; and He asks for our loving remembrance. He says, "Remember Me when I am gone. Observe this feast in memory of Me." What infinite condescension on His part! How wonderful that He who sits upon the throne above should appreciate the remembrance of poor sinners on earth! It shows how near He got to man, and what a tender interest He took in our welfare. It was for our sakes, not His own. He wished to bind us to Himself by the strongest of all ties—the bond of love. He loves us; and He has proved His love by dying for our sins. He expects us to love Him in return, and to prove our love by a life of holiness and obedience, and by a life of self-denial for the good of others.

The Lord Jesus also carries with Him our memorial —the marks of the cross, the print of the cruel nails. Hence He says, "I have engraven thee upon the palms of My hands." This is His pledge to us that He will not forget us. "Zion said, The Lord hath forsaken me; my God hath forgotten me. Can a woman forget her sucking child, that she should not have compassion upon the son of her womb? Yea; she may forget, yet will I not forget thee. Behold, I have graven thee upon the palms of My hands" (Isa. xlix. 14-16). In those marks I see how much I suffered for thee. You have not so suffered, and cannot so love, and, therefore, may forget. Wherefore I would have you reminded of My dying love by this memorial ordinance.

In the Lord's Supper we specially commemorate the death of Christ, because His death was the completion and consummation of His finished work. "As often as ye eat this bread and drink this cup, ye do show the Lord's death till He come." He wishes us to remember Him especially as the crucified Saviour. The Apostle Paul places special emphasis on this thought: "I determined not to know anything among you, save Jesus Christ and Him crucified." Jesus can be nothing to us apart from His death. By His death He redeemed us from death. "Ye have been redeemed by the precious blood of Christ." We must never lose sight of the shed blood. It is the blood of Christ that "cleanseth us from all sin" (1 John i. 7).

However, we must not rest content with the general belief that Christ died for sinners. We must mount up on the wings of faith and love to our personal relationship, and say, "He died for me." Then He will come to us, and fill us with His own fulness, cleansing us from every stain of sin, making us holy, and restful, and happy.

In the Lord's Supper we have also set forth the idea of fellowship—not only communion with Christ, but communion with one another. By becoming one with Jesus we become one with each other. If we come to the Lord's Table in the spirit of true disciples, we shall love as brethren; we shall cherish no envious, or uncharitable, or unkind feelings; we shall resolve to do all in our power to promote the happiness of each other. If we have been born again we are all members of Christ's family, and belong to the household of faith. This new relation to one another brings new responsibilities and new duties: "By this shall all men know that ye are My disciples, if ye have love one to another."

.At the Lord's Table our first thought must be of the Master of the feast, and our supreme love must be centred on Him. But from Jesus as the centre our love must radiate to all our fellow-believers and fellow-heirs to the heavenly inheritance. They share in Jesus' love, and they should share in ours. Come to this sacred feast in this spirit, and you shall have the Master's welcome, and shall hear Him say: "Eat, O friends; yea, drink abundantly, O beloved."

VII.

DEALING WITH DOUBT.

"And when they saw Him, they worshipped Him; but some doubted."—MATT. xxviii. 17.

IT is a fact that must be recognized that there are many at the present time who have considerable difficulty with much that is revealed in the Word of God. Apart altogether from flippant unbelievers, bent on destructive criticism, anxious only to throw discredit on the Bible without supplying anything in its place, there are many earnest, thoughtful men engaged in honest inquiry—in fact, they are driven to it by the very thoroughness of their nature—who have real difficulties, and who deserve respectful attention. There are difficulties which, if not removed, must surely lead to settled doubt.

The time is for ever gone—and let us be thankful that it is gone—when the teachers of the Church can afford to push aside honest inquiry, and stifle difficulties, and denounce the independent thought of the age. The man who refuses to set his foot down until he sees and feels the solid rock, is safer and has far greater reverence for truth, than the easy-going professor, who believes and acts in accordance with the teaching of his spiritual guide without ever taking the trouble to think for himself. The man who questions, and inquires, and investigates until he can accept revealed truth intelligently, is the very man who in the end becomes a pillar in the Church and helpful to others. The Lord Jesus did not denounce Thomas because he demanded visible and certain evidence of the reality of His resurrection. He did what every true sympathetic teacher would do— He gratified a natural and most commendable desire on the part of Thomas to obtain certain knowledge on a matter of such vital importance.

Doubts and difficulties in religious matters must be fairly and honestly met, and candidly dealt with. They cannot be got rid of by pooh-poohing them, or by letting them alone. They thrust themselves upon young thoughtful minds unsought and unwelcomed. And yet how often do we hear it said to such troubled souls, "Why do you trouble yourselves about such things?" A physician might as well say to a person in sickness, "Why do you have pain?" and expect him, by a mere effort of will, to shake off disease. If you would remove the pain, you must remove the cause of it. And it is the same with doubt and difficulty about religion. You must deal, not with doubt merely, but with the cause of it. If the intellect demands clearer knowledge, then by all means let clearer knowledge be given. That is the first step.

You may not be able to make every point clear to the intellect, for there are certain spiritual truths that can be received only by the heart—the spiritual faculty— and can be known only in experience; such, for example, as the joy and peace that follow the felt sense of sins forgiven. But when by patient, honest inquiry you satisfy the intellect on one point and another, then you begin to feel assured that sufficient information will remove all your difficulties one by one, and you will then struggle on patiently and hopefully until you have conquered every difficulty and banished every doubt.

Take, for example, a man who has difficulty about the grand central fact of Christianity—the Resurrection of Christ. He asks himself the question, How do I know that it ever took place? He is told that the inspired word of God says He rose. But his difficulties about Inspiration are as great as about the Resurrection of Christ, and he is not helped in the least. Neither do you help him by saying, "You must believe or be lost," for you cannot compel the assent of the intellect. How are you to meet his difficulty? Certainly not by denouncing him as an unbeliever. That is a method too often adopted by ill-informed teachers who know little about Theology, and less about human hearts and their difficulties—a method which most surely drives thoughtful men away from the Church, and from the Bible, and from Christ, instead of leading them into light, and liberty, and peace.

The Resurrection of Christ is a fact, an historical fact, and, as such, it can be proved like any other fact in history. You do not require to believe that the Evangelists, and Paul, and Peter were inspired before you can accept their testimony in regard to the Crucifixion, and Resurrection, and Ascension of Christ, and the institution of the Lord's Supper, and the formation of the Christian Church. You have only to give them credit for common honesty, such as you give to any reliable historian, as Josephus, or Julius Cæsar, or any other who lived and wrote about the same time.

Notwithstanding all that has been written against Christ and the Christian religion, there is not a candid well-informed man to-day who does not admit that the four Gospels are a record of facts, and are substantially accurate. And not only so, but we have the testimony of contemporary heathen writers and the enemies of Christ in abundance, confirming in every important particular the record in the Gospels. And, moreover, we have the Christian Church built upon the risen Christ. If Christ did not rise it is utterly inconceivable that the disciples should have invented a lie, and have founded a religion upon it, and have exposed themselves to persecution and loss of property during their whole life for nothing, and less than nothing. Then, again, within a few weeks after the Resurrection we find multitudes joining the little band; and a great company of the priests, who had publicly opposed Christ during His life, have become "obedient to the faith." Now these men knew whether Christ rose or not. Like Thomas, mere sentiment would not have satisfied them. They must have had most conclusive evidence.

Thus we can establish the Resurrection of Christ on purely historical grounds, so that it can be received by the intellect intelligently and cordially. And in this way—namely, by satisfying honest inquiry—not only is belief made easy, but doubt is made impossible.

But the Resurrection of Christ, once established, carries with it other great truths, such as His divinity and the infallibility of His teaching. He possessed more than human wisdom; for He foretold His own death and resurrection. "Destroy this temple, and I will raise it up in three days." Here is Divine wisdom. No mere man would have dared to utter such a prediction. He also said, "I have power to lay down My life, and I have power to take it again." Therefore He rose by the exercise of His own power. He had power over death during His earthly life, and now in death He has still power over death. Here is Divine power. The Resurrection of Christ, therefore, once established, carries with it His divinity—His Divine wisdom and Divine power. And His divinity carries with it the infallibility of His teaching.

And now what have we got? Having established His divinity and the infallibility of His teaching, we have a short and easy method to prove that the Bible is the Word of God, and the expression of the Will of God. Christ, possessing Divine wisdom, and never erring in a single statement, declares that the Old Testament prophets spoke by the Holy Ghost, or that God spoke through them. He quoted "the Law, the Prophets, and the Psalms"—which included the whole Old Testament as we now have it—as the Word of God. This stamps the whole Old Testament with Divine authority.

He also promised to guide the Apostles in what they were to record: "When the Spirit of truth is come, He will guide you into all truth. . . . He shall teach you all things, and bring all things to your remembrance whatsoever I have said to you. . . . And He will show you things to come" (John xiv. 26; xvi. 13). As a matter of fact, this promise was fulfilled when they received the baptism of the Holy Ghost on the day of Pentecost, and "spake with other tongues, as the Spirit gave them utterance." The fulfilment of this promise, confirmed as it was by signs and miracles, stamps the teaching of the Apostles with the imprimatur of God. Thus we see that in dealing with doubt and difficulty respecting doctrine and belief, the first thing to be done is to satisfy the intellect about the historical Christ and the great facts of His life. Once establish the Resurrection of Christ as an historical fact, and you have also established His divinity and the inspiration of the Bible. Hence we conclude that in our teaching and in our beliefs, Christ, the personal historical Christ, must be the grand centre and citadel of our faith.

Doctrine may be difficult, but the personal Christ is easily apprehended; and by believing in Christ difficulties about doctrine very soon vanish. Hence Jesus says, "If any man will do My will he shall know of the doctrine whether it be of God" (John vii. 17). See how this truth is brought out in that touching incident which followed His promulgation of some of his most startling doctrines. Many who came and listened occasionally to His teaching were staggered at His claim to be "the living bread that came down from heaven" (John vi. 51); and that only by eating His flesh and drinking His blood could they obtain eternal life. They were offended, and said, "This is a hard saying, who can hear it?" And they went back, and walked no more with Him. It is worthy of note that He expressed no surprise at their conduct. He evidently expected it, and apparently regarded it as the most natural thing for mere listeners to do. He seemed to have recognized the grand truth, that His doctrine cannot be understood and received apart from His life. This thought comes out more clearly in what follows. He turned to the twelve, and said, "Will ye also go away?" As if He had said, I can understand how those who regard Me simply as a Teacher should stumble at these mysterious truths, but you who know Me as a Friend, you who have seen My life, My love, My power, My fellowship with the Father, will ye also go away? See, too, how Peter takes up this thought, and works it out to the strengthening of his faith: "Lord, to whom shall we go? Thou hast the words of eternal life. And we believe and are sure that Thou art the Christ, the Son of the living God."

The twelve would have the same intellectual difficulty as the people of Capernaum about "eating His flesh, and drinking His blood"; but they had found comfort, and hope, and strength in His teaching and fellowship. They had found in their experience that He was satisfying their soul-longings, and was giving a new zest to life; and they were not going to lose these blessings on account of some things in His teaching hard to be understood. I have no doubt but, like sensible men, with a modest estimation of their own abilities that was becoming, they would blame themselves and not the doctrine. The shallow-hearted critics of Capernaum listened only with the intellect, and intellect was baffled. The inner circle of the twelve attended with the heart as well; and the ties of personal affection were too strong to be severed by any difficulties about doctrine that was above their comprehension. They were willing reverently to wait for further light; and in due time the further light came, and with it satisfaction and intellectual rest. And many trusting Christians have a similar experience. From this line of thought we find that the personal historical Christ may be apprehended, and loved, and trusted, even when the intellect is baffled in its efforts to comprehend difficult doctrines found in the Bible.

We should never forget in dealing with difficulties, whether in ourselves or in others, that nowhere is it said, "Believe all the doctrines and statements in the Bible, and thou shalt be saved"; but, "Believe on the Lord Jesus Christ, and thou shalt be saved." Christ is the centre of the Christian religion, and the object of our faith.

In addressing the Jewish Rabbis, Christ Himself puts this thought very clearly: "Ye search the Scriptures, for in them ye think ye have eternal life, and they are they indeed which testify of Me, and ye will not come unto Me that ye might have life" (John v. 39). They sought peace and reconciliation with God by the study of doctrine, instead of by coming to Christ. A man may search the Scriptures, he may be thoroughly familiar with the Bible, and be able to accept its doctrines and harmonize its statements—in other words, he may be thoroughly orthodox—and yet he may not have personally accepted Christ as his Saviour. This was the condition of the Jewish Rabbis whom Jesus addressed. On the other hand, a man may be personally drawn to Christ, and love Him, and trust Him, and be saved, and yet have difficulties about many statements in the Bible—and especially about certain interpretations of theologians. There is scarcely a difficult text in the Bible about which eminent Christian men do not hold different opinions. This simply proves that our knowledge of Biblical truth is not yet perfect, that we need more light. However, all Christian men, although they may differ on many minor points, have no difficulty in agreeing about the great central truths of Christianity. They are so plainly revealed that they do not admit of any difference of opinion. The enemies of Christianity are fond of pointing to the divisions in the Christian Church, with the object of showing that the different sections in the Church hold very different views of Christianity. But take those sections that are at the very opposite poles of thought,—take the Romanist and Ritualist, on the one hand, and the Evangelical Presbyterian and Methodist on the other,—and see how they agree as to the historical facts of Christianity. They all agree that Jesus came to this world, lived a holy life, healed the sick, raised the dead, died on the cross for the sins of others, rose again the third day, ascended to heaven, and will come again in great glory, and be the Judge of quick and dead. They all believe that He instituted the Lord's Supper, that by His Spirit He dwells in the hearts of those who love Him, giving them a new life and power over sin. They all believe that the Bible is the Word of God, that holy men of old spoke as they were moved by the Holy Ghost. They all believe that Christ was Divine, and that He is the Saviour of all who put their trust in Him.

God, in His great goodness, has made everything that is essential to salvation so plain, that "he may run that readeth it"; and in His wisdom He has left many things obscure to invite and compel close and earnest study—things, too, that are not to be revealed until the last times. The earnest student of Scripture, therefore, ought not to be discouraged when he finds many things in the Bible hard to be understood, but remember that his soul's salvation does not depend upon a clear apprehension of everything contained in the Bible, but upon the personal acceptance of Christ, and devoted attachment to Him as Saviour, and Helper, and Friend.

It is very commonly assumed that the Bible, as a whole, is the foundation of Christianity; and the enemies of the Christian religion imagine that if they can detect any inconsistencies or contradictions in the Bible, they have, as a matter of course, demolished Christianity. But Christ, and not the Bible, is the foundation of Christianity and the citadel of our faith. When men come to you, therefore, and tell you that it is absurd to believe that Joshua was able by his command to cause the sun to stand still and prolong the natural day till Israel vanquished the enemy; or to believe that Jonah could exist for three days in the belly of the whale, your simple answer is, " I am not asked to believe in Joshua or in Jonah, but in Jesus." If you can answer the objector on his own ground, and show that there is no real difficulty in such events, so much the better. But if you cannot you are entitled to say, Christ is the foundation of my hopes. " Other foundation can no man lay than that is laid, which is Jesus Christ." Your objections do not touch the Rock upon which we Christians have planted our feet. Are you prepared to find any flaws in His character ? Are you competent to correct and improve His teaching ?

Have you wisdom enough and genius enough to originate a better plan of salvation than that which He introduced ? Can you communicate to helpless, tried, tempted souls the power over sin and temptation that He gives to those that love Him ? Can you provide a scheme of redemption that will at the same time uphold the holiness of God, and yet allow Him to extend mercy and pardon to those who have transgressed His law ? Can you develop a system of philosophy that will lift up the fallen, and restore the prodigal to the paths of virtue ? Can you enable the dying to meet the King of terrors in peace, and light up for them the valley of the shadow of death ? Can you give to them any words of comfort that will compare with the precious words of my Lord, " In My Father's house are many mansions. . . . I go to prepare a place for you ".; " Let not your heart be troubled, neither let it be afraid " ? If you cannot provide all these helps and all these comforts as a substitute for my Saviour and my Bible, then I must cling to my Rock, Christ Jesus, with all the mystery that surrounds His birth and mission, with all the difficulties that cling to His death and resurrection, and with all the glory and comfort attached to His ascension and intercession. And I must cling to the precious promises of the Bible that so fully meet my every need and my every desire, notwithstanding the difficult passages scattered up and down in its pages. If you thus take your stand upon Christ —His life, His character, His teaching, His death and resurrection—you will soon find that all doubts and difficulties have vanished from your mind, like morning mists before the rising sun.

VIII.

PENTECOSTAL PRAYING AND PREACHING.

"And when they had prayed the place was shaken where they were assembled together ; and they were all filled with the Holy Ghost, and they spake the word of God with boldness."—ACTS iv. 31.

THE early history of the Christian Church is full of interest and instruction. For fascinating interest no story of adventure can compare with it. For deeds of noble heroism the world has never produced men like Peter, and John, and Paul. The story of their heroic lives thrills us and inspires us as no work of fiction could possibly do. If you have a longing for the marvellous, here you have signs and wonders far transcending the boldest flights of imagination. If you want to see the sublime in character—and this is certainly the highest form of sublimity—you have it in the fearlessness and faithfulness of these brave, heroic men of God, defying danger and even death that they may do God's will, and bring blessing and salvation to their fellow-men. There is no record of valour and heroism in all history that can compare with the unwavering and persistent courage of these holy men. And the moral sublimity of their lives is immensely heightened when we remember that they braved the rage of enemies and the power of fanatical rulers, not for their own sake, not to promote selfish ends, not to minister to their own ambition, not for any earthly reward, but to obey God, and bring blessing to the world. It is a marvellous sight, seen nowhere outside of Christianity.

The ambition of conquest and the desire for fame prompted Alexander the Great, and Cæsar, and Charlemagne, and Napoleon, and others to do and to dare much; and the world has called them heroes. But the fact that they braved dangers, not for duty, not for liberating the oppressed, nor to make the world brighter, and happier, and better, but from greed of power and for purely personal ends, greatly detracts from the moral value of their courage. They were indeed brave men and skilful generals, but their lives were not sublime. Selfishness and sublimity are never found together. But these early disciples give up home comforts, and endure hardships and imprisonment and scourging that others may be brought out of darkness into the light, and liberty, and joy of the Gospel. It is this spirit of self-denial and self-sacrifice alone that can give true dignity and sublimity to life. It proves that the life is linked on to divinity— that the power of Christ rests upon the men, lifting them up far above those who know not God, and care not for Christ's example.

Now where shall we seek the explanation of this wonderful power as seen in these humble men? Do we not find it in the fact that they were men of prayer— that they held close and constant fellowship with God —that they did His will and sought His guidance in everything? Yes; this is the grand secret of their boldness and power, and the only explanation of their noble self-sacrificing lives. They pray to God, and God answers their prayer. They live with God, and God lives in them. They are in perfect sympathy with God, and they feel the quickening touch of His Spirit. God, by His Spirit, holds fellowship with their spirits, clothing them with Divine power. Herein we see the strength of Christianity. It invests men with a power not their own—power over sin, power to endure hardships, and power over men. That such is the case is abundantly attested by the lives of these early Christians; and every holy man has proved it in his own experience. To all such the power of prayer is not simply a matter of faith, but a matter of positive knowledge.

The value of prayer is seen also in the fact that Christ prayed on every great emergency, besides habitually retiring for prolonged seasons of communion with God. These men perform mighty works, but never in their own name. They always obtain power direct from God. The lame man is healed "in the name of Jesus Christ of Nazareth"; and he gives praise to God for the blessing received. The Apostles will take no credit to themselves: "Ye men of Israel, why marvel ye at this? or why look ye so earnestly on us, as though by our own power or holiness we had made this man to walk?" (Acts iii. 12.) Men who practise magic and perform wonders by their own skill, are never found attributing the power and giving the glory to another. Christianity alone does this.

The matter of their prayer also is worthy of special notice, as it proves them to be utterly unselfish. They do not pray for personal safety, or deliverance from danger. That seems to be a matter of no concern to them. " Lord, grant unto Thy servants that with all boldness they may speak Thy Word . . . and that signs and wonders may be done by the name of Thy holy Child Jesus." They ask for courage. They ask God to make them heroes. How conscious they were of their own weakness! How much they felt their need of Divine help in witnessing for Christ! They had not forgotten the words of the Lord Jesus: " Without Me ye can do nothing " (John xv. 5) " Abide in Me, and I in you." So they are careful to abide in Christ by faith, and prayer, and holy fellowship ; and they become heroes—mighty men of valour, strong in the Lord and in the power of His might. " They were all filled with the Holy Ghost, and they spake the word of God with boldness." And this, all in answer to earnest believing prayer. Surely there could be no more convincing evidence of the power of prayer.

And what a beautifully instructive lesson we have here ! When they were in difficulty or in danger, and knew not what to do, at once they lay the whole matter before God in prayer, proving that they had no doubt as to the efficacy of prayer.

The subject-matter of their prayer is most instructive. They do not pray for everything they can think of. They go at once to the point. They tell God that they are threatened, and they ask for strength to enable them to be faithful. They lay no plans. They hold no conference as to the best methods to be adopted. They leave all with God, knowing that He will guide them in the right way. They do not need human counsel when they are sure of God's direction. They say, in effect: "Lord, we are Thine; we are ready to do Thy will; we are ready to suffer for Thy name; do Thou guide us and give us strength to endure." They were ready to make any sacrifice of goods, of comfort, of reputation, of life even, so that the Lord Jesus might be magnified before men. Here, then, is the grand secret of their marvellous power. They were men of prayer, and faith, and self-sacrifice, having no other aim or desire than to do God's will; and God fills their hearts with joy and gladness, and clothes them with power. They ask for boldness to speak for Christ, not to fight their enemies, not to raise a revolution by stirring up the people against their rulers; but "boldness to speak Thy Word." The one overmastering desire in their hearts is to have courage and opportunity to tell their fellow-men what great things the Lord had done for them.

One of God's greatest gifts to man is the gift of speech. Among living creatures man only possesses speech. Where there is soul there is speech. In this respect man is made in the image of God. And when the image of God in us, lost by the fall, is restored in the new birth, we ought to have our speech sanctified and consecrated to God. Our tongues should be loosed to speak for Christ. The first impulse of a new-born soul is to speak to others of a Saviour's love, and to persuade them to come to Him. This is a never-failing proof of the new life in the heart; and it is the grand qualification, as it is our commission, for preaching the Gospel. Prayer and the gift of the Holy Ghost necessarily precede preaching. That is God's order, as seen in the history of the Church of Christ in Pentecostal times. First, the patient waiting in prayer and faith for the baptism of the Spirit. Then, but not till then, the preaching with power. Jesus Himself received the baptism of the Holy Ghost before He formally entered upon His public ministry. So it was with the disciples. They had to tarry at Jerusalem until they were "endued with power from on high.' There were prayer and pleading, earnest wrestling with God for power and courage; but there was no aggressive work—no testimony for Christ, no pleading with men, no persuasive preaching of the word. They had first to receive before they could give. There was, first, prayer with one accord in one place. There was perfect harmony and goodwill—all waiting and praying for the same blessing. They attempted to do nothing, they could do nothing, in the way of teaching, and preaching, and testifying until they were endued with power. But now their united prayer is answered. They receive the baptism of the Spirit, and they are ready to preach the Word of salvation. Peter stands up and addresses the astonished multitude. He at once plants his feet upon the Prophets and the Psalms. He goes to the promises of the Word. He reminds them of the prophecy of Joel and points to its fulfilment. He does not attempt to argue the matter. He simply quotes the prophecy and promise, and points to the historical fact, known to them all, as the fulfilment of the prophecy. And then with marvellous courage and power he brings home to them the terrible guilt of crucifying the Messiah: "Let all the house of Israel know assuredly that God hath made that same Jesus, whom ye crucified, both Lord and Christ." That is brave language ; but from whom ? Is the preacher the same who quailed like a coward a few days before in the presence of a servant maid, and with trembling lips denied his Lord ? Is the Peter of Pentecostal power the Peter of Pilate's hall ? The same indeed, and yet not the same. He is no longer tremulous with fear ; but, filled with holy fire, he presses home the tremendous accusation, and charges them with the murder of the Holy One of God. Their terrible crime is brought home to their consciences by the Holy Spirit. They are pricked in their hearts, and cry out in deepest anxiety, "Men and brethren, what shall we do ? "

Now let it be noted that this was the first sermon preached in the newly-organized Church. It may, therefore, safely be taken as a model of what preaching ought to be. First, it was founded on the Word of God and the historical facts of Christianity. Second, it presented Christ as the Saviour of the world. And third, it brought home to their consciences what was wrong in their lives, and they were pricked in their hearts. If the pulpit is to maintain its power it must give prominence to these three things. God cannot give His blessing where His Word and His Son are not magnified. It is the Word of God, and not the word of man, that is "quick, and powerful, and sharper than any two-edged sword, piercing even to the dividing asunder of soul and spirit, and is a discerner of the thoughts and intents of the heart." When the Apostles preached, they preached the Word of God ; and it was the Word that was with power. If preaching at any time loses its power, it is because Christ and His Word and Spirit are not honoured. God will honour them that honour Him. When preaching has ceased to be a power, as has often been the case in nominally Christian Churches, it is no proof that the Gospel has lost its power. Preaching has lost its power, because it leaves out the Gospel. Pentecostal preaching, which honours Christ and the Word of God, will always have power over men.

When a man is in earnest about his soul's salvation it is not fine phrases and faultless rhetoric that he wants. He must have the sure Word of God to rest upon. That only can inspire confidence. An earnest man is not going to rest his hopes for eternity upon the word of a man, however true and holy he may be. He wants to know God's mind on the matter, and that can be found only in His Word. No words of man, however tender and sympathetic, can take the place of God's Word in comforting human hearts.

But Pentecostal preaching also magnified Christ. A little study of the history of the early Christian Church, as recorded in the Acts of the Apostles, will convince any one that the burden of the Apostles' teaching and preaching was Christ crucified and Christ risen. "Daily in the temple and in every house they ceased not to teach and preach Jesus Christ" (Acts v. 42). The sole crime for which Stephen, the first martyr, was stoned, was preaching Jesus and the Resurrection.

But, further, Pentecostal preaching was pointed and piercing. Peter brought home to his hearers their particular sin so pointedly and so powerfully that they were pricked in their hearts, and cried out, "Men and brethren, what shall we do?" When Stephen preached his powerful sermon which cost him his life, his hearers "were cut to the heart, and gnashed on him with their teeth" (Acts vii. 54). This conviction of the heart is the result which the preacher must always seek; for there can be no conversion, and no reformation of life, until there is conviction of sin. This can be accomplished only by the Word of God brought home with power to the heart by the Spirit of God. A man must be convinced that he is a sinner and needs a Saviour, before he can be persuaded to accept Christ. And if Christ is not accepted as our Saviour from sin—from the love and power of sin— He can be nothing to us. All men are sinners; and, as such, they are lost, condemned, and need to be saved. Hence they must be told that "the Son of man came to seek and to save that which was lost." The preaching that falls short of this fails altogether.

It is characteristic of Pentecostal preaching that the Apostles did not prophesy smooth words to the people. They did not seek to please men, but to save them. Above all things they were faithful to their trust. Whether men will hear, or whether they will forbear, it is the preacher's duty to bring them face to face with their particular sins and shortcomings. Peter, in the first part of his powerful address, takes the shed blood of Christ, as it were, and pours it in a scorching flood upon the heads of those who rejected Him. And then, when their terrible sin is brought home to their consciences, he at once presents the same blood as the blood of blessing. The blood that was shed *by* them is now presented as the blood shed *for* them. Their relation to the blood is changed the moment they see their error and repent of the sin of rejecting the Saviour. Before it was Christ crucified *by* them ; now it is Christ crucified *for* them. Before they were guilty of the blood of Christ; now the blood of Christ washes away their guilt. In the one case it is trampling under foot the Son of God, and doing despite unto the Spirit of grace. In the other it is lovingly and gratefully accepting Christ as Saviour, and Helper, and Friend.

This, then, was the sum and substance of the Apostle's preaching. They preached Christ crucified and Christ risen, and "through Him the resurrection of the dead " (Acts iv. 2).

What an elevating effect it must have had upon the people to be convinced by indubitable proofs of their own personal immortality—that this life was not all of life—that man was nobler, grander, better than the beasts that perish. The Sadducees were doing all in their power to destroy the hope and belief in a future life, just as the Pharisees had laboured to make religion a thing merely of outward ritual and ceremony. Christ and the Apostles infused new life and power into religion by making it a thing of the heart, and by making it take in the future as well as the present life.

The Apostles did not seek merely to please their hearers. Their great aim was to teach truth—truth about God, truth about Christ, truth about man's own conduct and needs, truth about the future life. Above all, they magnified Christ in their preaching, and gave Him the glory of all their wonderful work "Give me a penny," said a poor cripple to Peter and

John at the Beautiful Gate of the Temple. They reply, "In the name of Jesus Christ of Nazareth, rise up and walk." He enters the temple walking, and leaping, and praising God. At once the Apostles disclaim the possession of any miracle-working power of their own. They magnify Christ before men. They declare that the work was not theirs, but God's. They will not allow anything to withdraw the eyes of the astonished multitude from Christ.

When Da Vinci, the distinguished artist, finished his celebrated picture, The Last Supper, he took a friend to see it before exhibiting it in public. "Exquisite!" exclaimed his friend; "that wine-cup seems to stand out from the table like solid, glittering silver!" The devout artist, instead of being complimented, instantly took his brush and dashed out the cup, saying, "I meant that the figure of Christ should be the most striking part of the picture. I cannot allow anything to come between the eye of the beholder and my Lord." So it was with the apostles. The eyes of all were directed to Christ. And so it must always be if the strength of Christianity is to be judged by the power of preaching. If we would see Pentecostal power we must have Pentecostal preaching. Our preaching must have Christ as its central and most prominent figure. Nothing but a lifted-up Christ can permanently attract men. "I, if I be lifted up, will draw all men unto Me." And nothing but the power of the Holy Spirit can convince men of their need of Christ. Hence we must preach the Word, present Christ, and pray for the power of the Spirit.

IX.

THE MYSTERY OF GOD.

"Clouds and darkness are round about Him."—PSALM xcvii. 2.

OUR first thoughts of God are always thoughts of wonder and awe. Clouds and darkness are round about Him. His mode of existence is to us a profound mystery. I have no doubt but it is God's will that it should be so. First impressions are always lasting; and our early thoughts of God, so full of mystery and wonder, help all through life to keep us humble and reverent. Although God has chosen to give us a very full revelation of His will in His Word, and a perfect revelation of His heart in the love and tenderness of His Son Jesus Christ, yet He has not chosen to unveil all the mystery of His being. God does not wish to reveal to us here and now all His majesty and glory. Throughout the Bible, and in the book of Psalms especially, we see how language struggles to utter a full description of God; at one time going down to the depth of darkness, and again mounting up to the light of heaven: "He made darkness His secret place." "Clouds and darkness are round about Him." And again, " Who coverest Thyself with light as with a garment." Darkness and Light! They seem at first sight to be contradictory. But the more we ponder these expressions the more do we see them to be true. Such language clearly implies that the human tongue cannot utter all of God. It means that in some aspects of His nature He is revealed to us, while in other aspects He is hidden. It means that the mode of God's existence is above the comprehension of man. God is greater than we know. And so it must ever be. The infinite God must ever be beyond the grasp of finite creatures, else He would not be God. If man could know all of God, then God would not be greater than man. It is the glory of the Bible that it sets forth a God far above any of His creatures. Heathen religions strive to bring their gods down to the level of weak and erring mortals, clothing them with human passions, and even with low vices. But one of the grand proofs that the Bible is God's Word—His own revelation of Himself—is that it never panders to the corrupt tastes and desires of men. It presents to us a pure and holy God, a righteous and just God, a God of majesty and glory; and yet a God so condescending that weak, erring mortals are encouraged to draw near to Him. Little by little He reveals Himself to our opening natures, letting us see as much of His glory and goodness as we are capable of taking in.

However fully God may have revealed Himself in His Word and in His Son, our apprehension of God must always be just in proportion as we have taken on His image. "The pure in heart shall see God" (Matt. v. 8). Where there is sin and selfishness the vision of God is obscured. But those who live in the love and fear of God, and hold fellowship with Him, will be always receiving new and wondrous revelations of His glory and perfections, as well as of His love and constant care.

To profound and reverent minds the study of God must always afford fresh interest, because we are always learning more and more of His perfections, and of His wondrous condescension to our weakness, and of His marvellous patience with us in our waywardness and shortcomings. It is one of the glories of Revelation that it reveals to us a God infinite in His perfections and boundless in His love. We do not want, if we could, to bring God down to our own level. Take away the mystery from God, and He will, in a large measure, lose His charm for us. Despoil Christ of His divinity, and make Him a mere man, deny His miracles of healing, and convert the story of His marvellous life and profound teaching into a mere myth, as Rationalists have attempted in vain to do, and you take away all interest in the study of His life, as well as all value from His death upon the Cross.

God has chosen to clothe Himself with mystery as well as with light; and they lose much who attempt to remove the cloud of mystery from His being, in order, as they think, to make God more intelligible to men. If we bring God down to man's low level we cannot worship and adore Him. It is because God is so far above us in His love and perfections that the thought of God has such a marvellous power over our life and conduct. It is just because we can never exhaust His perfections that we can study God all the days of our life with increasing interest and enthusiasm. Awe and mystery—some unfathomed depths—are necessary to reverence, and are essential to continued love and regard. Our deepest, truest, most abiding love is called forth towards those who have new depths in their nature for us to explore; and if there are no such depths there we soon tire of their friendship. Life in their company soon becomes monotonous, and fails to give pleasure. The friend whom we can truly love, and whose companionship we can ever enjoy, is the one in whose noble heart we are continually finding new depths, as little by little we are permitted to draw nearer and nearer And each new revelation of his worth and goodness fills us with new wonder and delight. Every new discovery affords us new and increasing pleasure. The friends that wear well are those in whose nature there is this element of mystery—whose lives are not all on the surface, who have hidden resources of love, and goodness, and wisdom, from which we can continually draw.

No one wants to explore all the depths of a noble nature at the first interview. We wish to feel that at each successive interview there will be new discoveries, and, therefore, new pleasures for us. For the same reason, I would not, if I could, remove the mystery from God, or explore all the depths of His nature in this present life, just as I do not wish to know at once all the depths of love and goodness in my friend. I delight in the thought that all through the eternal ages, while enjoying intimate fellowship with God, we shall go on learning more and more about the mystery of His being, the perfections of His nature, the wisdom and love of all His purposes and plans, and His dealings with us here in training us for fellowship with Him, and fitting us to receive new revelations of His glory and goodness. It is in love and wisdom, therefore, that God clothes Himself in mystery. We would not remove the clouds and darkness, if we could.

God not only does not, but He cannot, fully reveal Himself to our finite faculties. He would first require to endow us with infinite faculties. We cannot fully reveal ourselves to a child with its present capacities. To him "clouds and darkness" are about all our profounder moods. To a man, our equal, it is all clear. To him we are "clothed with light, as with a garment." But it is not so with the child. To him our profounder moods and nobler pleasures are shrouded in darkness. We must not expect, therefore, that in our present state, with our imperfect, finite capacities, and these blunted by sin, we can comprehend all of God. His mode of Existence as Trinity in Unity, His ability to be everywhere present, His capability of loving the unlovely without being contaminated by that love, may all seem to us to be shrouded in darkness; but to higher, purer intelligences, and to us in a higher and holier state, they may all seem as clear as the light of day.

God exists; God is real; God is light; God is love; God is good;—these are great truths, and our inability fully to comprehend them does not alter the facts. The sun exists; the sun is real; the sun is light; and although the untutored mind cannot understand how the sun can go on for centuries, burning and giving out light and heat, still the fact remains all the same. The existence of the sun does not depend upon our ability to comprehend its mode of existence; neither does the existence of God depend upon our ability fully to comprehend Him.

If we seek to know God by means of the intellect alone we must certainly fail. Human Reason is powerless to comprehend God. God can be known by us only through Revelation and experience. If we seek to know God through the intellect and by the exercise of reason He will be to us as clouds and darkness. But if we seek to know Him through the revelation which He has given of Himself in His Word, and in His Son, and in His personal dealings with those who love Him, we shall soon find that "at the brightness that was before Him His thick clouds passed," and all will be clearly revealed. If we would know God as He is, we must be willing to use the helps He has given us. We must study His Word and the life of His Son, and we must experience the power and enjoy the presence of His Spirit. What would we think of a man who undertook to study the stars, and yet refused the aid afforded by the telescope? The exercise of his own unaided powers would never give him a knowledge of Astronomy. If a man would study the heavenly bodies to any purpose, he must accept and use the helps which Science has placed within his reach. And so it is with every branch of science and knowledge. We must not trust to our own reason and powers of observation merely, but use all the helps we can obtain.

We pity or despise the man who in our day refuses

the help of science, and insists on the belief of the ancients that the earth is stationary, and that the sun revolves around it every day. He uses his eye only, and trusts to appearances, and because the sun seems to revolve around the earth, he believes it does so, although it involves the absurdity of the sun bounding through space at the rate of nearly half a million miles a minute. And so it is in reference to our knowledge of God. If we refuse to make use of the helps placed within our reach we must remain in ignorance of Him, and our beliefs respecting Him will be only crude absurdities. We cannot comprehend God, any more than Astronomy, by our own unaided reason. God has provided helps for us, and if we would have accurate knowledge of Him, we must use these helps in a reverent spirit. The man who refuses to take God's Word, and the life and teaching of His Son, and the help of His Spirit, in his search to know God, has no right to express an opinion about God. If he is ignorant of these helps through no fault of his own we pity him. If he is wilfully ignorant we ignore him. We must come from under the clouds and darkness of ignorance and prejudice before we can truly know God. Until we learn to study Him in His Word, and in His Son, and by the help of His Spirit, clouds and darkness will be round about Him.

God, to most men, is a mystery. Clouds and darkness are round about Him. Will the time ever come when the mystery shall be taken away—when to us He will be "clothed with light as with a garment"? Many in our day speak of God as if that time had already come. They talk flippantly of God, as if they knew all about

Him. But, in an older and more reverent age, men stood in awe of God, and acknowledged that He was greater than they knew.

There are others—very good people perhaps—who seem to think that, if God is to be loved and trusted, they must make Him very simple and easily comprehended, and take away from Him all that is mysterious and awe-inspiring. But this is a hindrance to worship, and not a help. The object of our reverence and worship must be recognized by us as superior to ourselves. We cannot worship and adore one who is regarded merely as our equal. We may love, and trust, and admire, but we cannot worship him.

There was a time when God was represented as so full of terrible majesty that men were afraid to draw near to Him, and, therefore, could not love Him with that intimate affection which would enable them to tell Him all their troubles, and trials, and sorrows. Instead of complying with the exhortation, "Stand in awe, and sin not," they stood in awe, and loved not. That was carrying the feeling of reverence and worship too far. It was virtually shutting out God from their lives and from their love. Others, in their endeavour to guard against this danger, have gone to the opposite extreme, and would take away from God everything of majesty and mystery—everything that inspires awe and reverence. The danger of such teaching is that it tends to bring God down to man's own level, and, therefore, to bring man into too familiar terms with God. They soon come to think that they have a right to reason with God, and to set up their wisdom against His in the details of duty. Now this is a most dangerous position to take up; and it never could be taken up, if men did not, in their own minds, strip God of all those glorious and majestic attributes which inspire awe, and reverence, and the feeling of worship. Both extremes are dangerous. We must not invest God with such terrible majesty as to make it difficult to come to Him for help and guidance in every time of need, making love, and trust, and confidence impossible. And we must retain as much of majesty, and mystery, and glory in our conception of God as to compel our reverence and worship. We cannot truly and pro-. foundly love one whom we do not in some degree reverence, and regard as our superior, in some respects at least.

This principle holds good even in human loves. Each must see in the other some traits of character superior to those traits in themselves. The woman must see strength, courage, manliness, nobleness of mind, high moral qualities, or superiority of some kind, in the man, giving a tinge of reverence to her love, if it is to be deep, and true, and abiding. The man must see in the woman true feminine qualities— gentleness, affection, patience, tenderness, sympathy, or some other excellence in which she excels him— enabling him to add to his love admiration and respect. True, deep, profound love requires to have in it the element of reverence, whether the object of our love be human or Divine. Therefore, if we take away from God all elements of majesty, and mystery, and superiority, we thereby make strong, trustful love impossible. While, therefore, in all His tender attributes of love, and mercy, and pity, and sympathy towards us, God clothes Himself with light, still, as regards His grander attributes of holiness, justice, wisdom, power, "clouds and darkness are round about Him."

Not only in this life, but in heaven also, there will be mystery—mysteries and glories which will be our study throughout the eternal ages, thereby greatly enhancing our pleasure and enjoyment. There will be a fuller revelation of God in the future life. Revelation, however, is not a complete unveiling of God, but rather a changing of the veil that covers Him. Under the Old Testament Dispensation God was veiled, when He appeared to man, by a radiant, fire-like brightness, so that Moses and others did not get a full vision of God. Then again, when God revealed Himself in Christ, His glory was veiled by a human body. In heaven we shall have fuller and clearer revelations of God; but the nearer we get to Him the more wonderful will He appear to us for ever. Many things, however, that are under clouds and darkness to us now, will be clothed with light then. Light will be thrown, no doubt, upon the mode of God's existence as Father, Son, and Spirit. We know now *that* He thus exists; we may know then *how* He thus exists. The mystery may be made plain. It has been revealed to us already with sufficient clearness to assure us of the fact of the Trinity. In God the Father we see our Creator and Father, governing, training, leading us. In Christ the Son we see our Brother and Friend, living with us our human life, suffering for us, and showing us how we may overcome and be crowned with victory. In the Holy Spirit we have an ever-present spiritual presence inspiring us, guiding, helping, comforting us. We thus may know *that* God exists as a Trinity—Three in One —Father, Brother, Comforter. How He thus exists He has not yet revealed. We know the comforting fact, and that is enough for us at present. When God sees that we need more, and can bear more, He will reveal more. At present we may rest satisfied with the promise that in the future life "we shall see Him as He is," and know even as we are known.

So it is with God's omnipresence—His capability of being everywhere present. Intellect struggles with the problem, and is baffled: How can God be everywhere at the same time? But, once receive the Spirit as Comforter into your own heart, and ever after you know that He is with you. Other believers know that He is with them also as an abiding presence. Now you have, in this practical way, solved the problem. God can be present in more than one place at the same time. You know as a fact that He can be personally present with all His faithful followers. That is enough. You need not puzzle yourself with the mystery, *how* He can do this.

It is the same also with another difficulty: How can God love the unlovely, and not be contaminated with that love? You say that you cannot do it; and your reason refuses to admit that God can do it. But here, again, we know it as a fact, and that is enough for us now. Christ loved sinners. He loved us, and remained pure and free from sin. If you ask, How can God do this? the answer is, God is greater than we know. "Clouds and darkness are round about Him;" mercy and peace go before His face. If we thus study God in the light of the several revelations which He has given us in His Word, in His Son, and in His personal dealings with us by His Spirit, we shall soon obtain such a knowledge of Him as will fill us not only with wonder and awe, but with gratitude, and joy, and praise.

However, although God has been graciously pleased thus to reveal Himself to our wondering eyes, and to come out from under the clouds and darkness, and to "cover Himself with light as with a garment," still He has not removed all the mystery from His being. The incarnation of Christ helped much to reveal God. While the human body, in one sense, veiled the Divine glory, it also helped to utter it. Men could now look upon God, and they could see more of God, when veiled, than they could see of God unveiled. It was so with the disciples while Christ was with them on earth. While by toil, and weariness, and suffering He seemed to be veiling His glory, He was really uttering it. This was true especially in His death, where His Godhead, for the time, seemed not only veiled, but eclipsed. But the veiling of His glory for the moment was really the unveiling of it. It was but laying aside the earthly body that He might put on a glorious body, which more fitly uttered His divinity. By His death and resurrection He "clothed Himself with light as with a garment." Before His death His disciples loved Him dearly. However, after His resurrection, their love is not only deepened, but it is of another kind—holier, more reverent, more profound. It is mingled with mystery and awe. They hesitate to touch Him. They fear to ask Him who and what He is. The new garment of a glorified body is a new revelation; while it veils His glory, it also utters it.

Still the mystery is not wholly removed. If we would truly know Christ our love to Him must go on deepening day by day. We must get clearer heart-revelations of Him. We cannot know Him by disrobing Him of His divinity and mystery, but by reverently gazing upon His Divine glory veiled and uttered by His true humanity. Then our love will necessarily take on the element of reverence and awe, and thus become deep, and profound, and enduring.

X.

GOD IN THE LIGHT: THE TRINITY.

"God, who commanded the light to shine out of darkness, hath shined in our hearts, to give the light of the knowledge of the glory of God in the face of Jesus Christ."—2 COR. iv. 6.

IN the previous chapter we discussed THE MYSTERY OF GOD—God in the thick darkness. We are now to meditate upon God revealed—GOD IN THE LIGHT. We have seen that if we approach God by means of the intellect alone—by unaided human reason—clouds and darkness will be round about Him. No man, by searching, can find out God. The infinite God must ever be beyond the comprehension of finite minds, else He would not be God. Modern Rationalism, therefore, which would bring all truth to the touchstone of human reason, has no standing ground in all matters pertaining to God. We might as well deprive a bird of its wings, and then expect it to fly, as to expect a man to know God without the help of His Spirit, and the revelation which He has given us in His Word, and in the life of His Son.

We have also seen that the clearness of our vision of God will be just in proportion as we have taken on His image. We cannot reveal our knowledge of mathematics, or of any science, to one who has no knowledge of that science. We must first lead him step by step along the path over which we have gone, else our stores of learning must ever remain hidden from him. A man must in some measure have taken on your image—must in some measure have become like you—before you can fully reveal yourself to him.

The same law holds good in reference to the emotions of the heart. We cannot reveal our power of loving to one who does not love us. We cannot reveal our power of sympathy to one who has never been touched by pity. We cannot reveal our love of holiness, our love of God, our love of souls, to one who has had no experience of these emotions. We are frustrated in our efforts to reveal ourselves by his inexperience and incapacity. The ignorant and impure mind shuts itself out from the light, and love, and knowledge of hearts that are more ennobled and more refined. And so must it ever be in reference to our knowledge of God. We must, in some measure, have taken on His image— we must love what He loves, we must love *as* He loves, before He can fully reveal Himself to us. The revelations which God has given of Himself in His Word, and in His Son, and in His personal dealings with us in providence and by His Spirit, are all intended to bring us so near to God, and to make us so like God, that He can reveal Himself to us in all His marvellous love, and sympathy, and wisdom, and beauty.

The Apostle in the context clearly recognizes the fact that men's minds may be so blinded by the god of this world—by the love of the world, its pleasures and vices—that the light of the knowledge of the glory of

God cannot be seen. "The god of this world hath blinded the minds of them which believe not, lest the light of the Gospel of the glory of Christ, who is the image of God, should shine unto them" (2 Cor. iv. 4).

He also sets forth another great truth, teaching us that by our own unaided efforts we cannot see the glory of God's goodness. God must shine in our hearts in order to give us "the light (illumination) of the knowledge of the glory of God." He shines in our hearts by His Spirit. We cannot possibly know God except He enlightens our minds by the quickening touch of His Holy Spirit. If the sun did not shine upon us we could know but little about it. It would be impossible to give any intelligible idea of the sun— its glorious appearance, its heat, its light, its life-giving and health-imparting power—to a man who had been brought up in a dungeon, and had never seen the sun. To know the sun we must see it and feel its power. So to know God He must shine in our hearts. We must feel the comforting, warming, life-giving power of His Spirit. Paul knew no other way of knowing God. With all his study of the Hebrew Scriptures, with all his knowledge as a learned Jewish Rabbi, he did not know God until Jesus appeared to him on the way to Damascus, and the great light shone round about him, and the Spirit of God touched his spirit and removed the veil from his eyes. He is, therefore, giving a simple narrative of his own personal experience when he says, " God, who commanded the light to shine out of darkness, hath shined in our hearts to give the light of the knowledge of the glory of God in the face of Jesus Christ."

GOD IN THE LIGHT: THE TRINITY. 103

God, by His Spirit, reveals Himself to human hearts. The Holy Spirit is more than "the Comforter." He is also the Revealer. The Lord Jesus said of Him, "When He is come He will take of the things that are Mine, and will show them unto you" (John xvi. 15). It must be remembered, therefore, that we cannot know the Father or the Son except by the direct help of the Holy Spirit shining in our hearts.

The Apostle further teaches that God cannot be fully known apart from Christ. " God hath shined in our hearts to give the light of the knowledge of the glory of God *in the face of Jesus Christ*" ; " No man knoweth the Father save the Son, and he to whomsoever the Son will reveal Him " (Matt. xi. 27). It is a great and comforting truth that Jesus came to die for our sins, taking them away, "nailing them to His cross." But we must never lose sight of the fact that an essential part of His mission to earth was to reveal the Father. They lose much who lose sight of either of these great truths. If Jesus had not taken away our sins, we could never meet God in peace. Our sins, as a great mountain, would stand between us and our God. We could never see anything but His justice and terrible majesty. And, on the other hand, if we did not see Jesus drawing near to poor sinners, speaking words of kindly cheer, bearing tenderly with their shortcomings, healing their diseases, and forgiving their sins, we never could have believed that a holy and just God could love the sinner and freely forgive his sins. While, therefore, we must never lose sight of the cross, but ever look upon the death of Christ for us with wonder, and awe, and adoring love, still we must see in the life of Christ—His love, and tenderness, and sympathy—a true revelation of the heart of God. Apart from Christ we see God in the mystery of darkness. In Christ we see Him in the mystery of light.

The life of Christ and the cross of Christ do not wholly remove the mystery from the being of God; but they throw great light upon it, revealing much of His wisdom and love, as well as His holiness and justice.

> "No angel in the sky
> Can fully bear that sight;
> But downward bends his wondering eye
> At mysteries so bright."

The poet here, with true poetic instinct, grasps the correct idea of these glorious mysteries. "Mysteries so bright!" In Christ and His cross the mystery of darkness becomes the mystery of light. Light is thrown upon the mystery of God, but the mystery is not wholly removed. The mystery of God brightens wonderfully to our view in the life and cross of Christ. In the gift of the Holy Spirit this glorious mystery becomes brighter still; for the touch of the Holy Spirit is God shining in the heart, giving light and knowledge. There is not only an experimental knowledge of the presence and power of God's Spirit in the heart, but the spiritual faculty is illuminated.

What man wants, in order to get clearer views of God, is not so much a fuller revelation, a clearer unveiling of God, as inward illumination—a quickening of the spiritual sense, the opening of the eye of the soul. This is the work of the Holy Spirit. It is only when the Spirit of God touches and quickens our spiritual faculty that we are able "to see the King in His beauty." By no other means can the eye of the soul be opened and strengthened so as to behold the glory of God.

It was not until after the baptism of the Spirit on the day of Pentecost that the disciples had clear ideas of Christ and His mission. He had been with them, teaching them, and inspiring them by His presence and example; still they had no true conception of His greatness and glory. They even undertook to advise Him, to reason with Him, and to differ from Him. They saw His human goodness, but His Divine glory was veiled—veiled to them, because their eyes were not opened to behold Him. And God is veiled in mystery and darkness to many now, just because they do not let God in upon their life, because they do not let God shine in their hearts, by His Spirit, to give the light of the knowledge of the glory of God in the face of Jesus Christ.

Many who say that they believe in God, and profess to love Him, are like the savages who had a sun-dial presented to them. In their great desire to do honour to this wonderful thing that could tell them the time of day, they built a roof over it. But if that dial was ever to be of any use, they would have to break down the roof and let the sun shine upon it. So we must break down the roof, and remove every barrier, and let God shine in upon our life. This is the first step to seeing His glory, and removing the mystery and darkness that are round about Him.

Whatever mystery there may be in the doctrine of the Trinity—in God as Father, Son, and Holy Spirit—

it lets in a glorious flood of light upon the being of God, and His relation to us. Apart from the revelation of God given to us in Christ, the awful majesty of God would be crushing and confounding, as in the case of the children of Israel at the giving of the law: "They said unto Moses, Speak thou with us, and we will hear; but let not God speak with us, lest we die. . . . And the people stood afar off; and Moses drew near unto the thick darkness where God was" (Exod. xx. 19, 21). It is only "in the face of Jesus Christ" that we can look upon the glory of God.

I do not wonder that men are found who deny the doctrine of the Trinity—men who do not accept the divinity of Christ and the personality of the Holy Spirit. Such views are the natural outcome of human reason, of the endeavour of the unaided intellect to grasp the infinitely wise and infinitely loving God. God cannot be grasped by the intellect. Human reason cannot see the necessity of the Divine Redeemer dying for the sins of men. Reason cannot comprehend the personality, and presence, and power of the Holy Spirit. Speaking of these great central truths of Christianity the Apostle says, "The preaching of the cross is to them that perish foolishness, but unto us who are saved it is the power of God" (1 Cor. i. 18). "The natural man receiveth not the things of the Spirit of God, for they are foolishness unto him ; neither can he know them, because they are spiritually discerned" (1 Cor. ii. 14). Paul knew, from his own experience, that unregenerated men can see nothing but foolishness in the doctrines of Christianity. The only true antidote to intellectual difficulties is to experience the quickening power of the Holy Spirit, and to accept Jesus as Saviour and Sin-bearer. The moment we do this we have the evidence in ourselves— a felt experience of the power and blessedness of fellowship with Christ: " He that believeth on the Son of God hath the witness in himself" (1 John v. 10). Paul, as a bitter opponent of Christianity, was not convinced by the powerful arguments of Stephen, although they were sealed with his blood. Not until he saw Christ, and felt the power of His Spirit, could he be persuaded to believe that the religion of Jesus had any claim on his regard.

Suppose you were to go to a person who did not know you sufficiently well to know that you were incapable of making a false statement, and tell him that a king, or some person far above you in rank or position, had given you many costly gifts, and many proofs of personal love and regard, and he resolutely refused to believe a word of your story, how would you undertake to convince him? You might show him the gifts bearing the stamp of royalty. You might tell him many things the king had said to you, things which no one else would be likely to say. But if he were of a critical or sceptical turn of mind, he would resist all such arguments. Costly gifts might be obtained in some other way. The stamp of royalty might be forged. All these proofs of affectionate regard may have been got up for the occasion, or may be the result of an abnormal mental hallucination. The sceptical mind will find an abundance of arguments to resist truth that it is not willing to receive. Now how could you bring conviction home to such a mind? Is

there no way in which you can make your own words
good? Is there no method by which you can remove
the false impression from his sceptical mind? I know
of only one method; but it is an effectual one. You
say to him, "I am not the only one among humble
people who has received such tokens of affectionate
regard. The king bestows similar favours upon all
who love him; and he will do the same for you, if you
come to him." "What! Will the king give *me* such
costly gifts, and such proofs of his love?" "Most
certainly he will," you reply, "if you will agree to
accept them on his terms." "Indeed! What are his
terms?" "Perfect love and perfect self-surrender."
He goes to the king, receives the promised blessings
and gifts; and what is the result? Does he say of his
own gifts, "They may have come from some other
source, and my joy and happiness may, after all, be only
a mental hallucination"? Ah, no! All his sceptical
thoughts go to the winds. He has seen the king;
he has heard his gracious words; he has shared his
love; and now he can never again doubt the goodness,
and love, and liberality of the king. Nay, more; he
ceases not to declare with earnestness and power what
a loving friend and helper he has in the king. So
personal experience of God's love and goodness, personal experience of Christ lifting up the burden of
unforgiven sin from our troubled hearts, personal
experience of the comforting and sustaining power of
the Holy Spirit, is the one sure evidence to our anxious,
questioning minds that Father, Son, and Holy Spirit—
the one only true God—are one in love to men, one in
purpose and effort in blessing mankind, as they are one

in will, in essence, in power, and in glory. It is when the Holy Spirit shines upon our hearts, enlightening the darkness, and enabling us to see God in the face of Jesus Christ, that the mystery of darkness is converted into the mystery of light. It is not the removal of the mystery, but the brightening of it. Even when seen "in the face of Jesus Christ" there will still be unfathomable depths in the being of God, in His purposes and plans, and in His marvellous love and wisdom, which will engage our thoughts, and elicit our wonder and admiration throughout the eternal ages.

The existence of God as Trinity in Unity has many parallels in Nature. We have a beautiful illustration in the plant—Root, Stem, Sap—all performing distinct functions, and yet a complete unity, each being necessary to the others. The Root, like the Father, is unseen, but is essential to the Stem. The Stem gives visibility to the Root, and bears the branches, and can say, "I and my Father, the Root, are one." The Sap is the life of both Root and Stem,—the bond of union, making both one. So the Holy Spirit is the life of Father and Son, and the bond of union, making them one. Thus Father, Son, and Holy Spirit make one God, just as Root, Stem, and Sap make one plant. By carrying the illustration further we see what point there is in the words of Jesus, "I am the Vine, ye are the branches." A branch that is united to the vine partakes of its sap, its life. It is fed by the sap of the vine, which flows from the root, through the stem, to all the branches. The sap is the life of the branches, and the bond of union making them one with the stem and root. So the Holy Spirit, proceeding from the

Father, through the Son, is the life of all true believers, and the bond of union making them one with Christ. It is because the Holy Spirit is "the Spirit of Christ" that the Apostle, whose body was "the temple of the Holy Ghost," could say, "Christ liveth in me," and could claim Christ as his life : "When Christ, who is our life, shall appear." In Christ and the Spirit God is no longer seen in the mystery of darkness, but in the mystery of light.

To the heathen mind God is mysterious because He is shrouded in clouds and darkness. He is awful and mysterious, like the thunder and the storm. To the devout believer, God is also mysterious; He is above his comprehension; but He is mysterious like the sun —mysterious because radiant with light and glory. Go to the earnest heathen, who has intelligence enough to rise to the idea of one God, but who has no revelation of God in Christ, and whisper in his ear the name of GOD. He is puzzled, and gazes into the profound darkness, and says, "Yes, I know there is a God above us, but I cannot find Him; I cannot know Him." Go to the humble and unlettered Christian, and ask him about God, and he looks up to the brightness, and says, "Yes, He is my Father, my Saviour, my ever-present Friend and Comforter. He loves me, and I love Him. In the darkness and in the light He is with me as the joy and light of my life, my Guide and my Keeper. He is to me the chief among ten thousand, the altogether lovely. He is greater than I know, yet He condescends to dwell in my heart."

The nearer we get to God, and the more constant our fellowship with Him, the more will we see in Him to call forth our wonder, and to fill us with reverence and awe. Great and reverent souls will not talk flippantly of God, nor claim to be able to pronounce upon the mystery of His being, or to declare the mode of His existence to be other than that which He has revealed to us in His Word, and in His Son, and by the personal presence and power of His Spirit. Those who persistently refuse to accept the revelation which He has been pleased to give of Himself, must, like the untutored savage, be content to have God shrouded in the mystery of darkness. And we, who have received, and who delight to accept the clearer light of Revelation, must not rest satisfied with merely believing the doctrines about God and Christ as revealed in His Word. We must daily seek the enlightenment and purifying power of the Holy Spirit. We must come before God with humble, contrite hearts, seeking to be cleansed from all sin. We must yield up our hearts to Him in reverent love, and our wills in cheerful self-surrender. We must take Jesus to be our personal Saviour, not only from the punishment of sin, but also from the love of sin and the power of sin. We must do His will with delight, loving what He loves, and hating what He hates. We must open the door of our hearts to the Saviour who stands knocking without—the golden gate of love, through which alone He can enter. Then He will be to us, not clouds, and darkness, and terrible majesty, but " the Lord will be to us an everlasting light, and our God our glory." By His Spirit He will constantly shine in our hearts, and "give us the light of the knowledge of the glory of God in the face of Jesus Christ."

XI.

CHRIST IN THE FLESH: THE INCARNATION.

"Jesus, who, being in the form of God, counted not equality with God a thing to be graspingly retained; but emptied Himself, taking the form of a servant, being made in the likeness of men . . . and becoming obedient unto death."—PHIL. ii. 6-8.

IN this wonderful passage we get a profound insight into the depth of Christ's humiliation, consequent upon His consenting to become the Redeemer of man. He, who was the eternal God, co-equal with the Father in power, and wisdom, and glory, for the time disrobes Himself of these high distinctions, assumes the form of frail humanity, submits to take the position of a servant in obedience and submission, that He may become, in His human life, a perfect example for humanity, and by His death expiate their sins on the cross. The human mind cannot fathom the awful deep of that *Kenosis*,—that emptying,—nor say how far, for the time, He laid aside His divinity, to be taken on again as He grew in wisdom and grace and resisted temptation. The one thing certain is that the Incarnation was made possible by His laying aside, for the time, the outward manifestation of His Divine glory and majesty. The expression cannot mean less than this. He also retained all that was essential to a true conception of Godhead. In becoming Man He did not cease to be God. He was throughout His earthly life the God-man. A true Divine nature and a real human nature were united in "the Man Christ Jesus." In this union we have the mystery of His Being. We know *that* it is, we do not know *how* it is. It is the union of two natures in one Person, not of two persons in one nature.

The union was such that there was no commingling or confusion of the Divine nature with the human nature. The human nature was not deified and endowed with Divine attributes by being taken into conjunction with the Divine nature. The human body of Christ, for example, was not lifted up out of the sphere of limitation, and endowed with the attribute of Omnipresence. We never find Jesus addressing the multitude in two places at the same time. In assuming human nature He necessarily assumed those limitations which are inherent in a real human body. His limitation in space, His gradual growth in wisdom, the entire subordination of His will to the Father's, afford most conclusive proof of His true humanity, greater even than His being hungry, and thirsty, and weary.

As the human nature of Christ was not lifted up above a true humanity by its union with the Divine, thus becoming something else than a real human nature, so the Divine nature was not degraded by its union with the human. By becoming the God-man Jesus did not become less than God, although for the time there was a veiling of His Divine glory and majesty. If it be asked, How can these things be? the answer is, They are proved by the facts of His life. Our conception of His Being, however difficult it may be to our intellectual grasp, must be founded upon fact. No conscientious student of the life of Christ can come to any other conclusion than that He was both the Son of Man and the Son of God. His divinity was as real as His humanity. He read the secret thoughts of men's hearts. He spake as never man spake, a marvellous power attending His words. He healed all manner of disease with a word. He raised the dead. Only God could do such mighty works.

Christ Himself was the first Christian. His earthly life was meant to be the type of all true Christian life — a life truly human, and yet directed and inspired by the Divine Spirit. He passed through all the stages of life from infancy up to manhood. He was tempted in all points like as we are. In childhood He was subject to His parents. Throughout life He was always submissive to the will of the Father. His life was lived in closest contact with men; and He was not ashamed to call them brethren. He entered into the life of humanity, rejoicing in the joys of men, and weeping with those who wept. How literally true are the words of St. John : " The Word was made flesh, and dwelt among us "!

If the Saviour of man had dwelt apart from men, and had never experienced humiliation, hunger, pain, weariness, sorrow, temptation; if He had never felt the deep soul-agony of being rejected and despised by those whom He came to benefit and bless; if He had merely hovered like an angel over this world of sin, without mingling with the sinning multitude,—then His pure unselfish life would be, to those longing to walk in His footsteps, only a hollow mockery, and could not possibly become to erring mortals a source of stimulus and strength. But the great and precious truth of the Incarnation is, that His human life was real. His humiliation was real; His joys and sorrows were real; His struggles and temptations were real; and His triumph over the tempter was real. In His spotless, sinless life, therefore, we see that sin may be resisted and overcome in the flesh.

True, as we have seen, He was something more than flesh. Mere human nature in itself could not overcome as He overcame. He was "the Word"—the Christ. Divinity was allied to humanity. In Him we see a real human nature made strong by the power of God, and preserved from any approach to selfishness or sin. And in a very real sense the same is true of those who are truly united to Christ and regenerated by the Spirit. We thus become "partakers of the Divine nature" (2 Peter i. 4). Paul could say, "I no longer live, but Christ liveth in me; and the life which I now live in the flesh I live by the faith of the Son of God, who loved me and gave Himself for me" (Gal. ii. 20). In like manner every true disciple of Christ may be "strengthened with might by His Spirit in the inner man."

In seeking to imitate His life and to walk in His footsteps, we must, like Paul, have the power of Christ resting upon us. If our bodies are the temples of His Holy Spirit, we will throw off the pollutions of the world, as the rays of the rising sun fling back the darkness of night.

If we would know and realize what the faith of

Christ can do for us to keep us pure and holy amid surrounding wickedness, we must clearly grasp the truth that the religion of Jesus is not merely a thing of this world, to be estimated as we estimate mere human agencies. It is from above. Its power is Divine power. Christ was not only *born*, He *came*. He was "the Word" before He was "made flesh." In Christ, therefore, the gulf between God and man was bridged. Heaven and earth met in the Christ. Divinity and humanity found a meeting place in Christ. Therefore God and man can meet in Christ. In this lies the priceless value of the Incarnation. God can dwell in the human heart. If I know that in Christ divinity can dwell in humanity, then I know that God can dwell in human hearts now. And this is precisely what every human soul, struggling against sin, and striving to keep clear of the world's defilements, wants—the clear conviction that there is a spiritual world, a spiritual life, and spiritual fellowship; that, while we live, and labour, and struggle in the natural world, we may also live in a spiritual world, and enjoy close and constant fellowship with the Father of our spirits.

When we read, "The Word was made flesh," it must be noted that it is not mere mystic teaching, but the plain and pointed assertion of an actual historical fact. It was a real appearing of God in the flesh. It was a real assertion of the possible union of divinity and humanity. And what comfort and hope this fact gives to the human soul struggling into light and liberty! God cares for man, and came to seek and to save him. God has dwelt with man, and therefore may dwell with him still. There is nothing that can make a man really strong, and that can enable him to triumph over temptation and sinful habits, but the felt sense of God's presence. It is spiritual strength which we need to enable us to overcome in the stern battle of life; for our enemies are spiritual. Let a man maintain spiritual fellowship with God, and he will be strong and healthy, morally and spiritually. He will hurl back temptation without an effort and with scarcely a thought, just as the man of vigorous health and abundant vitality can walk in the midst of disease with perfect security. A felt sense of the continual presence of God in the heart is the true health and vitality of the human soul. One might as well try to set the ocean on fire by hurling burning coals into it, as to try to pollute the heart that is full of the love and presence of God. The Holy Spirit, of which water is the scriptural emblem, instantly quenches "all the fiery darts of the wicked one," and we are made "more than conquerors" over every foe, "through Him who loved us, and washed us from our sins in His own blood."

To be pure in heart and strong for duty there must be this personal relation between the soul and the Saviour. Each one must have the Spirit of God indwelling. This profound and almost bewildering thought is made possible to the grasp of faith when we see, in the whole life of Jesus, His personal love for individual souls. He not only loved humanity in the mass, He loved each human soul. He talks to the woman of Samaria at Jacob's well, and unfolds to a congregation of one the great mysteries of Divine truth as fully and as faithfully as if He had been preaching to thousands. When a poor fallen woman is brought before Him to be condemned, by a pointed home-thrust He drives her enemies from His presence that He may talk to her alone: " He who is without *the* sin—the same sin—let him first cast a stone at her." And His love and His methods are the same now. By His Spirit He comes to us one by one, drawing us to Himself, speaking to us in whispered tones of love and earnest entreaty, filling us with marvellous peace, giving us courage and power in the presence of danger and temptation, and filling us with such a sense of His comforting presence that we become one with Him in love, and aim, and desire. His presence fills us with such blessedness, and peace, and conscious power that His favour is more precious to us than even life itself; and the one grand aim and endeavour of our lives will be so to live in holiness and purity, that we may ever enjoy His presence, and continually bask in the sunlight of His love.

The Incarnation of Christ is practically lost upon us until we see His whole life's love condensed into the one act of self-sacrifice on the cross. The soul, full of wonder, and gratitude, and joy at such a marvellous exhibition of love and condescension, now gladly yields up all to Jesus in willing self-surrender. And oh! the joy and gratitude of that heart when it finds that Christ accepts the poor offering as gladly as it was given. Now it is its own no longer, but Christ's. And yet it is more really its own than ever it was before. Before it was a bond-slave either to sin or to the law, but now it is Christ's willing servant, and not merely a servant, but a son and heir—an heir of God and a joint-heir with Christ to all the joys and privileges of close and constant fellowship with God. Such a soul, whether in life or in death, is one with its Saviour, and can confidently say with the Apostle, "To me to live is Christ, and to die is gain" (Phil. i. 21). And now, with its new life and new loves, it will pass unharmed through the moral contagion of earth. Yea, more; that soul which heretofore needed a physician for its ailments, and a surgeon to bind up its wounds, will now become a physician for others. It will become a minister of mercy, and will go forth into the world, no longer fearing its contagion and corruption, but bringing healing and health to the sin-sick, courage and hope to the desponding, and balm and benediction for all woes.

By such a consecration of our lives to the service of Christ and our fellow-men, after having "washed our robes, and made them white in the blood of the Lamb," we will not only be saved from the world's spots and stains, but we will have heaven begun in our hearts— we will enjoy a sweet foretaste of the glory and felicity of the future life in the land that knows no shadow, no sorrow, and no sin.

The ultimate issue of the Incarnation was to bring about the union of all true believers with Christ. How meagre the life and work of Christ appear when He is represented only as an example—a pattern life for men to imitate. His holy life is indeed important as well as His death, for He thus became "our obedience"; but it is only a part of His redemptive work. He "became obedient *up to death*."

No theory of the Atonement which leaves out the

death and resurrection of Christ is in the least degree entitled to respect; for Jesus said, "I have power to lay down My life, and I have power to take it again. This commandment have I received from My Father"; and again, "The good Shepherd giveth His life for the sheep" (John x. 11, 18); "The Son of Man came not to be ministered unto, but to minister, and to give His life a ransom for many" (Matt. xx. 28). He also declares that He is "the resurrection and the life."

In virtue of our union with Christ through the indwelling of His Spirit we become "partakers of the Divine nature," and we are reckoned to have been one with Him in all His life's work, and one with Him in His death and resurrection-life. This union is effected only in the New Birth. Hence the significance of the words of the Lord Jesus, "Except a man be born of water and of the Spirit he cannot enter the kingdom of God" (John iii. 5). The New Birth, or Regeneration, takes place, by the power of the Holy Spirit, the moment the heart yields itself up to God in perfect love, and trust, and self-surrender. It is Christ coming by His Spirit in resurrection-life and power. Hence Jesus said, "Whosoever liveth and believeth in Me shall never die" (John xi. 26). This new life is the life of Christ in the heart. It is Christ returning to humanity, and by His Spirit dwelling in human hearts with Divine power. The Incarnation makes this glorious mystery possible to faith; for He who possessed a real human body during His earthly ministry, still retaining His Divine power and wisdom, can now dwell in human hearts without any lowering of His essential dignity and glory. And the moment that we believe that our bodies *may* become "the temples of the Holy Ghost," and gladly accept the proffered blessing, and open the door of the heart to the waiting Saviour, that moment we shall have personal experience of "a peace that passeth all understanding," "a joy that is unspeakable and full of glory." We shall now have the witness in ourselves that Christ can dwell in the human heart, giving a new life and new loves, new aims and aspirations, new peace and new power—power to hold fellowship with God, power over sin, and power in service. This, then, is the true solution of the mysterious union of the human and Divine.

XII.

CHRIST IN THE WILDERNESS: THE TEMPTATION.

"Then was Jesus led up of the Spirit into the wilderness to be tempted of the devil. And when He had fasted forty days and forty nights He afterward hungered."—MATT. iv. 1, 2.

THE Temptation of Christ is one of the most wonderful incidents in all history. It strikes us as marvellous, and as almost transcending belief, that He who was truly God should thus submit Himself to be tried and tempted by the devil on the very threshold of His public ministry. But in God's modes of procedure there must always be mystery. His ways are past finding out. If we are truly reverent, and are willing to acknowledge that God is greater than we know, then we will be prepared to find that in providing a remedy for sin, as well as in the introduction of sin into the world, His mode of procedure is above our finite comprehension. For wise purposes God permitted the tempter to assail the first representatives of the human race; and also in wisdom and in love to man He permitted the devil to tempt and try the ideal Representative of humanity.

In the verses immediately preceding our text we have the record of Christ's baptism, and the descent of the Holy Spirit upon Him. This was His call and consecration to the office of Priest and Redeemer of man. He had completed the statutory age for entering the office of priest. The priest had to be thirty years of age. The priest had to be "washed with water" (Exod. xl. 12); "sprinkled with water of purifying" (Numb. viii. 7). The priest had also to be anointed, as the sign of receiving the Holy Spirit. Jesus had now fulfilled all these obligations. He was thirty years of age; He received the sprinkled water of purifying at His baptism by John at Jordan; and He received the baptism of the Holy Ghost. And now, "being full of the Holy Ghost, He returned from Jordan, and was led by the Spirit into the wilderness" (Luke iv. 1).

On entering upon His life's work it was meet that He should pass through a great inward crisis by which the human will would become entirely subordinated to the Divine Spirit. Hence it is recorded that He was "led up"—that is, borne away, transported—"by the Spirit." Again He is said to have been "driven" by the Spirit into the wilderness. Under these strong forms of expression it is clearly indicated that the human will was directed and controlled by the Divine Spirit. As in Christ, so in all Christian workers, this is the first qualification for service—a perfect readiness to be led by the Spirit in all that we do and say, an entire subjection of the human will to the Divine will.

As Jesus was truly human, there was necessarily a real human progress in the unfolding of His powers. He increased in wisdom, in stature, and in grace— namely, in the threefold department of His nature, in body, soul, and spirit. "The child grew, and waxed strong in spirit, filled with wisdom; and the grace of God was upon Him" (Luke ii. 40). Possessed of a human nature in union with the Divine nature, His human powers had to be unfolded under human conditions of progress. This is a thought to be carefully noted, if we would clearly comprehend the Temptation. As early as the age of twelve we find Him discussing knotty questions of Theology with the learned doctors of the law, and being conscious of a Divine call to be about His Father's business. But, with these exceptions, we find no early record of mature powers in virtue of His divinity, but a gradual growth and unfolding of all the natural powers of the human soul. This fact must be remembered, else we will be in danger of losing sight of His true humanity, and the reality of His temptations, and toil, and agony, and suffering, as those invariably do who accustom themselves to think exclusively of His divinity and miraculous power.

Now that the Holy Spirit has descended upon Him, a wondrous transformation is wrought in His inner consciousness. With the Spirit comes a voice, and with the voice a new power; and He feels the Messianic forces heaving in His breast. The voice from heaven, "This is My beloved Son, hear ye Him," is His commission and call to commence His life's work. Now all the great movings of spirit attendant upon such a call—the shrinking, the self-sacrifice, the inspiration of hope, the agony of anxiety—would break in upon Him like the rolling and the surging of the waves of the sea. There was, no doubt, the same kind

CHRIST IN THE WILDERNESS.

of commotion in His heart that is felt by every truly noble and upright man when called to consecrate himself to the Lord, and to devote his life and all that he has to His service. All that was human in Him would instinctively shrink from the tremendous responsibility of the work which He had undertaken. This feeling would be met by the surging tide of love and joy—love to man, and "the joy of bringing many sons to glory"; and the effect upon His Spirit is such that every faculty groans with the pressure, and sways and moans like a forest in a storm. The Divine Spirit is upon Him, and He does what He must. He does not *go;* He yields Himself up *to be led*—to be driven by the Spirit into the first stage of His work.

This experience of the Master ought to be most comforting to all who are called upon to pass through similar conflicts, when they know that even sinless humanity required to pass through a terrible struggle and wrestling with the spirit of evil in order to be fitted for the work of blessing men. Like Him, we have to pass through the struggle alone. He is led by the Spirit into the wilderness away from the contact of men. We, too, must have retirement for the struggle with no one near us but God.

His inward commotion so completely absorbed His whole soul, that for forty days He seemed altogether unconscious of the needs of the body. It would seem to have been an involuntary fast. Apparently He had no consciousness of hunger, and perhaps no consciousness of time, until the inner conflict was ended. It was not until "after He had fasted forty days" that He hungered. The human organization is such, that under great nervous tension and mental stress the body may be sustained without food for a much longer period than when in its natural and normal state. Therefore, no miraculous sustaining power is necessary to account for this prolonged abstinence from food. Others, both in ancient and in modern times, have fasted as long.

But what was the Christ doing in this long solitude and silence in the wilderness? To say that He was fasting is not a full answer to this inquiry. The fast certainly was total,—"He did eat nothing,"—and not from food alone, but also from society and from worship in the synagogue. He was entirely isolated from the world, and was altogether alone in the dreary desert— alone with God. There was no one present to furnish a graphic report of the unique experiences of those forty days—the struggles, the shrinking, the yearning, the submission, the final triumph. And He has chosen to report only the closing scene, usually called the Temptation, which must have taken place at the end of the forty days. Here alone the veil is lifted.

However, we may know that He was not purposely afflicting Himself with penances of hunger and starvation. We may know that He was not wrestling with the question whether or not He would undertake the work to which He had been called. We may know that He was not bewailing His sins, for He was then, as ever, the Sinless One. Then, what was He doing, and why was He there?

To arrive at an intelligent conception of the experiences of this time it must be borne in mind that He had a nature in part humanly derived; and, so far, a broken, frail nature. He took upon Him "the likeness of the flesh that had sinned" (Rom. viii. 3). That flesh—namely, human nature—by sin came under the curse of the law. He is now not merely in the world; He is in the flesh. In Him, as in all of us, the flesh would strive to obtain the mastery over the spirit. And there would come to Him, as there comes to all men, a time when the permanent supremacy of the flesh or the spirit must be definitely and for ever settled. He did not, indeed, have any sinful habits to overcome; but the pure human soul would shrink back in horrid recoil and revulsion from the shame, the humiliation, the hate, the wrong, the woe, the curse, which He inherited as the Son of Man, and assumed as the Sin-bearer for the world. So He must have retirement that He may wrestle with this feeling, until, with complete resignation, He can consent to veil His Divine glory and His equality with God while He bears the sins of humanity and the shame of the cross. The cross, and the nails, and the physical suffering could hardly seem terrible to Him; but to be numbered with transgressors, to be accounted an impostor and a malefactor, to be rejected by those for whose salvation He yearned, and for whom He was ready to lay down His life—*that* was a trial from which God Himself might well shrink. There is nothing so revolting to a pure upright soul as to be made the subject of scandal and reproach, and then to find that the lie or the calumny is believed, and he is despised and rejected by those who ought to defend his integrity and purity of life. The agony of crucifixion is as nothing to this. And it was such a trial that the Lord Jesus was now passing through; for the whole of His earthly life was present to His mind during these anxious days.

Human nature is keenly sensitive to suffering, and His human nature would naturally recoil from the lot of suffering to which He was called. But the soul-struggle would be the most trying. His call, which was now upon Him, was a call to self-denial, and self-sacrifice, and submission, and He was fully conscious of it. The fact that He was Divine did not make Him superior to suffering. He had assumed human nature as it is, and we know that it is weak for suffering. The flesh is not heroic. It is the spirit in man that makes the hero. The flesh shrinks from being hated of all men—shrinks from dying, and especially from dying under a curse. He knew that He was tending towards the cross; for in one of His earliest discourses He speaks of being "lifted up." This instinctive shrinking from the suffering and shame, from the cross and the curse, must now be overcome. The flesh must be entirely subordinated to the spirit before He can enter successfully upon His life's work. The struggle would be severe, but it must be decisive; and it must be won in solitude, with the Divine Spirit alone to help, and the spirit of evil to oppose.

Then, again, at the moment of His call and consecration, there would come upon Him another kind of inward commotion, arising from the fact that He had taken the world upon His love. How differently we feel towards any person the moment we undertake for them, making their case our own! Jesus, in entering upon His work as the Saviour of men, must make Himself one with those whom He is to redeem—to live for them, suffer for them, die for them. Love always undertakes to suffer for those beloved. The mother suffers for her child. The patriot lays down his life for his country. The Christian martyr seals his testimony with his blood. It is this moral suffering that now comes upon the Christ; and it comes in an intensity and agony proportionate to the strength and compass of His love. Physical suffering bears no comparison with such soul-agony as this.

In addition to this physical and moral suffering which was present to His mind, He must have been profoundly engaged in unfolding and maturing the plan of His life's work, as the world's Redeemer. True there was a Divine plan ready for Him, prepared before the creation and fall of man; for, in the purpose of God, He was "the Lamb slain from the foundation of the world." But He, as man, as One who had to grow in wisdom, must think it out, step by step, in all its parts, according to human methods of thought and arrangement. In consenting to become man He consented to be unfolded gradually in body and mind. His plan, therefore, must be carefully and profoundly thought out in order to be mastered in detail.

He has already studied the Messianic prophecies, and, no doubt, had a deeper spiritual insight into their meaning than even the prophets who wrote them; still the plan of His work must be thought out in detail: what He shall do and teach; what He shall suffer; when He shall suffer; how He shall suffer; by whom shall He organize; how many bosom friends shall He have; what shall His relation be to a worldly Church and worldly-minded teachers; shall He permit popular demonstrations in His favour, or shall He forbid all such manifestations of approval? Forty days in the wilderness! It is a long time. Yes, a long time to fast; but short enough for all the wrestling and planning through which He was called to pass, as a necessary preparation for entering upon the sublime work of the world's redemption. What a world of thought would be crowded into those forty days! After such mental toil, and soul-wrestling, and bodily abstinence, is it any wonder that the God-man hungered? And what a hungering it would be! What exhaustion of body, and what sinking of spirit! If there ever was a weak moment in His life surely it was the present moment.

Now is the tempter's opportunity; and he readily avails himself of it: "If Thou be the Son of God, command that this stone become a loaf." The point of this temptation lay in the suggestion that it seemed wholly inconsistent for the Son of God, who possessed all power, to suffer from hunger. What will the people say of One who professes to be the Messiah, if He allows Himself to suffer bodily privation? By all means work a miracle, if Thou canst. Display creative power, and thus establish Thy Messiahship. The people expect such a wonder-working Messiah, and if you are politic you will conform to their expectations.

It would seem as if Satan had already perverted the expectations of the Jewish people concerning the Messiah for the very purpose of turning aside the Messiah Himself. And in all probability the influence of these perverted views upon the mind of Jesus would give rise to an inward struggle; for they must be rejected.

Many suppose that Satan had employed some of the chief priests, as his instruments, to tempt Christ to undertake the part of a worldly Messiah, and to set up an earthly kingdom; and that they waited upon Him for that purpose when He had emerged from the wilderness at the end of the forty days. This seems in every way probable. Satan, by God's permission, had the power of entering into the serpent to tempt Eve. He also entered into Judas before the betrayal. The devil certainly has the power of operating directly on the human mind by evil suggestion; and he is also permitted by God to employ human agents to carry out his designs.

John the Baptist had already declared to the deputation from the Sanhedrim that the Messiah had come, and that Jesus was the Son of God. It was the Baptist's duty to point out the Messiah to the people, and especially to the representatives of the people. They had come to ask him, and he must have given a truthful reply. It is altogether probable, therefore, that the chief priests would endeavour to persuade Him to set up an earthly kingdom, and become the Priest-king of God's chosen people. But Christ had a grander mission to fulfil; He had come to be the Saviour of man, not simply the Ruler and Deliverer of a single nation. Therefore, He must reject their counsel, and thereby incur their enmity and opposition. If this supposition be correct, it may, to some extent, account for the malignant opposition of the Scribes and Pharisees throughout His ministry. If He declined their counsel they would do all in their power to thwart His projects in order to make success impossible without their aid. The suggestion also to convert a stone into a loaf would seem to indicate that the temptation came through a Jewish channel. It was characteristic of the Jew to seek a sign—some display of power—as an attestation of Messiahship: " What sign showest Thou unto us?" (John ii. 18). " Master, we would see a sign from Thee " (Matt. xii. 38).

In the second temptation, when Jesus was placed upon the pinnacle of the temple, the chief priests may again have been the mouthpiece of Satan. The pinnacle, or wing, being within the temple, and a sacred part, the high priest alone would have access to it. Another sign in attestation of His Divine commission is demanded: "Cast Thyself down, and let the wondering multitude behold the attending angels bearing Thee up in their hands; and then we will present Thee to the people as the promised Messiah." This would seem to be the point of the temptation.

In the third temptation it is hardly possible that the chief priests had a part. It is most probable that after the scene in the temple Jesus retired to a high mountain near Jerusalem, and here the tempter assails Him directly. He does not address Jesus as the Son of God, but sets himself up as God, and claims the worship of Christ—homage, at least, though not necessarily adoration. Here Satan appears in his true character, as the enemy and rival of God, and Jesus treats him accordingly: " Get thee hence, Satan; for it is written, Thou shalt worship the Lord thy God, and Him only shalt thou serve " (Matt. iv. 10). In the first and second temptation Jesus dealt with him according to his assumed character, as one who seemed anxious to promote the mission of the Messiah. Now, however, He meets the pretensions of Satan to absolute power and universal dominion by asserting His own superior authority. He addresses the tempter by the name Satan, indicating that He clearly sees through his false pretensions. Professing to promote Christ's Messiahship, he is really an adversary, as the name Satan signifies.

In these temptations we see the presumption and the persistency of Satan. He is bold enough to try his wiles even upon the Son of God. He persists in his attempt, although foiled in the first and second assault. He exhibits also almost incredible impudence; for the last temptation clearly indicates that he believed that the Messiah Himself had His price at which His virtue and fidelity might be bought. It is scarcely necessary to observe that Satan's liberal promise to give the kingdoms of this world and all their glory to Christ was a lie, like all his promises; for he proffers what is not his to give. No truer designation of the devil can be given than "the father of lies."

Looking at the temptation of Christ as a whole, we see in it an exact parallel to the temptation in the Garden of Eden. There was in both a threefold temptation, touching and testing every department of human nature. These the Apostle John summarizes as, "The lust of the flesh, the lust of the eyes, and the vainglory of life" (1 John ii. 16). Eve saw that the tree was good for food. Here was a desire for bodily gratification—a wish to eat what God had forbidden. This was the first temptation presented to Christ—a proposal to satisfy the cravings of the body in a forbidden way; for it seemed to be the one restriction placed upon Christ that He never wrought a miracle to satisfy His own personal wants, or for gaining personal glory. The second temptation was to personal pride, or vanity—a desire to appear great, to be looked at with wonder and admiration. This feeling the Apostle designates "the lust of the eyes." The third temptation was to worldly ambition—to possess commanding power and universal rule before God's time. So Eve was ambitious to become as God Himself. To her also the devil's promise was a lie. He promised her fellowship with God in knowledge and enjoyment. He promised more abundant life. The result, however, was misery, shame, suffering, death.

In all these temptations there is an element of truth in the devil's lies. Christ is to enter into His Messianic inheritance, but it is to be different in character—earthly instead of spiritual; and different also in time—*at once*, instead of having to wait and suffer. It is this *immediateness* that makes the devil's bait so alluring to many. The means and the manner, too, are different. He is to employ Satanic agency instead of Divine power. He will employ magic, and live upon stones instead of bread; and, by demon-worship, command the homage of the world.

As we see in this wonderful and thrilling narrative the devil's subtle methods of tempting, let us also learn from Christ the true method of resisting temptation. He fought the tempter with a text. Three times He says, "IT IS WRITTEN." Like Him, if we would come off victorious, we must be skilful in wielding the sword of the Spirit, which is the Word of God.

XIII.

CHRIST IN THE GARDEN: THE AGONY.

" My soul is exceeding sorrowful, even unto death."—MATT. xxvi. 38.

THE Garden of Gethsemane has ever been dear to the Christian heart on account of the scene described in our text. It is a most touching and memorable scene, and so strange and marvellous that we but seldom realize how real it was to the Sufferer. It is night. The traitor is away on his mission of betrayal. The Lord has left Jerusalem with the eleven disciples. He descends from the city into the dark vale of cypresses, where once the fire blazed in which the abominations of idolatry were consumed. Here He crosses the brook Kedron, over which King David passed, barefoot and in sackcloth, when fleeing from his rebellious son Absalom. The very path which He trod would naturally suggest treachery and betrayal. Solemn, yet calm and peaceful, with perhaps a touch of depression in His countenance, He arrives at the Garden of Gethsemane, at the base of the Mount of Olives. Here gigantic olive-trees to this very day point out the very spot where the suffering Saviour wept, and prayed, and agonized for the redemption of fallen humanity. This peaceful enclosure was a spot to which He had often resorted after the labours of the day in the city. How He loved quiet, and retirement, and cleanliness, and a pure atmosphere. By His example He would seem to teach how impossible it is to be morally strong amid the din, and crowding, and filth of low city life. " He went, as He was wont, to the Mount of Olives."

Every one in that little company must have observed how His soul was oppressed; and they would be prepared to hear Him say with deep emotion on their arrival, "Sit ye here, while I go and pray yonder." He takes the three who can best understand the scene, Peter, and James, and John, to be witnesses of the solemn experiences of that hour, and to watch, lest they, not He, should be surprised and alarmed : " My soul is exceeding sorrowful, tarry ye here and watch." It was of paramount importance to His future Church that there should be competent witnesses of that solemn and sublime scene.

The purely human feeling of the need of affectionate fellowship would also cause Him to desire to have some of His trusted friends near to Him. Solitude increases the feeling of horror. Companionship makes conflict comparatively easy. Here, then, we see His true humanity asserting itself: " Do not leave Me; do not sleep; stay near by and watch with Me." He goes forward a few steps and falls upon His face, the Eastern posture of extreme sorrow and anguish, crying, " O My Father, if it be possible, let this cup pass from Me!" He does it a second time, more earnestly, and a third time, when His earnestness amounts to agony : "And, being in an agony, He prayed more earnestly;

and His sweat became as it were great drops of blood falling down upon the ground" (Luke xxii. 44).

The agony—the heart-anguish—was so intense that there were forced out through the pores of the skin large drops resembling blood. This bloody perspiration takes place in the human body only under the most intense agony. The bite of a poisonous serpent and certain painful affections have produced it. In Christ it was produced by extreme mental anguish.

The first natural inquiry, therefore, is, Whence and why this terrible crisis of anguish and agony? We are not to suppose that He is under God's wrath, or that He has lost the Father's love and favour. Never was He doing the Father's will more faithfully. Never was He more beloved by God. He is now, as ever, "The Beloved Son"; and God proves His love by sending an angel to strengthen Him.

Some have supposed that His agony at the present moment, when there was no immediate danger, would be out of place on mere human principles, and, therefore, it must have been caused by some mysterious judicial infliction, or by the withdrawal of the Father's favour. However, it is not until He comes to the cross that He feels forsaken by God. God does not send His angels to strengthen and support those whom He forsakes; and only a short time previous He comforted Himself in the assurance, " Therefore doth My Father love Me, because I lay down My life for the sheep." And further, when He says, three times repeated, in His prayer, " Not as I will, but as Thou wilt," He surely expresses the strongest possible confidence in God and perfect repose in His love. And yet further, before He leaves the precincts of the garden He formally declares His confidence in the Father's love and favour, "Thinkest thou that I cannot pray to My Father, and He shall even now send Me more than twelve legions of angels?" (Matt, xxvi. 53.) The whole account affords the most decisive proof that He does not for a moment imagine that God has withdrawn His favour.

The momentary disturbing of the perfect harmony between His human will and the will of the Father must be ascribed, in part at least, to that human infirmity necessarily attached to His state of humiliation. The prompt and spontaneous submission, as expressed in each prayer, shows that there was no taint of rebellion on His part, but perfect resignation to the Father's will. It was not the result of moral weakness, but rather the struggle with the human will to subordinate it to God's will and purpose. In carrying out God's purpose and plan for the redemption of man, in finishing the work given Him to do, it was necessary that He should submit to a terrible and ignominious death, by which He was to manifest His perfect obedience to the Father's will. From such a trial all that was human in Him would naturally recoil in inconceivable horror. However, although the human soul was burdened, and almost crushed by the weight of woe which He was enduring, yet the spirit of Christ, in all His conflicts, maintained the consciousness of Sonship, and close and constant fellowship with the Father.

Possessing a real human nature,—a nature that is naturally sensitive and weak for suffering,—we ought to expect from Him the cry, "Father, save Me from this hour!" But see how the instinctive cry of nature is checked: "Now is My soul troubled, and what shall I say?" Shall I say, "Father, save Me from this hour? Nay; for this cause came I unto this hour. *Father, glorify Thy name.*" This prompt submission proves that "He learned obedience by the things which He suffered." He had to sacrifice His human will, His shrinking, His sense of humiliation, on the altar of duty. In Him, as in us, this is the triumph of faith : " Not My will, but Thine, be done."

To possess a nature that needs to be sacrificed is not sinful. It is a God-given nature, and therefore good. But the sin consists in refusing to sacrifice it in obedience to God's command. The fact that human nature has desires and longings that are not in accordance with God's will makes conflict and struggle inevitable —the human soul in conflict with the Divine will. In the Temptation and in the Agony Jesus had this conflict, yet without sin; for He never gratified any desire, nor refused to submit to any suffering or humiliation, in opposition to the will of the Father.

The highest and holiest life is not the life that knows no conflict, but the life that marches steadily on in the midst of conflict, turning every trial into a triumph. If we meet with no trials and temptations in our path, we can have no triumphs; and the crown of rejoicing is given "to him that overcometh," and he is made "a pillar in the temple of God." Paul, in recording his own experience, does not thank God for escaping trial, but joyfully exclaims, " Now thanks be unto God, who always causeth us to triumph in Christ" (2 Cor. ii. 14).

As Jesus received power from the Father at the time to perform His mighty works, so He also learned the Father's will in reference to the cup of suffering at the time ; and apparently He had to wait patiently in order to make sure that no escape was possible. But when, by the Father's continued silence, He was satisfied that the world's redemption depended upon His drinking the cup to its bitter dregs, He expresses His ready compliance with the Father's purpose in words of peculiar beauty and pathos : " My Father, if this cup may not pass from Me, except I drink it, Thy will be done !' The struggle is ended. He is assured that the pathway of suffering is the pathway of duty ; and He rises at once to the consciousness and joy of certain victory.

The Agony in the garden was not the result of fear. Jesus was not afraid to die. He had power to lay down His life, and He had power to take it again ; and He laid it down cheerfully for the joy of bringing many sons to glory. It cannot be supposed for a moment that a Being of such transcendent goodness and majesty could be shaken and unnerved by fear of any kind. The fact that the blood oozed through the pores of the skin is a proof that the agony was not the result of fear ; for in fear the blood is driven inward, and leaves a deadly pallor over the surface. In the case of Christ the blood is driven outward. And yet there are those who affirm that this incident proves that He was only a man, and a very weak one, sadly lacking in manly courage. It is worthy of note that it is not said that He was filled with fear, but that He was "exceeding sorrowful," a very different emotion. Heart-anguish has been known to produce bloody perspiration, as in the case of Charles IX. of France, who agonized on his death-bed, and was filled with horror and dismay as he fully realized his awful guilt for consenting to massacre the French Protestants on St. Bartholomew's Day. The agony of Jesus was not the agony of fear.

How, then, shall we account for this terrible agony? Here is the Son of God, confessedly the world's greatest benefactor; One who has never had to acknowledge sin, or fault, or failure; perfect in His life; facing every sort of danger in His works of mercy; One who has shown the most perfect trust in God; carrying with Him, too, throughout His ministry, the consciousness that He must die, and in the end refusing to be protected by force; and yet He is somehow the subject of extreme anguish and agony at the near prospect of death. Well may we ask, How can this be; and how can we account for it?

Now it seems clear that His agony could not be merely human. If only the human in Him was suffering, could He not have endured calmly like Socrates and others? As, on account of His divinity, His love was deeper and more intense than mere human love, so His anguish and agony would be more intense, and, when in full play, would necessarily give a tremendous shock to the human organism. It was as the God-man that He agonized in Gethsemane.

But can divinity suffer? Is there any sensibility in God that can experience anguish and agony? We are apt to think that God is superior to suffering. He could not, of course, experience physical pain. But we read of God being "grieved at His heart"; "The Lord pitieth them that fear Him." To pity another is, in some measure, to suffer with him. Nothing is more certain than that God can suffer. He suffered in giving up His well-beloved Son to die for the human race. It is one of the perfections of Godhead that it can suffer ; and in any moral being the capability of suffering will be in proportion to his goodness. When God undertook fully to reveal Himself to man, He did not appear in kingly majesty and glory, but in the suffering Saviour. There is, therefore, some true sense in which God's perfection requires Him to be a suffering God. But He is not, on that account, unhappy. A noble nature finds its highest happiness in self-denial for the good of others. Christ Himself, as the Captain of our salvation, was made perfect through suffering. He was thereby fitted to become a sympathetic Saviour ; and by His sufferings and triumphs, He proved that human nature, when directed and controlled by the Divine Spirit, may triumph all along the line, without ever succumbing to temptation, or being crushed by suffering. The Divine nature, therefore, may suffer without suffering loss, or becoming thereby less than perfect.

What, then, was the cause of the agony of the God-man, Christ Jesus ? We think His pure nature would recoil with something like horror, not from the thought of dying, but from dying as an impostor, and being rejected by those whom He longed to bless and save. This thought would well-nigh crush Him ; for He knew that, as they now rejected His love, so in all ages there would be many to do the same, and His yearning love for man would not meet its full reward. He is not afraid to die ; but His pure human soul shrinks back in awful recoil at the madness and fury that are ready to burst upon Him; at the madness of men to reject such a benefactor, and to trample upon Divine love itself. It is an appalling thought. Man, who was made in God's image; man, whose nature He had assumed; man, whom He came to redeem and save, going to crucify their Divine Friend! He thinks not of Himself merely; His heart is agonizing for the souls of men. Having assumed a human nature He would naturally have a tender regard for man—a love far transcending a patriot's feeling for his country, or a brother's feeling for one of his father's children.

His incarnation made Him, in a very real sense, one with man; and, man being under the curse, He, as bearing the sin of men, came under it too; and He will not by a miracle push aside the liability He has assumed as the Sin-bearer and Saviour of man. This He cannot do; for it is an essential part of God's redemptive plan that Christ should offer such a tribute of respect to God's retributive order in punishing sin that His law will be honoured and magnified before men, in such a way as to profoundly impress them with its propriety and necessity. Sin is inseparably linked to suffering, and the Sin-bearer and Redeemer from sin must therefore suffer. By this voluntary submission of Christ to man's curse, or lot of penalty, a sting of conviction will be sharpened against sin that will start a new sense of the righteousness of God's law and the retributive order of God's government in the hearts of all mankind. For if God's sinless Son, in coming into contact with the world's sin, must suffer, and agonize, and die, surely it will ever be believed that suffering is inseparably linked with sin. Therefore Christ's love to man and His love for God's law made it impossible for Him to turn aside from the path of suffering.

Every form of love—motherhood, fatherhood, friendship, patriotism, philanthropy—carries with it its burden of anxiety, and anguish, and agony, according to the strength of love, and according to the want or woe of the object loved. Moses carried this burden: "I am not able to bear all this people alone; for it is too heavy for me." Paul had a similar experience: 'I have great heaviness and continual sorrow in my heart . . . for my brethren, my kinsmen according to the flesh." He could even wish himself anathema from Christ for their sakes. He would be willing for a time to endure the withdrawal of Christ's comforting presence, as Jesus endured for a time the hiding of the Father's face, if thereby His brethren might be saved. There is no burden so heavy as the burden of souls. Love must always bear its burden of sorrow. We must bear this thought in mind if we would fully understand the scene in Gethsemane, and truly interpret the anguish and agony of the suffering Saviour.

This pathetic incident in the life of our Lord has its lesson for us all; for we are called upon to walk in His steps. As certainly as the Master's love is in us, as surely will His burden rest upon us. If our hearts become pure as He is pure, we will be shocked and revolted at the wrath and wrong of evildoers. In so far as we have love, and pity, and sympathy for others, we will have the anxiety and agony that necessarily accompany these emotions. If we have the Master's spirit, we will also in our measure have the Master's burden. We will have the fellowship of suffering, as well as the fellowship of joy and victory. And if we would have fellowship with Him in victory over temptation and trial, we must, like Him, cheerfully submit to the Father's will in all things. We must be willing to suffer with Christ rather than disobey God, remembering, however, for our comfort, that in all our anxiety, and anguish, and agony God loves us dearly. If He cannot answer our cry for deliverance, if He cannot wisely remove the cup of sorrow, He will assuredly give us strength to bear it, and thus make us stronger for life. "And there appeared unto Him an angel from heaven strengthening Him."

XIV

CHRIST ON THE MOUNT: THE TRANSFIGURATION.

"And, behold, there talked with Him two men, which were Moses and Elijah; who appeared in glory, and spake of His decease which He was about to accomplish at Jerusalem."—LUKE ix. 30, 31.

IN this sublime incident in the life of the God-man we have brought together the glory of heaven and the shame of the cross. Here the Transfiguration and the Crucifixion touch each other. Jesus was transfigured in the presence of the three disciples; and Moses and Elijah appeared and talked with Him of His decease which He was about to accomplish at Jerusalem. Between the Transfiguration and the Crucifixion there is a close connection, the one being preparatory to the other. At the Transfiguration Jesus touched the highest point in His earthly life; as at the Cross He touched the lowest point in His humiliation. This glorious Transfiguration, and the heaven-sent messengers, and the Voice, "This is My beloved Son, in whom I am well pleased; hear ye Him," prove conclusively that He had now attained to the highest heights of holiness. In virtue of that personal holiness He had a right in His human body, transfigured and glorified, to enter heaven, like Enoch, Moses, and Elijah, without passing through the avenue of death. Death, as the wages of sin, had no claim upon the sinless Saviour. He was perfectly conscious of His own sinlessness. We never hear from Him in any of His discourses or prayers, not even during the agony in the garden, any expressions of regret, or repentance, or remorse; and He can fearlessly confront His bitterest enemies with the challenge, "Which of you convinceth Me of sin?" Such a life does not require, for its own sake, to pass into heaven through the avenue of death, much less through the humiliation and shame of the cross.

Man, at his creation, was promised life on condition that he should obey God and recognize his dependence upon Him. He was left free to choose the path of obedience and dependence, or the path of independence and self-assertion. The pathway to glory led through temptation and moral progress; so that by continued resistance of temptation his free will would become confirmed in loyalty to God's will. He would thus advance from a state of mere innocence to the higher state of holiness. Then, by a glorious transformation of the bodily organism, such as took place in the bodies of Enoch, Moses, and Elijah, the final step would be taken from the state of holiness to a state of glory and the full vision of God.

Jesus had now, by resisting temptation, by unwavering obedience, by the entire surrender of His own will, and by the consecration of all His powers to God, attained to that summit of holiness, which, according to the original law of human life, entitled Him to a glorious transformation and an abundant entrance into the heavenly state. The Transfiguration, with the attendant messengers and the Shekinah-cloud, was at once the proof and the attestation of heaven that such was His due. The human in Him was now so thoroughly subjected to the Divine Spirit, that the inner light and glory shone in glorious effulgence through the body, so that the fashion of his countenance was altered, and His face did shine as the sun, and even His raiment became bright as the light. Such a glorious mode of departure is His by right, if He will only claim it. The heavenly messengers are ready to accompany Him. The chariot of fire—the Shekinah-cloud—is waiting to receive Him, and to bear Him to the heavenly mansions. There is no doubt but Jesus had the refusal of this triumphant mode of departure, as the just reward of his holy, consecrated life.

There comes now another testing time in His life. Will He enter heaven now, and leave behind Him those whom He came to redeem ? Will the everlasting doors now lift up their heads that the King of glory may come in, and then for ever close against a lost and helpless world ? If He enters now He must enter alone. Will He, therefore, live for self or for others ? Will He, once for all, prove to the world that there is no joy like the joy of doing good, and that His love for man is stronger than death—stronger even than the attraction and the joys of heaven ? The whole matter is deliberately weighed. In the presence of the Shekinah-cloud,—the visible token of God's presence,—and the open heaven, and the resplendent glory, He talks with Moses and Elijah of the decease which He should, according to the plan of redemption, accomplish at Jerusalem. The pathway to glory is open to Him ; but, see, He chooses the pathway to the cross. He will not grasp the crown, although, by resisting temptation, by prompt obedience, by cheerful self-surrender, by loving ministry, He has attained to the highest heights of human perfection ; and, therefore, is entitled to the highest reward that heaven has to bestow.

But why does He turn away His eye from the crown, and fix it upon the cross ? Why does He decline to enter the opened heaven, and go back to earth with its sorrow, and suffering, and shame ? Why must the heavenly escort return to heaven from the peaks of Hermon, and, after many days, come back on the same mission to meet the risen Lord on Olivet ? There is but one answer to these questions. *The redemption of man could not possibly be effected without the death of the Redeemer.* If His death was not absolutely necessary to the salvation of men, on every principle of right and justice He ought to have entered heaven now. This is the one conclusive reply to those who make the Atonement of Christ consist merely in His example and moral influence upon men, and ignore the necessity of His death upon the cross. The question, WHY DID HE DIE ? has but one possible answer : " Without the shedding of blood there is no remission." " It pleased the Father that in Him should all fulness dwell ; and, through Him, to reconcile all things unto Himself, having made peace through the blood of His cross " (Col. i. 20). Therefore the cross cannot be avoided, if man is to be redeemed.

In talking of His decease—His mode of departure from the world—Moses and Elijah, representing the Law and the Prophets, would naturally refer to the Paschal Lamb and the Blood of the Passover, and such clear prophetic statements as, " The Lord hath laid on Him the iniquity of us all. . . . He was wounded for our transgressions ; He was bruised for our iniquities ; the chastisement of our peace was upon Him, and by His stripes we are healed " (Isa. liv. 5, 6). Thus the mind of the Lord Jesus would be assured that the path of suffering was the appointed path for the Redeemer of man ; and He would be nerved and strengthened to submit to the terrible lot of shame and suffering to which He was called.

From this time forward Jesus carries with Him the clear consciousness that He must die; and He now communicates the startling intelligence to His faithful and confidential friends : "As they were coming down from the mountain He charged them that they should tell no man what things they had seen, until the Son of Man should have risen again from the dead" (Mark ix. 9). And now He tells them plainly that the Son of Man came " to give His life a ransom for many " (Matt. xx. 28). From this time the language respecting the fact and the purpose of His death is unmistakably clear : " I lay down My life for the sheep " ; " No man taketh it from Me, but I lay it down of Myself. I have power to lay it down, and I have power to take it again " (John x. 15, 18). At the last Supper He lifts the veil, and all is clear : " 'This is My blood of the new covenant, which is shed for many for the remission of sins " (Matt. xxvi. 28). From such language it is abundantly evident that Jesus regarded Himself as, in a very real sense, the representative of man, and knew that sin could be forgiven only by the shedding of His blood.

In His perfectly holy life humanity touched its highest

point. Adam was man at his beginning; Jesus was man at his climax—man at his best. He was the perfect ideal man made in the image of God. He proved in His human life that the moral constitution given to man was good; that man, by the help of the Divine Spirit, might resist temptation, and advance to perfect holiness, and thus be fitted for eternal fellowship with God. Jesus thus became the pattern man, the model of what life ought to be. He took man's place, and, through all the stages from infancy up to manhood, lived man's life; and by the marvellous power of His matchless love He became the living centre and source of a new life for man. However, in order that He may be present in the hearts of all His disciples as a new life and inspiration, He must lay aside the human body, which during His life on earth necessarily restricted Him in His movements, and limited Him to a particular locality. Therefore His death would serve a double purpose. His life, voluntarily given, would be a ransom for the life of man, forfeited by sin; so that God could forgive "the sins that are past" without seeming to make light of sin. And, having laid aside the earthly tabernacle, He could come by His Spirit and dwell in the hearts of all who love Him as a new life, a new spiritual power, thus enabling men to mount up to God in holy aspiration, and to enjoy close and constant fellowship with Him; so that "the peace of God might be shed abroad in our hearts through the Holy Ghost given unto us." Therefore, both for man's redemption and for the manifestation of His own power in the hearts of men, it was necessary that His path should lead to the cross.

In the early part of the human life of Jesus the feeling of Sonship was most prominent before His mind: "Wist ye not that I must be about *My Father's* business?" "Make not *My Father's* house a house of merchandise." But from the Transfiguration onward He is fully conscious of His Messiahship. And, as the Messiah and Redeemer of man, He consents to accept the lot of suffering, and to be numbered with transgressors. He cheerfully consents to lay aside for a time the rights of Sonship, and to endure the hiding of the Father's face, in order to become the Substitute and Sin-bearer for man. Now the cross is full in view, and He does not hesitate to submit to it with all its shame and woe. And yet it is not done without a struggle. In all the great epochs of His life there was struggle, with conflict, always ending, however, in complete victory. It was so in the wilderness. It was so at the Transfiguration. It was so at Gethsemane. And it is so on Calvary, to which He is now approaching. There was conflict, crowned with victory, at every stage in His progress through life. And the conflict was as real as the victory. He has taken the place of sinful humanity; and, in rendering homage to God's holy law, which man had trampled under foot, He cannot escape from the cross and the curse, which are necessarily linked to transgression. He will magnify the law, and make it honourable. He will show to all generations that "the commandment is holy, just, and good"—that God's law, demanding obedience from man, is not arbitrary, but necessary. He will show to the world that God cannot surrender his authority and right to rule—that, if man will not yield to love, he must yield to power, and be made to suffer. The law of God must be upheld in its integrity till the conscience of man freely acknowledges its claim to respect, and the will of man gladly accepts it as the only rule of life. This truth is self-evident, when the law of God is recognized as the verbal expression of the will of God. To trample on God's law, or to make light of its requirements, is to oppose our will to God's, and to assert our independence of Him. If such self-assertion were permitted there could be no harmony between man and God, and all moral government would be at an end. Therefore the work of Jesus was necessarily twofold. He had to uphold the law of God by a life of perfect submission to God's will in all things, as well as to give His life as a ransom for those whom He came to save. If the holiest, and wisest, and greatest of all who have ever appeared in human form cheerfully submits to God's will, and honours and magnifies God's law, surely it will ever be acknowledged that the law of God is necessary and good for man. If Jesus, in offering His tribute of respect to God's law, does not hesitate to bear in His own body the suffering due to sin, it must ever be admitted that a holy and just God, having a world of moral beings to govern, cannot let persistent sin go unpunished.

How real the Saviour's sufferings were is evident from the agony in Gethsemane, and from the cry on the cross. There is no meaning in the agony, and there is no accounting for the cry, " My God, My God, why hast Thou forsaken Me ?" except the God-man is suffering for sin. The Transfiguration proved that He was prepared to enter into glory without passing through the avenue of death. He did not suffer for any sin of His own. Then why the agonizing cry? Why the awful feeling of desertion? Why the temporary hiding of the Father's face? Why the momentary withdrawal of the Father's comforting presence? Whether the human mind can comprehend it or not, the experience was terribly real to the Sufferer. God forsaken by God! This is the mystery of mysteries. How can we account for it? The agony of soul must have been intense; for on no other supposition could this startling cry have been possible. Although He was at this moment beloved by God, and was faithfully doing the Father's will, and although all heaven was looking on approvingly, yet He must have felt at this awful crisis that He was indeed forsaken by God. His human heart experienced a real desertion; but by faith His spirit kept clinging to God. God is still to Him "My God." His consciousness of doing the Father's will enabled Him to struggle successfully against the feeling of desertion, although to all that was human in Him that feeling was terribly real. The cry was not so much a cry of weakness as a cry of faith.

But how was this feeling of desertion possible to the sinless Sufferer? Such a feeling is possible only to one who is bearing sin. It must ever remain true that he who is separated from sin necessarily holds fellowship with God: "If we walk in the light as He is in the light, we have fellowship one with another"— that is, we with God. We know as a fact in our own experience that while we are conscious of bearing our sins we feel forsaken by God. We are haunted continually by the terrible feeling of alienation. Only sin can produce this feeling of conscious alienation. But Jesus had no sin of His own to account for this feeling of desertion. Therefore it follows that He must have been bearing the sins of others. We cannot possibly account for His cry of anguish in any other way.

In the scourging, and buffeting, and mocking, and piercing, and smiting, we have further confirmation of the fact that the Sufferer was a Sin-bearer. A holy God could not permit innocence so to suffer, except there was a profound and mysterious meaning in it all. There is but one answer to all His sufferings: not for Himself, but for others, He is left to feel forsaken. Not for Himself, but for others, He endures the curse and the cross.

XV.

CHRIST ON THE CROSS: SIN AND ATONEMENT.

"For Christ also hath once suffered for sins, the just for the unjust, that He might bring us to God."—1 PETER iii. 18.

EVERYWHERE in Scripture sin is recognized as a fact requiring to be dealt with. The alienation of the sinner from God is also recognized as a fact, making reconciliation necessary. Sin and alienation, as facts, are also known in human experience. To meet the fact of sin and alienation we want a salvation and reconciliation which may also be known as a fact in our own experience. Otherwise peace in the presence of God would be for ever impossible. The life of Christ in the world is a fact; and so is the Atonement, which has been effected by the holy life, obedience, death, and resurrection of the God-man, Christ Jesus. Reconciliation with God, through faith and union to Christ, may also be known as a fact in human experience. And so may salvation from sin—not simply from the punishment of sin, but also from the love of sin and the power of sin.

The mighty problem of evil, with its far-reaching consequences, has its difficulties. Why should a good God, possessing all power, have permitted it? Could not infinite wisdom have devised a moral constitution for man, in which sin would have been impossible? Most certainly He could. However, even God could not have prevented sin in man as he is now constituted; for sin is the result of man's free choice. Human evil originated in the misuse of that freedom with which the Creator graciously endowed the creature.

God could have prevented sin by denying to man Intelligence; for if man, like the dumb animals, could not understand God's command, then the violation of it would not be sin. God could have prevented sin by denying to man Conscience, the knowledge of right and wrong. Animals may injure and hurt each other. They do not know that it is wrong; and it is not sin to them. God could have prevented sin by denying to man Free Will. If man was not free to choose as he pleased, he would not be responsible for his acts; and, therefore, no act of his would be sin. God could have prevented sin (but not evil) by giving man no law, or rule of life—by allowing every man to be a law unto himself; for where there is no law there can be no transgression.

However, it is a fact easily demonstrated that man has been made on the best possible model. Had he been denied any or all of these—Intelligence, Conscience, Free Will, or a good law—he would be infinitely inferior to what he is with his present moral constitution. God gave to man the best possible moral constitution, and in it sin was possible. He made man in His own image, possessed of Intelligence, Freedom, and a knowledge of right and wrong; and, possessing these gifts, it was possible for him to choose the wrong. God, therefore, could not *wisely* have prevented sin.

His wisdom appears in the permission of sin. His goodness and love are shown in the provision which He has made to overcome it, and to deliver man from its power, in the Atonement and the New Birth. Let no man, therefore, rashly blame God for permitting sin, until he fully understands God's entire scheme concerning man.

The Fall of man was not owing to any blunder on the part of the Creator in making man. Nor was the Atonement of Christ an after-thought to correct that blunder, as some seem to imagine. The Atonement was a part of God's original plan, and was devised before man was created. Hence the Redeemer of man is spoken of as "the Lamb slain from the foundation of the world." It is thus clearly proved that God anticipated the Fall, and made provision for it in the counsels of eternity.

At present, however, we are dealing with facts—Sin as a fact, and the Atonement as a fact. In all sin there is wilful disobedience to God, if not deliberate defiance of God. When a man wilfully disobeys God, he says in effect, "God, Thou art not true, Thou wilt not punish"; or, "God, Thou art not able, Thou canst not punish." Therefore, when a man has wilfully violated God's law, he is necessarily out of harmony with God; and something must be done to bring about satisfactory relations between God and man, or else there cannot be peace. What must be done? Man must certainly be brought into harmony with the law of God. He must acquire similarity of feeling with God. He must learn to love what God loves, and to hate what God hates. But even such a change of heart and desire does not cover the past. Hence an atonement, a covering, must be provided for the sins of the past—for the disobedience, the disloyalty, the defiance of God. The human heart, as well as the law of God, demands such an atonement before there can be peace. The human heart could not possibly believe that God could forgive deliberate sin, except the majesty of the law had been upheld in the person of Christ. He, by bearing the full penalty of transgression, showed that sin could not be forgiven in any easy, off-hand manner. To do so would be to remove all moral distinctions. The transgressor would be treated as if he had never transgressed. The Holy and Just One would be seen to trample on His own law. But Christ, by His sinless life and vicarious death, "magnified the law, and made it honourable." This was the need and purpose of the Atonement, and not to soothe the feelings of an angry God.

The love of God to man was before the Atonement; and the Atonement was the outcome of Divine love. The Atonement of Christ is not the ground and cause of God's love to His people; but the reverse is true. God's love to man is the ground and cause of the Atonement. "God so loved the world that He gave His only-begotten Son." It must be remembered that Sin and Salvation have a very wide range, affecting not only our relation to God, but also our knowledge of God in the tender, gracious, forgiving attributes of His nature.

The effects of sin upon man are twofold. First, there is the *guilt* of sin, exposing him to the penalty laid upon transgression. By the guilt of sin is meant *the obligation to give satisfaction to the violated law.* For this, man wanted a Redeemer who had not Himself incurred the penalty, and who could, therefore, pay a full ransom for the life of man forfeited by sin. But, secondly, sin is *personal pollution.* By sin the heart and affections become corrupted. Hence the soul that has sinned wants renewal,—new loves, new desires, new purposes, new aspirations,—bringing it into harmony with God's law. This need is provided for in the New Birth and by union to Christ. By the Redemption of Christ and the regenerating and sanctifying power of the Holy Spirit, man is lifted up to a higher and safer platform than that upon which he stood before he had sinned. He is not only confirmed in love and loyalty to God by the deliberate choice of the will in turning to God and accepting Christ as Saviour and Lord ; but he has the experience and bitterness of sin, as a powerful motive to deter from future sin ; and he has also the promise of Christ to keep him from finally falling away : " I give unto My sheep eternal life, and they shall never perish."

By Sin and Redemption we also have a fuller and clearer Revelation of God. Had it not been for sin, man could never have had such a marvellous display of love, on the part of God, as was manifested in the life and death of the Lord Jesus Christ. It is only in Christ that man can learn that God can love the unlovely, and that He is " longsuffering and gracious, forgiving iniquity, transgression, and sin." And the love of God, perceived by man, is the one great power by which his stubborn and rebellious will is broken and brought into harmony with God's will, so that ever after God is loved supremely. " We love Him, because He first loved us."

In Redemption, too, we see the power of God to new-create, and to snatch His creature man from the powers of evil. It is a fact abundantly attested by human experience, that, by the indwelling of the Holy Spirit, man is delivered from the love of sin and the power of sin. He is radically changed ; so that he really becomes "a new creature "—a " partaker of the Divine nature "—with a heart and will in perfect sympathy with God. Hence it is seen that the complete plan of Salvation includes both Redemption and Regeneration. Redemption alone could not save man without Regeneration : for, if man was not " renewed in the spirit of his mind," he would be daily adding to his past transgressions, so that pardon for the ˙past would avail him nothing. Power to lead a holy life is absolutely necessary to inward peace ; for without holiness there can be no fellowship with God. To enjoy peace and fellowship with God we must "walk in the light as He is in the light" (1 John i. 7). This is a truth known also in human experience. Therefore in order to abiding peace there must be regeneration—renewal.

But, further, Regeneration without Redemption cannot give peace to the soul that has sinned. Take a practical illustration. A man has committed a crime. By and by he comes to loathe that crime. He is a reformed man, thoroughly resolved never to transgress again. But can he have peace if no atonement is made, if no satisfaction is given to the law which he has violated ? No ; he feels that he is a condemned man. Even if the hounds of justice were not on his track, his conscience would give him no peace. Now how shall he find peace in the presence of conscience and his past record? Sorrow for his sin does not give peace. Reformation, the determination to live a good life, does not give peace. No amount of reformation can give peace in view of sin committed. Neither can lapse of time give peace. In the absence of satisfaction conscience forbodes punishment. He may hate and loathe the sin, yet conscience forbodes punishment. So long as God lives, and conscience, and memory, he cannot have peace until he knows and believes that his past sins have been atoned for. Hence we see that Conscience demands just such an atonement as the Scriptures declare has been provided. And yet men, who do not think closely, and who never get to the heart of things, are continually exclaiming, " If a man repents, and reforms, and leads a good life, what do you want with atonement?" Such men seem to imagine that atonement is intended merely to soothe the feelings of an outraged Deity. But, as we have seen, atonement, satisfaction for sin, is necessary for the sinner's sake; and without it he cannot have peace. If a man convicted of crime serves his term of punishment, he is no longer afraid of the officers of justice. Or if a friend pays the fine for him he is at peace. The law has been satisfied, and has no further claim upon him. Peace has been obtained by upholding and fulfilling the claims of the law; and on no other conditions could peace be obtained. So it is impossible for us to feel at peace in God's presence until we know and believe that atonement has been made and accepted for us. Until such time, the voice of conscience, which is the voice of God within, will insist upon satisfaciton being made.

It will not do to say, "Could not a merciful God forgive, and receive back to favour, a reformed sinner, although he has not accepted Christ as his Saviour and Redeemer? If God could have taken man back to fellowship with Himself without the death of Christ, He certainly would have done so. By sin man forfeited his life. "The wages of sin is death." Life only could redeem life. It must be sinless life, as well as rational and immortal life, that is to redeem man. So God Himself must die; and God did die.

The Lord Jesus possessed pre-eminent personal qualifications for making atonement for a fallen world. Being the infinite God, there was value in His life and sufferings. Being sinless, He could die for others, the law having no claim upon His life. Having freely offered Himself there was no injustice in the innocent suffering for the guilty. He did it cheerfully, gladly, for the joy set before Him in bringing many sons to glory. Being truly man as well as God, atonement was made in the same nature that had sinned. Wherefore, no anxious soul need fear that the atonement of Christ is not sufficient. It is such as God can accept, for He Himself has provided it. Like all God's works, it is perfect.

However, the grand difficulty to be faced and met was not so much a legal as a moral difficulty. How could the Holy God hold communion with a fallen creature? How could the Holy One take the unholy into His arms and still remain pure? It was a real difficulty. It would seem to ignore all moral distinctions. The righteous and wicked would seem to be treated alike. The holy and just God would appear to men to violate His own law. There must, therefore, be a penalty exacted. Atonement must be made by the sinner, or by a Substitute. There must be death for evil-doing, as well as mercy for the penitent sinner. Otherwise sin would be encouraged. By the death of Christ on the cross the terrible death-bringing and death-deserving power of sin would be revealed. Innocence would not be confounded with sinfulness, and yet the fallen would be lifted up—the lost would be saved.

But it may be asked, Could not God, by the exercise of His omnipotent power, have produced goodness and loyalty in the heart even of man fallen, apart altogether from the death of Christ upon the cross? But force, compulsion, is out of the question, seeing that the needed salvation is largely a moral result, which can be brought about only by moral means and motives. The will of man cannot be constrained; it must act freely. Love and loyalty to God cannot be compelled. It is of the very essence of love that it be spontaneous. Outward compliance with God's law, if secured by force, without securing the obedience of the heart, or love to the law, would not be salvation; for there can be no salvation without reconciliation. If there remains in the heart any secret enmity to the law of God, there is enmity to God Himself. The law is not obeyed until it is loved; and he who loves the Lawgiver will also love His law, which is but the expression of His will. Therefore there must be a profound moral impression made upon fallen man so as to touch the heart and move it to love God. But love only can produce love; therefore it was necessary that God should make a display of His love sufficient to convince men that He seeks their highest good and happiness. Thus "God commendeth His own love to us, in that, while we were yet sinners, Christ died for us" (Rom. v. 8).

During His life, and on the cross, Christ encountered two kinds of suffering, mental and physical. Mental suffering, which includes burdened feeling and wounded sensibility, is not called suffering in the New Testament. We find it couched in such language as "being grieved," as at the hardness of men's hearts; being "burdened in spirit," as in sympathy and loving concern; "being troubled in spirit," or "being in an agony," or being "exceeding sorrowful," as in the garden of Gethsemane. Hence, when it is said that "Christ hath once suffered for sins," the reference is clearly to His sufferings on the cross. These sufferings, however, were both mental and physical. Heart-sorrow is much intenser than mere bodily pain; and Christ's physical suffering, even on the cross, was but little compared with the anguish and agony of heart which He endured through being numbered with transgressors, and by being rejected by those whom He longed to save. The fact that, when His side was pierced, there flowed out mingled blood and water, proves that His heart was literally rent by grief. The physical suffering was very real; but it was the heart-anguish that crushed Him in the end.

Now such suffering for sin, and at the hands of

sinners, in the person of the Holy and Just One, was needed to impress men with the exceeding sinfulness of sin, and to convince men of the marvellous love of God in making provision for its forgiveness. Thus man, in turning away with loathing from sin, is encouraged to come to God seeking forgiveness and reconciliation. Christ suffered for sin "*that He might bring us to God*"; "Who His own self carried up our sins in His body to the tree, that we, having died unto sins, might live unto righteousness" (1 Peter ii. 24).

By the death of Christ for sin the way is opened for man to return to God. Reconciliation is made possible. And there is also presented to man in the marvellous love of the Saviour the strongest possible motive to live unto righteousness. By bearing the world's bitter curse Jesus proclaimed the sanctity of law and justice, as well as His tender interest in man. And it is just this that gives His life, and teaching, and death such marvellous power over men's hearts and consciences. In this respect Christ, as the Author of salvation, as their Leader in bringing many sons to glory, was made perfect through suffering,—perfect, not in His personal character, for He was that without suffering; but perfect in His official competency—perfect as having got power over men by His sufferings; so that, drawn to Him by His great love to them, they will gladly follow Him as their Leader, and love Him as their Redeemer and Friend.

At the cross mercy and truth met together. Mercy was made possible, and truth was honoured in the one act; so that now God can be just—can be seen by men to be a just God—and yet the justifier of Him who believeth in Jesus. (Rom. iii. 26.) The cross, therefore, as the culmination and completion of Christ's redemptive work, makes reconciliation possible, and man is thereby restored to all the privileges of Sonship.

XVI.

CHRIST IN THE HEART: SANCTIFICATION.

"For if, when we were enemies, we were reconciled to God by the death of His Son, much more being reconciled, we shall be saved by His life."—ROM. v. 10.

IN this passage the Apostle clearly distinguishes between reconciliation and complete salvation. Reconciliation is effected by the death of Christ; but we are saved by His life. We are saved from the love of sin and the power of sin *by the life of Christ in the heart*, lifting us up above the desires of the flesh, filling us with holy longings and aspirations, and clothing us with power to resist evil in all its forms.

By the life of Christ here is meant, not His public life in the presence of men, given for our example and imitation, but the power of His resurrection-life in the hearts of those who are truly united to Him by faith. The Apostle Paul, in narrating his own experience, makes his meaning clear: "I am crucified with Christ, and I no longer live; but Christ liveth in me" (Gal. ii. 20). So also in his prayer to God for the converts at Ephesus: "I bow my knees unto the Father of our Lord Jesus Christ, that He would grant you, according to the riches of His glory, to be strengthened with might by His Spirit in the inner man, that Christ may dwell in your hearts by faith" (Eph. iii. 17).

While, therefore, our reconciliation with God and the forgiveness of past sin are effected by the Atonement made by Christ, appropriated by faith on our part, complete salvation from sin can be effected only by the life of Christ in the heart. The new life of fellowship with Christ becomes possible the moment faith lays hold of the Saviour. The human heart no longer shrinks back in terror from a holy God; for, in Christ, God is seen as reconciled. Provision has been made for all past transgressions. The love that made this provision for sin necessarily draws the heart toward God; and so soon as God is seen and recognized as a loving Father and Friend, the heart is opened to receive the Saviour who is waiting for admittance: " Behold, I stand at the door and knock; if any man hear My voice and open the door, I will come in to him, and will sup with him and he with Me" (Rev. iii. 20). Christ, by His Spirit, enters the heart, and a life of conscious fellowship is begun. From that moment the believer can claim, with Paul, that the power of Christ rests upon him. Under this power the human will breaks altogether with sin, and the foundation of sanctification is laid—heart-holiness is experienced.

By the acceptance of Christ as Redeemer the sinner recognizes the justice of the law and the righteousness of God in laying the penalty of death upon sin. He sees sin as God sees it, as rebellion against God, as deserving death. By accepting Christ he admits that he cannot work out a righteousness of his own so as to merit the favour of God. This recognition of the death-deserving nature of sin means the death of sin in the heart. It will be no longer loved, but loathed.

It will be cast out as an enemy. The justice of the law in punishing sin being now recognized, the sentence of death does not require to be carried out against the transgressor. The death penalty is remitted. Man is permitted to breathe the invigorating air of reconciliation. He is introduced into a state of grace, and enjoys the favour of God and the help of His Spirit. He is now a probationer for glory. He is "justified from all things from which he could not be justified by the law of Moses" the moment he accepts Christ as the Redeemer from sin.

Now he starts life anew. The past is left behind, with its burden of conscious guilt and anxiety. He faces the trials and temptations of life with a light heart, and with the consciousness of victory. A strange peace fills his whole soul. There is no worrying, fretting care. He has complete control over self—over temper, and appetite, and passion. He is a new man. "Old things have passed away; behold, all things have become new" (2 Cor. v. 17). Now his "life is hid with Christ in God." He becomes strong as Christ is strong; for the power of Christ is resting upon him. Sin has not only lost its charm, but also its power over him. For with Christ in the heart sin is necessarily cast out.

Jesus, by His holiness and obedience, brought human nature up to its perfect ideal; and by His death upon the cross He honoured and fulfilled the claims of the law which sinful man had outraged. In both cases He did for man what man had failed to do for himself. The believer who gladly and gratefully accepts this twofold work of Christ, and rests upon it, thereby gives a pledge that the life of Christ will be reproduced in Him. Like the Apostle, he says in effect, "To me to live is Christ." God can now reckon to him the whole atoning work of Christ as if it had actually been done by Himself. He is now of one mind with Christ with regard to the demerit of sin and the need of holiness; therefore Christ can hold fellowship with him, dwelling in him as a new life. And by the power of Christ in the heart the will is brought into sympathy with God's will, with holiness as the result. He is now dead to sin. Sin has lost its power over him. And, since by Christ's life and death the law has been upheld and honoured, God can now accept the sinner's death *to sin* instead of his death *for sin*. Thus pardon becomes possible on the basis of a new life begun in the heart, the finished work of Christ being its procuring cause.

The faith that secures pardon also unites the believer to Christ. It is a belief of the heart. (Rom. x. 10.) It is not simply an assent of the intellect to historic truth about Christ, or to doctrine. It is the free and glad consent of the heart, as the seat of the will and affections, to love God supremely and to delight in His will. The moment the soul lays hold upon Christ as Saviour, and thus secures pardon for all the past, that moment the life of holiness is begun. God could not pronounce the sinner just on any other terms. He who is justified must both forsake and loathe all sin. The faith that justifies carries with it a new heart and a holy life. By bearing this fact in mind it is easy to reconcile those passages of Scripture that speak of salvation as being granted to faith, with other passages that speak of a judgment according to works. There is no true faith that is not accompanied by good works —by a life of holiness and obedience. Faith always obeys God. The faithful Abraham, in offering up Isaac, obeyed. The faithful Moses at the Red Sea promptly obeyed the command, "Speak unto the people that they go forward." The faithful priests that bore the ark at Jordan went forward to the margin of the overflowing river, proving their faith by their deeds. If we would obtain pardon through Christ's work for us, we must also experience the power of Christ's life in us. We must love what He loves. We must obey as He obeyed. We must yield up our own will in cheerful self-surrender to God's will. We must, by a life of self-denial and self-sacrifice, reproduce the life of Christ on earth. If we are branches in the true Vine, we will bear vine-fruit.

Faith in Christ as our personal Saviour secures the forgiveness of all the past: "By Him all that believe are justified from all things from which ye could not be justified by the law of Moses" (Acts xiii. 39). Here it is taught that the only moral condition necessary to the forgiveness of sins is simple faith. But this great act of grace on God's part, in freely forgiving the sins that are past, is only a preparatory step to the renewal of the life. The forgiven soul at once commences to take on the likeness of Christ. The ultimate object of the work of Christ is to produce holiness in the heart of the believer, the forgiveness of sin being but a part of the means necessary to that end—a step in the progress. God reckons the sinner righteous who accepts Christ; but the acceptance of Christ must be such as to change the whole current of the life, so that he who was reckoned righteous will become actually righteous through the life of Christ in the heart. The cultivation and perfecting of holiness and Christlikeness are the works according to which believers will be finally judged.

By such a line of thought it is seen that there is no contradiction between those passages of Scripture which teach justification by faith, and those that speak of judgment according to works. The apparent conflict disappears so soon as it is noted that justification by faith refers to the entrance upon the spiritual life, and judgment according to works to the use which is made of our opportunities for perfecting holiness and taking on the image of Christ. God deals with that portion of our life which precedes the acceptance of Christ by graciously forgiving it; but He deals with what follows the acceptance of Christ by judging it. The reason of this is evident. Before the acceptance of Christ, and the peace and joy that accompany forgiveness, the sinner has no personal experience of the power of Christ, and the blessedness of fellowship with Him; therefore his opposition to Christ may be excused and forgiven on the same ground that Paul claimed forgiveness for his persistent opposition to Christ—" because he did it ignorantly in unbelief." But so soon as a man has experienced the sweets of forgiveness and the joy and power of fellowship with Christ, he is without excuse; he sins against light and knowledge; he deliberately invites God's judgment if he goes back to his old sins. If a man will not, by the power of Christ resting upon him, be saved *from* his sins, God cannot save him *in* his sins. If a man wil. not co-operate with the Spirit of God in producing holiness of heart and life, he proves thereby that he is not in sympathy with God. His faith is not genuine; for it does not unite him to Christ: " He that is joined to the Lord is one spirit " (1 Cor. vi. 17). There is, therefore, the human side and the Divine side in the work of sanctification. We must "work out our own salvation" while God at the same time "works in us both to will and to do "—to direct our wills and to give the power to perform.

In justification faith rests upon the finished work of Christ—His holy life, obedience, and death. The sinner, with Christ, acknowledges that suffering and death are the necessary consequences of sin. He justifies the law of God which inflicts death for evildoing. As Christ upheld the righteousness of the law by dying for the sins of men, so the justified believer will seek to uphold the law of God by living up to its requirements. As by Christ's holy life and vicarious death the law of God was honoured *for* him, so now, by a life of personal holiness, the law of God will be honoured *in* him. But if the life is not such as to honour God's law, then it must be judged by the law. Therefore, judgment according to works logically follows justification by faith.

Justifying faith is necessarily accompanied by the sanctification of the life. The moment the heart lays hold of Christ as Saviour and Sin-bearer the Divine Spirit touches the human spirit, and quickens it into a new life, bringing it into sympathy with God's will. Now God's law will not only be obeyed, but loved.

When God justifies the soul He endows it with the necessary power to lead a new life. If that power is not used it will be withdrawn. The Holy Spirit may be resisted so persistently as to be quenched. Hence the significance of the Apostle's exhortation: "Quench not the Spirit" (1 Thess. v. 19). Final justification cannot take place without holiness of heart and life; for "without holiness no man shall see the Lord" (Heb. xii. 14).

The whole of salvation, therefore, does not consist simply in the forgiveness of sins, just as the whole work of Christ is not summed up in the Atonement. By the atoning work of Christ we are reconciled to God, but we are saved by His life—by His life in us producing holiness and likeness to Himself. Here we have the Divine side of sanctification. Reconciliation, however, must precede the indwelling of Christ as a new and life-giving power. God cannot dwell in man while in a state of enmity. Hence it follows that the Atonement of Christ is the groundwork of Sanctification. Only those who accept Christ as Saviour and Sin-bearer can have His Spirit dwelling in them as a new life. So soon as we are reconciled to God, and all enmity on our part is removed, there is no longer any barrier to the inflow and indwelling of the Holy Spirit.

The death of Christ preceded the promise and gift of the Spirit; and the acceptance of Christ, as Redeemer and Reconciler, must precede the reception of the Spirit as a new life and as Comforter. By the Spirit of Christ dwelling in us as a life-giving power we at once obtain the victory over self, and sin, and Satan. The victory is won by Christ in us, just as He won the same victory in His own body over all the powers of evil. In His own human life He realized the ideal of what humanity ought to be ; and now He dwells in His people by His Spirit to bring their lives up to that ideal. This is an essential part of His work; for without it man could not be saved. It is in this sense that we are said to be *saved by His life*. We have now not only Christ's righteousness for us, in virtue of which past sin is forgiven, but also His righteousness in us ; for, " beholding as in a mirror the glory of the Lord, we are transformed into the same image " (2 Cor. iii. 18).

Christ lives in the believer by His Spirit; so that Sanctification is at one time ascribed to the life of Christ in the heart, and again to the power of the Holy Spirit. After His ascension Christ became the Dispenser of the Spirit ; so that the Holy Spirit may be said to proceed from the Father through the Son. "As the Father hath life in Himself, so hath He given to the Son to have life in Himself; and He hath given Him authority to execute judgment also, because He is the Son of Man" (John v. 26, 27). In the gift of eternal life, and in judgment, God deals with man through the Son, because He is the Son of Man. Seeing that the Father is God, but not man, there is necessarily a great gulf between them ; but Christ, being both God and man, can have personal dealings with man as well as with God. Hence it follows that we receive spiritual life direct from Christ through the power of His Spirit : "As I live by the Father, so he that eateth Me, even he shall live by Me." Our spiritual life, which is the gift of Christ, is also nourished by maintaining fellowship with Him. This text clearly points to the fact that our relation to Christ, as the source of spiritual life, is the same as His relation to the Father. And what does this mean? Surely this. As the Holy Spirit is the bond of union between the Father and the Son, and the life of both; so He is the bond of union between Christ and the believer, and the life of the believer.

But what does Jesus mean when He says, "I live by the Father"? He means that He lived by direct communication with the Father; that when He spoke or acted He yielded up His own will entirely to the Father's will. So to speak, the Father lived in Him, He being every moment perfectly pliant to the Father's hand. Now this is precisely the relation which must exist between the believer and Christ in the matter of sanctification. The human will must be entirely and cheerfully surrendered to the will of Christ. He must live in us in such a sense that He will act through us; so that we are really living the life which Christ directs, and virtually reproducing His life in the presence of men. The true ideal of Christian holiness and consecration cannot be brought below this standard.

But how is the human will to become completely subordinated to Christ's will? Only by the power of Christ resting upon us. If we can say with Paul, "Christ liveth in me," His love will so possess us, and His presence will so fill us, that every selfish wish and sinful desire will be entirely suppressed. We will cheerfully yield up ourselves to Him in perfect self-surrender that He may do for us, and in us, and by us, just as He pleases. When we have once experienced the blessedness of being led by Him, and the joy of holding communion with Him, all will be yielded up to Him, not only without a struggle, but with a calm confidence and a holy joy which will make the soul rich and strong for life. And this act of self-surrender will be entire and immediate. Christ is not gradually received into the heart, nor is sin gradually excluded from the life. The moment Christ is received the reigning power of sin is broken. " Whosoever is born of God doth not commit sin ; for His seed "—His Spirit as the seed-germ of the new life—" remaineth in him ; and he cannot sin, because he is born of God " (1 John iii. 9). When Christ comes with new-creating power the soul at once breaks with all sin. However, there is a sense in which sanctification is a process. As we receive new revelations of Christ and clearer views of holiness, we will exclude from our lives what before was permitted. But in all true Christian Consecration the soul at once condemns and casts out all that is known to be contrary to the mind of Christ.

This is the triumph of faith. With Christ living and reigning in the heart, faith can say with Him in every time of temptation, "Get thee hence, Satan"; and the discomfited tempter will immediately be foiled. Wherever Christ is, Satan is absolutely powerless. Only admit Christ to the heart, and yield up the body to be the temple and dwelling-place of His Spirit, and then the victory over self, and sin, and Satan is assured. Faith makes us one with Christ, and we become "more than conquerors through Him" (Rom. viii. 37). This inbred holiness, as the outcome of the life of Christ in the heart, is an essential part of salvation. It is the one sure evidence that the soul is meet for the inheritance of the saints.

Forgiveness and holiness, therefore, are the two grand elements in salvation; and both are secured to us by Christ—by His work *for* us, and by His work *in* us. By His obedience and death for sin He became our righteousness, on the ground of which past sin is freely forgiven, and we become reconciled to God. By His life in us He becomes our sanctification, on the ground of which we are finally justified. This would seem to be the full significance of the Apostle's words: "Reconciled to God by the death of His Son—saved by His life."

XVII.

THE MYSTERY OF SPIRITUAL LIFE.

"In Him was Life, and the Life was the Light of men."—JOHN i. 4.

THERE are two great mysteries in the world—the mystery of Life and the mystery of Death. Science finds no intelligible answer to the questions, How did man come into being, and, Why should he cease to be? Life, the most potent of all forces, and the most real of all realities, eludes the search of the scientist. We all come into the world endowed with this mysterious principle of Life. In virtue of it we think, and will, and act. It is the most real of all our possessions; and yet it is to us the mystery of mysteries. For centuries scientific men have been studying the Origin of Life with but meagre results. What is it? Whence does it come? Why does it depart? Where is the original Fountain of Life? One old Book only, and it making no profession to being scientific, although never out of harmony with scientific fact, had given for centuries any positive and final utterance on the subject: "The Lord God formed man of the dust of the ground, and breathed into his nostrils the spirit of life, and man became a living soul." Life from the ever-living God—that is the first and the last word of Revelation. And it is also the last word of

Science. Scientific men for ages have fought shy of Revelation. They collected their materials, made their observations, conducted their experiments, constructed their theories, and built up the several sciences, not only without the aid of Revelation, but by rigidly excluding it. The last word of Science, therefore, respecting the Mystery of Life cannot be said to have been influenced by the ancient Revelation. We are in a position, therefore, to-day to accept the testimony of Science, so far as it is in accord with the Old Book, as an independent witness to the facts concerning Life.

The Old Book teaches most explicitly that Life came from antecedent Life—that man became a living soul by receiving the gift of Life from the living God. Now Science, it must be noted, has not passively accepted this teaching; but, on the other hand, has laboured most assiduously to account for Life in a way, which, if established, would necessarily discredit the ancient Revelation. For years scientific men have earnestly striven to account for Life by Spontaneous Generation —that is, that dead matter could generate Life by natural processes, without receiving it direct from a living being. But to-day Science stands helpless in its endeavour to produce Life by Spontaneous Generation.

Professor Tyndall and others have proved, as conclusively as Science can prove anything, that all attempts to produce the Living from the Not-Living have utterly failed. The doctrine of Biogenesis—that Life only can produce Life—is to-day triumphant along the whole line. By no possible process in the realm of Nature can Life be spontaneously generated. And if we persist in getting at the origin of Life there is no resort left us but that it is the gift of Him who is the Eternal Life. If, as Professor Tyndall so positively affirms, "no shred of trustworthy experimental testimony exists to prove that life in our day has ever appeared independently of antecedent life," then we have every reason to believe that Life never did and never will spontaneously appear.

Now what is true of natural life is also true of Spiritual Life. As natural life is confessedly a gift, so Spiritual Life must necessarily be the gift of the Ever-Living One. *Omne vivum ex vivo*—only from Life can Life come—is true in the spiritual sphere as well as in the natural sphere. The necessity of Spiritual Life being communicated to us from a source outside ourselves, is greater than the necessity for natural life to be thus communicated, by as much as the Spiritual Life is of a higher order than the natural life. If the lower life cannot be spontaneously generated, much less can the higher. Hence it follows that man cannot endow himself with Spiritual Life.

How necessary, therefore, was this word of Revelation: "In Him was Life, and the Life was the Light of men." It is here taught that the Christ of God is the source and fountain of Life—of a Life superior to the life that men possessed. It is such Life as can become the Light of men. By becoming partakers of the Life which is His gift, men become illuminated; they receive new light, as well as a new life.

Man by disobedience lost communion with God; he placed himself out of harmony with God; he became alienated, separated from God. He lost Spiritual Life. The moment he ceased to hold communion with God he became spiritually dead. In the day he disobeyed God he died. He still possessed natural life, but spiritually he was dead. The body dies when it is separated from the spirit. Separation is death to the lower organism. So also spiritual death takes place when the spirit is separated from God and ceases to hold communion with Him. God still lives, but the spirit of man is dead to Him. "In the day that thou eatest thereof, thou shalt surely die." This was no empty, unmeaning threat. It was the calm and solemn announcement of an eternal law. To fall out of harmony with God, and lose His favour and fellowship, is to die. Death is separation, not a ceasing to be.

Separate a plant from that which nourished it—air, moisture, the soil, the sun—and it dies. The same is true of the animal creation. Separation from food and air is death. It is true also of the natural life of man. And the same law holds good of man's higher spiritual life. The Spiritual Life is nourished and sustained by fellowship with the Spirit of God: "He that eateth Me, even he shall live by Me" (John vi. 57). Interrupt that fellowship, and the man, having no spiritual nourishment, dies. "He that hath the Son hath Life, and he that hath not the Son of God hath not Life" (1 John v. 12). Live in sin, disobey God, and lose communion with Him, and spiritual death ensues by an eternal law. "To be carnally minded is death." And only the law of the Spirit of life in Christ Jesus can make us free from this law of sin and death (Rom. viii. 2). When by sin we come under the law of sin, which is death, we cannot be set free from this inexorable law, except by "the Spirit of life in Christ Jesus" coming to us, and restoring fellowship by casting out sin. "If ye through the Spirit do put to death the deeds of the body, ye shall live" (Rom. viii. 13).

With the will weakened by sin, and the heart alienated from God by having the affections misplaced, there is no hope for man in the struggle of life, unless Christ comes to him by His Spirit, regenerating the heart, renewing the will, and restoring fellowship. In Him is Life, and that Life must become the Light of man. In no other way can fallen man be lifted up.

It is a law of the different orders of life in the universe that the lower can be lifted up into the region of the higher, only by the higher taking it into union with itself. If plant life is to be lifted up into the higher sphere of animal life it cannot be done by force, and it cannot be done by contact merely; it can be effected only by union. The animal must take the vegetable to itself, and assimilate it to its own body. By the process of digestion and assimilation the animal communicates to the vegetable, now one with itself, a new life. The plant now shares with the animal in its life, and becomes a partaker of the animal's nature. So if man, who is living a mere natural life, is to be lifted up into the higher sphere of Spiritual Life, as possessed by Christ, Christ must take man's spirit into union with His own Spirit, and make man a partaker of His own Divine nature. Spiritual Life must come to man as a gift, an endowment. Man cannot, by any process of Evolution, by any process of unfolding and developing, rise of himself from his natural or psychical life into the higher Spiritual Life.

Life cannot originate by Spontaneous Generation; there must be antecedent life. Neither can Evolution produce a higher order of life. The plant cannot, by culture, be made to take on animal life, and endow itself with feeling and powers of locomotion. The animal cannot develop into a man with reason, conscience, and free will. Evolution may improve the species, but it cannot lift up the species out of its own order, or kingdom, into the one next above it.

Spiritual Life is a distinct order of life. And as life can come only from the touch of life, so Higher Life can come only from the touch of Higher Life. It follows, therefore, that if man is to be lifted up out of his natural life into the Higher Spiritual Life of fellowship with Christ, he must be touched by the Spirit of Christ; his will must become one with Christ's will; he must be truly united to Christ. Nothing less than a vital union can effect this great change. In Him is Life, and His Life is the Light of men. Thus we see the profound significance of the words of the Great Teacher, " I am come that they might have Life, and that they might have it more abundantly."

The one endowment that distinguishes man more than any other from the brute creation, and makes him great and Godlike, is his spiritual faculty—his capability of holding communion with God. This faculty was blunted and blighted by sin; and, having once lost its power of holding communion with God, it requires to be revivified before communion can be resumed. .A flower-seed may lie dormant in the earth for centuries if the necessary conditions of growth are not present. So man's spiritual faculty lies dormant until touched and quickened by the Divine Spirit. The seed requires moisture, warmth, and light to cause it to germinate and give signs of life; and it is interesting to note that water, fire, and light are used in Scripture as the best emblems of the Holy Spirit. As the seed lies dormant until it feels the warmth and power of the sun, so the spiritual faculty in man is dormant and inoperative until it feels the warmth and quickening power of the Spirit of God.

This fact, suggested by the analogy of Nature, is clearly taught by Scripture, and is also abundantly confirmed by human experience. "Ye must be born again—born of the Spirit," is but the pointed utterance of an eternal truth. No man can enter the kingdom of God—can attain to spiritual fellowship with God, except he is quickened by the Divine Spirit. The apparent harshness of this declaration is greatly softened when it is noted that it carries with it the gracious assurance, "Ye *may* be born again." Our communion with God, which had been interrupted by sin, may be restored. Man's blunted spiritual faculty may be quickened. From the eternal Fountain of Life he may receive more abundant life.

In order to enjoy communion with God and to participate in the joys and privileges of the kingdom of God man needs not only Spiritual Life, but Spiritual Light as well—inward illumination: "Except a man be born again he cannot *see* the kingdom of God." The spiritual eye, sealed by sin, must be opened before it can see the King in His beauty, and see God as a loving Father and Friend. Now provision is made for this need in Christ. By His Spirit dwelling in the heart He becomes not only the Life, but the Light of men. Regeneration brings light as well as life. This fact of Revelation is confirmed by our spiritual experience. The New Birth revolutionizes not only the life, but our views of God, of truth, of duty. It sheds a marvellous light upon our path. God is no longer in the "thick darkness"; He is Light, and in Him is no darkness at all. His commands, which seemed obscure and puzzling and perplexing before, become illuminated. We now see the spirit of the law, and not the mere letter. We are set free from the bondage of the law, by being brought into sympathy with it. This inward illumination which accompanies the new life is not only very real to those who have experienced it; but it is so transcendently glorious that language cannot convey any clear idea of its marvellous power. Paul passed through this experience. To him it was a real shining of God in the heart. "God, who said, Let the light shine out of darkness, hath shined in our hearts to give the light of the knowledge of the glory of God in the face of Jesus Christ" (2 Cor. iv. 6). He was conscious of possessing what he declares to be a "peace which passeth all understanding," and "a joy that is unspeakable and full of glory." He felt that he had the light of Christ within him, and the power of Christ resting upon him. Those who have passed through similar experiences—and such experiences are by no means rare—know that the tongue is helpless to utter any adequate description of this inner glory and illumination. There is new life, new light, new loves and longings, new aims and aspirations, new peace and joy, new power over sin, and new power in service. It is a "new creation." As Spontaneous Generation is unknown in Nature, so it is impossible as a way of entrance into the higher Spiritual Life. Christ is the only true source of Spiritual Life. Only those who can say with Paul, "Christ liveth in me," can attain to these higher experiences. No man by any process of growth or culture can lift himself out of the natural life into the Spiritual Life.

To those who have no experience of this new life it can be made known only by Revelation or by testimony. If they refuse these the path of knowledge is closed to them. "The natural man receiveth not the things of the Spirit of God, for they are foolishness unto him; neither can he know them, because they are spiritually discerned" (1 Cor. ii. 14). The natural man has his eye closed to spiritual beauty, and his heart closed to spiritual realities. We are amused at the child in the picture, looking up in wonderment at the kindly face of a favourite dog and saying, "CAN'T YOU TALK?" We know that it would require a miracle to endow the dog with intellectual powers that would enable him to enter into the thoughts of the child, and to express them in intelligible speech. And just as the dog would require to be specially endowed with intellectual powers to enable him to enter into the intellectual life of the child, so the natural man requires to be specially endowed with spiritual power before he can understand the mysteries of the Spiritual Life. The natural man cannot understand "the things of the Spirit of God" —spiritual truth, spiritual joy, spiritual power,—"but he that is spiritual discerneth all things, yet he himself is discerned of no man"(1 Cor. ii. 15). In these passages the Apostle is not simply teaching dogma; he is speaking of that which he knows from his own experience to be true. He had passed through the experience of the natural man, and knew only too well its painful limitations, and its utter inability to enter the spiritual sphere. He, above all others, is entitled to speak with authority on this subject; for no man ever strove more earnestly than he to lift himself up out of the natural life into the higher life of fellowship with God. And where Paul failed, all must certainly expect to fail.

It is evident, therefore, that human experience, as well as the analogies of life in Nature, proves most conclusively the necessity of Regeneration, if man is to be lifted up into the higher sphere of Spiritual Life. He who would know the things of the Spirit of God must be born of the Spirit. He must receive Christ both as the Life and the Light of men. Thus only can men become sons of God and enjoy fellowship with Him. "As many as received Him, to them gave He power to become the sons of God, even to them that believe on His name; who were born, not of blood, nor of the will of the flesh, nor of the will of man, but of God" (John i. 12, 13).

To all spiritual things the natural man is dead; and if he is to enter into the Spiritual Life at all, he must enter it as he entered upon the natural life—by being born. There is no other way. Nicodemus marvelled when Jesus said, "Ye must be born again"; and so men marvel now. However, the Great Teacher did not answer his marvelling mood by suggesting another method. He simply affirmed the great truth with uncompromising emphasis, assuring him that a spiritual birth was indispensable in order to enter the Spiritual Kingdom. This birth would take place the moment he looked to the crucified Saviour, and accepted Him as his Life and Light. Only by believing in Him could Life be obtained. To become spiritual, man must be born of the Spirit: "That which is born of the flesh is flesh, and that which is born of the Spirit is spirit" (John iii. 6). Here "the flesh" stands for human nature with its tendency to sin, in contrast to the spiritual nature imparted in the New Birth. In natural generation man receives natural life and a human nature. In Regeneration, or spiritual generation, he receives Spiritual Life, and becomes a "partaker of the Divine nature" (2 Peter i. 4). This is the only possible solution of the mystery of the Spiritual Life.

XVIII.

THE MYSTERY OF REGENERATION.

"The wind bloweth where it listeth, and thou hearest the sound thereof, but canst not tell whence it cometh, and whither it goeth : so is every one that is born of the Spirit."—JOHN iii. 8.

IN the previous chapter we have shown the necessity for Regeneration. The Lord Jesus proclaimed it : "Ye must be born again." The human heart demands it as the only possible way of entrance into the higher Spiritual Life and communion with God. No man has ever by his own unaided efforts lifted himself up out of the natural life, with its prevailing tendency to sin, into the higher life of holiness, and Christlikeness. This fact is abundantly attested by human experience. No spiritual man claims to have regenerated himself. Science, too, adds its testimony, and from the analogies of Life in Nature, points to the fact that Spiritual Life can originate only by the touch of the Ever-living Spirit.

The Word of God is most explicit in declaring that Eternal Life is the Gift of God : "The wages of sin is death ; but the free gift of God is eternal life in Christ Jesus our Lord" (Rom. vi. 23). "God hath given to us eternal life, and this life is in His Son. He that hath the Son hath life ; and he that hath not the Son of God hath not life" (1 John v. 11, 12).

Although the true Christian who has received the gift of Life, and has been regenerated by the quickening power of the Holy Spirit, and has experienced the blessed power of the Gospel, does not require any confirming testimony to the truth of God's Word; still the testimony of Science and human experience may be useful to those who are only groping their way into the light, and are feeling after God, if haply they may find Him. All such must cordially welcome anything and everything that throws a ray of light across their path. But these rays of light will be of no value unless they bring them to Christ, the only Source and Fountain of Light and Life.

The Great Teacher in our text clearly reveals to us the fact that the New Birth is a Mystery. It is something different and distinct from anything observed in the ordinary course of Nature, or experienced in the ordinary operations of the mind and heart. Regeneration is altogether a unique experience. The new Life is not only a new experience to the possessor, but is also mysterious even to himself. He knows that he possesses it, but he cannot explain to others how it is that it came to him. He is conscious of possessing a new life, and a new relation to God and to duty. He is a new creature. Old things have passed away, and all things have become new. The old sinful pleasures have lost their charm. God is seen to be reconciled. Duty becomes transfigured. The change is very real, and it is very marvellous. He who before marvelled that he *must* be born again, now marvels that he *is* born again. He is astonished beyond measure at the wonderful change that has been wrought in him. All in a moment the darkness has been dispelled, and his whole soul is flooded with light and joy. He is conscious now of holding close and intimate communion with God. He breathes the very atmosphere of heaven. The joy of the heart is seen in the countenance; is heard in the gentle tones of the voice; and is felt in the power to control temper, and appetite, and passion. The fact and the fruit of the new life are abundantly evident; still the manner of it is veiled in mystery. It is mysterious like the wind and the light. Its new-creating power is a fact known in experience, but how the change came about is not clear. This is Christ's own teaching on the subject, and it is in perfect accord with our own experience.

All life is mysterious. Science cannot explain it, or get at the origin of it. We know the fact. We know *that* it is; we do not know *how* it is. Revelation here comes to our aid. And if Revelation was ever necessary surely it is needed here. The origin of Spiritual Life is a subject of profound moment, affecting, as it does, the happiness and well-being of the whole human race. Only from Life can Life come; and only from " the Spirit of Life in Christ Jesus " can Spiritual Life come. " He that hath the Son hath Life.".

What, then, is Spiritual Life; and how does man come into the possession of it? Paul could say, " Christ liveth in me "; and, addressing believers, he claimed for them the same high privilege: " Christ in you the hope of glory " (Col. i. 27). " Know ye not your own selves, how that Jesus Christ is in you, except ye be reprobates? " (2 Cor. xiii. 5.) And again: " When Christ, *who is our life*, shall appear " (Col. iii. 4).

From such passages it is clear that Spiritual Life exists only in those in whom Christ dwells. Spiritual Life, therefore, is the life of Christ in the heart, communicated by the quickening touch of His Spirit.

But it may be asked, What conditions are necessary on our part in order to become partakers of this new life? Paul gives prominence to Faith and Love: "That Christ may dwell in your hearts by faith; that ye, being rooted and grounded in love, may be able, with all saints, to comprehend what is the length, and breadth, and depth, and height, and to know the love of Christ, which passeth knowledge, that ye might be filled with all the fulness of God" (Eph. iii. 17). There must be an actual heart-reception of Christ; and that is much more than simply acknowledging Him as the historical Messiah and infallible Teacher. The faith which worketh by love is a laying hold of Christ by the heart—a clinging to Him, and a trusting to Him alone for salvation. "If thou confess with thy mouth the Lord Jesus, and *believe in thine heart* that God raised Him from the dead, thou shalt be saved" (Rom. x. 9). It is heart-belief that unites the sinner to the Saviour, and sets up the Spiritual Life in the soul. The will and affections must be wholly turned towards Christ before He can take up His abode with us. "If a man love Me he will keep My words, and My Father will love him, and we will come unto him, and make our abode with him" (John xiv. 23). Such a faith as rests upon the finished work of Christ for acceptance with God, and such a love as yields up the will, affections, *all* to God, are the necessary conditions on man's part for receiving Christ as his life and salvation. Christ, by His Spirit, comes to such a heart, and dwells there as a new life—the Divine Spirit holding fellowship with the human spirit, endowing it with new forces, and fitting it for new joys.

It is evident, therefore, that spiritual generation, like natural generation, is an act. It is not a gradual unfolding of the natural powers, but an instantaneous quickening of the spiritual faculty, bringing it into conscious fellowship with God. In a moment of time he that receiveth Christ "passes out of death into life" (John v. 24). Before, he was spiritually dead—he had no communion with God. Now, by the quickening touch of the Holy Spirit, he receives new life, and communion is restored. He who was spiritually dead now lives—the lost is saved. If Regeneration be attributed to the Spirit of God, as the only source of Life, it must be instantaneous, like every act of generation. The steps that lead up to it may be gradual, and may extend over a lengthened period. So also after the New Life has dawned it may develop gradually. However, the preparatory steps—the burdened conscience, the earnest struggling after light, the abandonment of known sin, the chastened and subdued spirit—are not Regeneration. A man may pass through all these, and yet have no conscious fellowship with God and no Spiritual Life. In Regeneration, whether it comes, as in the case of Paul, with the impetuous rush and irresistible power of the whirlwind, or, as in many cases, like the gentle fanning of the evening breeze, the moment of contact between the Holy Spirit and the human spirit is a definite point of time. There is no such a thing in Scripture, in Science, or in human experience, as generation by a gradual process.

As the steps which lead up to Regeneration may be gradual, so there may be a gradual unfolding, a progressive development of the new life in the soul after Regeneration has taken place. However, it must be remembered that neither of these gradual processes is Regeneration, although they are often confounded with it. The one thing which, in modern times, has weakened Christianity more perhaps than anything else, is the growing tendency to ignore the necessity of Regeneration by the quickening touch of the Spirit of God. Dependence is placed upon a good moral life and a growing conformity to the law of God. But Nicodemus could not enter into life by such a method. Paul, too, strove most earnestly to perfect his life by similar means, and failed. We ourselves have also tried, and have hopelessly failed. Human experience, therefore, re-echoes the words of the Master, "Ye must be born again."

However, while the new life dawns suddenly, and comes more or less as a surprise, there will be growth, development, a pressing forward and a mounting upward. While we affirm that by no possible means can the natural life be evolved into the higher Spiritual Life without the quickening touch of the Spirit of God, still we insist upon the necessity of growth and progress in the Divine life. Paul, not considering himself to have attained to the highest heights of holiness, pressed forward towards the mark for the prize of the high calling of God in Christ Jesus (Phil. iii. 14); and we are "enjoined to grow in grace and in the knowledge of our Lord and Saviour Jesus Christ" (2 Peter iii. 18). There is no controversy about the necessity of growth and the continual unfolding and expansion of the powers of the soul. What Christ and Christianity insist upon is that the growth shall be in the line of the Spiritual Life, communicated in the New Birth, as distinguished from the unfolding of the natural life. Where there is life there is growth; and where there is Spiritual Life there will be spiritual growth. If an organism which is the vehicle of life fails to develop itself, it necessarily deteriorates. There is no standing still. Stagnation means death, decay, corruption. A plant that is neglected soon deteriorates. Flowering plants of all kinds are improved by culture, and by neglect soon degenerate into an inferior species. The same is true of animals and the human race. So also there must be growth and culture in the Spiritual Life: "If ye live after the flesh ye shall die" (Rom. viii. 13).

. Regeneration by the Spirit of God, and Justification by faith in the finished work of Christ, do not do away with the necessity of perfecting holiness in the fear of God; as some, anxious only to misrepresent the teaching of Christianity, persistently affirm. No secular evolutionist can insist more strenuously upon the necessity of uprightness of heart and integrity of life than Paul and every true representative of Christian teaching. The Christian is enjoined to put off the old man with his deeds—anger, wrath, malice, blasphemy, filthy communication, lying, envyings, murders, drunkenness, and every form of impurity, and to put on the new man, cultivating love, forbearance, forgiveness, patience, purity, and all the social virtues. Nowhere in the whole realm of literature have we inculcated such high-toned morality as in the Sermon on the Mount and in the Epistles of Paul. Christianity insists upon perfection, perfect likeness to Christ, as the ultimate goal to be attained. Therefore Regeneration and Justification by Faith are not substitutes for righteous living, but necessary steps to the entire sanctification of the life.

Man does not rise to his highest and best at a single bound. His best will never be attained during this earthly life. He will, if he preserves communion with God, go on progressing in knowledge and capabilities of enjoyment throughout the eternal ages. Christ Himself likened the kingdom of God in the heart to the gradual unfolding of the seed cast into the ground: " First the blade, then the ear, after that the full corn in the ear" (Mark iv. 28). There must always be development, otherwise there would be no life in the heart. However, Christ, always careful never to omit any essential point of detail in His parables, refers, first of all, to casting the *seed* into the ground. It is not the growth and development of the natural products of the soil, but of the seed. Any other growth would be but tares and weeds. So in all true spiritual growth and development the first concern must be to have the Divine seed planted in the soil of the human heart. The Holy Spirit alone is the seed-germ of all Spiritual Life.

Regeneration is the Divine side of the process of renewal, Conversion the human side. Regeneration is necessarily sudden, and comes as a surprise. Conversion, however, so far as it is the result of human effort, may be approached by gradual stages. And yet in Conversion the moment of turning and decision must always be a definite point of time. The work, viewed as a whole, may seem to be gradual and progressive; but the definite and decisive act of will, by which the soul accepts Christ and breaks with sin, is the real turning point. It will be found, moreover, to correspond with the moment of Regeneration. It is by the help of the Divine Spirit that the human will is enabled at that decisive moment to turn to God and embrace Christ as Saviour and Sin-bearer.

In many cases the point of turning is most marked. Under deep impression the whole soul is stirred to its deepest depths, and resolutely determines to lead a new life. From that moment the stubborn will is broken; self and sin are overcome; the man is a new creature. The work is so thorough, the new life is so real and unmistakable, the accompanying joy and peace are so glorious, that the day and the hour are indelibly impressed upon the mind, as by far the most important era in the whole life. In other cases the change, though real, is much less marked, just in proportion as the nature is less intense. A nature, constitutionally gentle and refined, may not experience the sudden arrest, the indescribable terror and agony of soul, the awful dread of doom, and the unspeakable anguish of despair. The downward path was gently trod; and although the march was not upward, it was scarcely downward. It was almost a life of balance. Coming to such a soul, the Spirit of God does not turn the nature upside down, and prostrate the soul in the dust, and fill it with dread alarms. The breath of heaven is gently breathed into such a soul. The new life dawns almost imperceptibly. The current of life is indeed changed, and now flows Godward and heavenward; but the moment of turning cannot be easily determined. Nevertheless there was a definite moment when, by the help of the Divine Spirit, the upward path was chosen, and the new life entered the soul. A boat in the harbour is bearing a precious freight of human souls. Gradually it is being borne out on the tide towards the sea. Presently the pace of the boat is slackened, for the tide has nearly ebbed. Now it stands still. No oar is lifted. As yet no effort is made by the party to bring the boat back. But the tide has turned, and a gentle breeze springs up with the returning tide. Now they are gradually borne back, and before they are aware they have made considerable progress on the homeward track. Friends on shore observed the point of turning more readily than the occupants of the boat. The time of turning was a definite moment, although those on board could not discern it. It is thus with what are called gradual conversions. In all cases there is a decisive moment when the soul enters upon the homeward and heavenward path, whether it is clearly recognized or not. The tide of gracious influences and the breath of the Divine Spirit may have been wafting them heavenwards for some time before they are distinctly conscious of any marked change in their lives; and hence they cannot say precisely at what moment they turned their back upon the world and set out for the Celestial City. But still the fact remains —the point of turning was definite and decisive.

It will not do, therefore, to decry sudden conversions as something abnormal and suspicious, and bordering on fanaticism. The beginning of Life must always be sudden and instantaneous. The moment a man opens the door of the heart and admits Christ, that moment he passes from death into life.

With respect to the origin of life, Biological Science is in perfect harmony with the teaching of Scripture. Life comes only from the touch of life. There is no such a thing in Nature as Spontaneous Generation. So Spiritual Life comes from the touch of the Spirit of God, and not by any process of Evolution.

XIX.

THE LAWS OF THE SPIRITUAL LIFE.

"Being confident of this very thing, that He who hath begun a good work in you will perform it until the day of Jesus Christ."—PHIL. i. 6.

SPIRITUAL Life is a growth, and the laws of its growth may be analysed and noted like the laws of a plant or any other living thing. If we wish to cultivate successfully any new and rare plant, we are careful to learn something regarding the laws of its life. We try to understand its nature—whether it requires light or shade, a cool or a warm atmosphere, and all other conditions of healthy life and growth. The skilled botanist who has studied the habits of the plant, is able to lay down the laws of its life, so that the gardener knows exactly how to treat it. But while the gardener attends to the general laws laid down for its culture, he also makes use of his own skill, and learns much as to the best treatment of the plant from his own observation.

The same is true of the Laws of the Spiritual Life. In the Word of God skilled spiritual botanists have laid down the general laws of healthy spiritual life and growth. These laws, or RULES OF HOLY LIVING, are our general instructions for the nurture of the Spiritual Life. But just as the gardener has to use his own knowledge, and find out much from his own observation and experience, so must it be with all those who are cultivating the garden of the soul. We must be able to vary our treatment according to the several stages of growth and progress in the Divine life.

This was the method adopted by the Apostle Paul. He says of those who were as yet but babes in Christ, "I have fed you with milk, and not with meat; for hitherto ye were not able to bear it." They were babes, but they were babes in Christ. They were Christian men,—believers in Christ,—but they were not *spiritual*. He says that there were divisions, and envyings, and strife among them; and thereby implies that those who become *spiritual* are able to rise above such things. In speaking of discipline in the Church, he clearly recognizes two classes of Christians, one class being spoken of as "spiritual": "Brethren, if a man be overtaken in a fault, ye which are spiritual restore such an one in the spirit of meekness." Thus we see that the true qualification for exercising rule in the Church is not learning, or position, or such qualifications as would fit a man for office in civil matters, but that maturity of Christian experience which the Apostle designates by the term "spiritual."

With reference to the Spiritual Life the text clearly teaches that it has a definite beginning, and that it is begun by God: "He that hath begun a good work in you will carry it on until the day of Christ Jesus." This good work—this inception of the Spiritual Life—not only begun by God, it is also carried on by Him; and this is the sure guarantee that, when begun, it will be perfected.

This text, therefore, takes in the whole life, from the date of the New Birth until we stand complete and glorified among the angel throng. And during the varied stages of that life what growth is perceptible! The aged saint, like Paul, "desiring to depart and to be with Christ," has a far larger and fuller life than when he set out·in the Christian race. He may not have the same buoyancy of spirits, the same intense enthusiasm, the same exuberant feelings, the same outspoken frankness; years have toned down these impulsive moods. But he has grown marvellously in the higher reaches of the soul. See what a peace sits enthroned upon his placid brow! See in what a kingly mood he meets temptation now! See how calmly and confidently he holds converse with his God! He walks with God. He talks with God. His life is hid with Christ in God. The fitful joy of early life has grown into a settled and all-pervading peace. The spasmodic efforts put forth during the brief impulses of enthusiasm have developed into a constant and almost unconscious influence for good. The impassioned address has given place to solemn and earnest entreaty. He has become a king among men, controlling self with scarcely an effort, and exerting an immense influence for good over his fellow-men. He was not always such, but he has grown.

This, then, is a most interesting subject: The unfolding of Christian character, and the laws which regulate it.

One of the most obvious laws of all true growth is, that each step in the progress is preparatory to the next step, and makes further growth possible. Just as in the erection of a building, one tier of stones is so placed and prepared as to receive the next tier; and so on until the building is complete. In Nature as well as in Art we have the same law. Look at the growing fruit. It is ripened by the direct action of the sun's rays producing a chemical change in the substance of the fruit; and every ray of the sun that ripens the apple makes it opener to further influence from the sun.

Now this is the law of the Spiritual Life. It is the method of all growth in the Divine life. Every step we take in the progress upwards fits us for taking a further step. We ascend the heights of holiness as we ascend the successive heights of a mountain range. We start at the bottom with a near eminence in view. Nothing is seen beyond it but the clear azure. But, when we attain to it, a further height is seen. And no sooner is it reached than we espy another, still towering above us, and so on in the ascending series. In the life of holiness we mount upwards in the same manner. Every step we take in the pathway of holiness enables us to see higher heights beyond us, which invite us to press onward and upward. And so will it be all through life. The more we see of the beauty of holiness, the more will our eyes be opened to see new beauties in the Divine life.

When we first gave our hearts to Christ we understood something of His wondrous love, and our hearts were opened to receive Him. But this step prepared us for something higher. We were filled with a longing desire to experience more of His fulness. This felt sense of the love and presence of Christ made us purer in heart and holier in life; and this purity created in us a holy longing for a higher degree of holiness and purity. And thus the work went on. Hence it follows, that if the Spiritual Life is healthy, there must necessarily be progress in holiness. The apple does not ripen to a certain degree, and then go back. If it is healthy, and maintains its connection with the tree, it will make steady progress towards maturity. So if the child of God maintains his connection with Christ he must be maturing in holiness, and self-control, and in all the Christian graces and virtues.

Another law of growth is that nourishment is indispensable. The growing plant requires to be fed, and so does the growing Christian. If the plant does not receive proper nourishment it will certainly fail to mature its fruit. It requires to be well rooted in the soil in order to take in its food. So the believer must be "rooted and grounded in love"—that is, of course, in love to Christ. It is love that binds us to Christ. Faith is dead, except it work by love. Love to Christ is the beginning of the Christian life; and it is increasing love to Christ that prompts us and enables us to take every onward and upward step in the life of holiness. The perfecting of this love between the soul and Christ brings to us here a sweet foretaste of the fuller, larger life in heaven, where there will be no clouds of selfishness and sin to obscure the bright beams of Divine love.

The plant, however, is not wholly fed through its roots. It derives a large portion of its food from the atmosphere that surrounds it. Every leaf has its scores of stomata, or mouths, through which it takes in the gases of the atmosphere as part of its food. It must also enjoy the direct influence of the sun's rays, else it cannot assimilate the food taken in from various sources. Here also there is an analogy between plant life and the Spiritual Life. While the Christian's first consideration is to remain rooted and grounded in Christ by a living, ever-acting faith, working by love, like the plant, he requires to be surrounded by an atmosphere capable of supplying nourishment. And if he cannot find such an atmosphere he must make it. By the study of God's Word, by prayer and meditation and Christian conversation, he must create an atmosphere which will nourish his Spiritual Life.

Then, again, as the plant seeks the sunlight, and cannot assimilate its food without it, so the child of God requires the energising force of the Holy Spirit to enable the soul to feed upon Christ and the Word of God. There are, therefore, these three points to be noted in the nurture of the Spiritual Life: 1. The believer must be rooted and grounded in Christ by a continuous faith, working by love,—that is, heart-union to Christ. 2. By prayer, and meditation, and holy conversation, and the study of God's Word, he must create for himself a healthy moral atmosphere. 3. He must have the constant presence and power of the Holy Spirit to enable him to take in and assimilate food that will nourish the Spiritual Life.

Another law of the Spiritual Life is that as a man advances in holiness it will be found that he has been feeding more and more upon doctrine, upon the great doctrinal truths of Scripture. No person who has not an intimate acquaintance with the great doctrines of Sin and Redemption, as set forth in the Word of God, can make any substantial progress in the Divine life. Faith cannot feed upon feeling. To be strong and helpful, faith must have a promise to rest upon. Faith must have a warrant for its hope and expectation, and that warrant is found only in the promises of God's Word.

In this effeminate age there is in many places a great aversion to doctrine and to creeds—to Scriptural truth definitely stated and arranged into a system. There are those, for example, who do not care to be found holding the doctrine of Total Depravity—that is, that man, in his sin, is wholly turned away from God. Now if a man does not believe that he is wholly a sinner there is not much hope of him ever becoming wholly a saint. He can never be made to realize that, apart from Christ, he cannot be saved. A man who does not believe that he is wholly turned away from God will not see the necessity of wholly turning to God. If he does not believe that, on account of indwelling sin, he is entirely lost, he will not see the necessity of coming to Christ, as helpless and lost, in order to be saved. And until a man does this he has not even started in the Divine life. Nothing but a profound sense of human depravity, of our own personal sinfulness, can cause us to feel the need of a personal Saviour. For no man is saved until he is saved from the love of sin and the power of sin, as well as from the punishment of sin. And he will never forsake his sins until he sees the exceeding sinfulness of sin. The man who does not believe that he is wholly ruined by sin will not feel the need of the Atonement of Christ; and if Christ did not come to make atonement for the sins of men, then why did He die? There could have been no moral purpose in His death. And hence it follows that if His death was not necessary as an essential part of the scheme of redemption, He could not have been Divine, or else He would have been able to prevent it. See, then, how closely one doctrine is linked on to another. And if one of these grand doctrines respecting Sin and Salvation is rejected, other fundamental doctrines are consequently either ignored or rejected also. If, therefore, we would be strong in faith, we must keep a firm hold of Scriptural doctrine.

To say that religion is character, and has nothing to do with doctrine, is only to raise a false issue. To decry doctrine in order to give prominence to character is as absurd as to say, It is not food we want, but health. You cannot have sound bodily health without wholesome food, and you cannot have spiritual health and spiritual growth without sound doctrine and cordial faith. Food is not health, and doctrinal truth is not holiness; but food is necessary to health, for if the body be not fed it will languish and die. So also will the soul languish if it be not fed on Divine truth.

It must be noted, however, that if we would grow in the Divine life, we must not merely believe the doctrines of Scripture, but so feed upon them that they will become, as it were, interwoven with our nature.

The reverent and growing Christian receives daily and ever-increasing strength as he is able to realize more and more fully God's presence and power, and God's constant care. " God with me," when so believed as a doctrine as to become a present realization, makes a man not only strong, but holy. No earnest man can wilfully commit sin, if at the moment he realizes that God is near. God's care, too, when fully realized, lifts us up above all worry, and anxiety, and fretfulness. God cares for me ; He leadeth me ; therefore all will be well. That is the way to transmute doctrine into life. And thus, what otherwise would seem to be merely dry doctrine, becomes to us the source of our greatest joy and strength. And so it is with all the doctrines of Scripture. They are the materials for building up our life. Let us remember, however, that we must use the materials in bringing our life into shape. A pile of huge stones, however beautifully squared and chiselled, does not make a temple. The stones must be brought together, each one in its proper place ; and then the spacious temple is seen standing out in all its fair proportions.

Doctrines are the materials for building up character. But merely to believe the doctrines without putting them into practice and moulding our lives by them, would be like admiring the collection of finely-chiselled stones without ever erecting the building. Here, then, is another Law of the Spiritual Life. In order to grow we must not simply believe that the great doctrines of Redemption are true, we must bring them to bear upon our life and conduct, living them out in our daily life. In this also Christ has left us an example. He lived out in His life every truth which He taught. When He said, "Take no anxious thought for to-morrow," He went about day by day without anxiety or fear of harm. When He said, "Lay not up for yourselves

THE LAWS OF THE SPIRITUAL LIFE. 211

treasures on earth," He Himself had no earthly possessions, and did not seek them.

Another very important Law of the Spiritual Life, and one which is a never-failing sign of spiritual growth, is what we might term THE TRANSFIGURATION OF DUTY. What I mean is this. As we come more and more into harmony with God, duty ceases to be done because we *must* do it, and becomes a delight. We say with the Psalmist, " I delight to do Thy will, O my God ; yea Thy law is within my heart."

To the young and immature Christian, duty is always hedged about by commandments. "Thou shalt" or " Thou shalt not" meets him at every step. He takes up the duties commanded, and sets himself manfully to do the will of God *because* it is the will of God, and because it is necessary to his peace. Duty is done, but done as a task, with the feeling that it is a burden, and with a sense of satisfaction when it is finished. This is, I think, the experience of very many Christians. For example, you feel it to be your duty to visit the members of your Sunday-school class, or a district in the town, or to engage in tract distribution, or some other form of Christian work. You love the Master, and you do not feel at rest until you are doing some kind of service in His vineyard. You undertake the work from a sense of duty, for you feel that an idle Christian has no right to expect any reward from the Master. You do the work, but it is done as a toil and a burden. But as you obtain richer experiences of the love of Christ, and become so like Christ as to be filled with an earnest longing for souls, duty will become transfigured to you. It will no longer be toilsome, but a delight. This change in your relation to duty is a sure evidence of spiritual growth, and a most certain proof that you are born of God.

Some of us can mark this change with great distinctness in our own lives, and in the character of our service; and we now feel what a poor, feeble service we rendered when duty was done because it must be done, rather than because we longed to do it. This great change—for it is a great change—proves that in disposition and in will we have come into harmony with God's will, and that is the only true test of mature Spiritual Life. Now we hear the voice of Jesus saying to us, as He said to His disciples, "Henceforth I call you not servants, but *friends.*" What a different thing it is to do anything for one you love, beside having to do it as a servant, because it must be done! The grand secret of Christianity, which so many miss, is KNOWING JESUS AS A FRIEND. "This is life eternal, that they might know Thee, the only true God, and Jesus Christ, whom Thou hast sent." That is the kernel of Christianity. That is the secret of a happy, triumphant Christian life. That is the secret of all spiritual growth. The Lord help every true believer to weave it into his every-day life and experience.

XX.

THE HIGHER LIFE OF HOLINESS.

"There remaineth yet very much land to be possessed."—JOSHUA xiii. 1.

THESE words express very concisely and very accurately the experience of many Christians— perhaps I might say, most Christians. Like the children of Israel, they have left for ever the land of bondage. They have set out on the Christian life. They have passed through the wilderness wanderings. Their faith has been tested and tried. They have proved God's love, and power, and readiness to help. They have crossed their Jordan, and have seen the stronghold of the enemy taken. They have entered the promised land,—the good land that is beyond Jordan,—but they have not subdued it. To them there remaineth yet very much land to be possessed.

We have already dwelt upon the importance of Regeneration as the only mode of entrance upon the Spiritual Life. But it must ever be remembered that entrance upon the Christian life is not all of the Christian life. Christian life is a progress, a growth. We must go on from one conquest to another, from one height of holiness to another. We must go on from victory to victory, subduing every evil desire and tendency, and "bringing into captivity every thought to the obedience of Christ" (2 Cor. x. 5).

There are various stages in the Divine life through which true believers pass. First, there is the stage of CONVICTION, through which all must pass—conviction of sin and sincere sorrow for it. Conviction of sin may be brought about in various ways. In some the feeling of alienation from God is so overpowering that they are constrained to cry out for mercy. They have a feeling of utter loneliness and desolation. Their soul, like David's, cries out for God, for the living God. Like a lost child that has wandered from home, life becomes intolerable—no rest, no comfort, no sense of security, no companionship. They are alone and desolate even when surrounded by sympathetic friends. They may not have committed any great sin. Like the young man who came to Jesus anxiously inquiring the way of life, they may be able to say of the commandments, "All these have I observed from my youth up." But still they are sick at heart, and feel that they are far off from God; and the language of their heart is, "Oh that I knew where I might find Him, I would come even unto His seat!" There is deep searching of heart. There is sincere and thorough reformation of life. Every known sin is abandoned. Every doubtful habit is given up. The conviction that works such reformation as that is surely from above. However, it is not all of the Christian life. It is but the initial stage—the first round on the ladder that reaches from earth to heaven.

Where conviction of sin is real—that is, produced by the striving of the Holy Spirit in the heart—it will invariably be accompanied by CONTRITION—a real heart-felt sorrow for sin as being contrary to the will of God. There will also be CONVERSION—a turning from all sin unto God, and an utter loathing of every form of sin, as that which interrupted communion with God and made inward peace impossible. No one has entered upon the Divine life who has not experienced conviction of sin, contrition for sin, and conversion from sin. Christ came to save His people, not *in* their sins, but *from* their sins. No man is saved until he is saved from sin; not simply from the punishment of sin, but also from the love of sin and the power of sin. The faith that saves purifies the heart and sanctifies the life. "They that are Christ's have crucified the flesh with the affections and lusts" (Gal. v. 24).

But it may be asked, Is any man able thus to stamp out sin, and crush the desire for gratifying evil passions and lusts, and indulging evil habits? There is but one answer—he cannot do it in his own strength. He must have Divine help. He must be born again. He must be united to Christ, and become a partaker of the Divine nature. (2 Peter i. 4.)

A nature is communicated only by a birth, or, more particularly, by generation. We received our human nature—the old Adam nature—in our first birth; and we become partakers of the Divine nature in the new birth by being born of the Divine Spirit. God alone can give life, and He only can give new life. No man, therefore, by his own unaided efforts, can change his nature and overcome sin. Hence, if man is to be saved from sinning, there must be not merely conviction, and contrition, and conversion,—that is, man's turning away from sin,—but regeneration as well. No man can be saved from the love of sin, and the power of sin, and the practice of sin, who is not born of God: "Whosoever is begotten of God doth not commit sin" (1 John iii. 9).

Now it is just here that so many, who are earnestly struggling after a higher and a holier life, come short. They do not realize their need of being born again. They imagine that by watchfulness and a resolute will they will be able to stem the tide of temptation, and in the end overcome in the struggle. However, the enemy proves too strong for them, and after repeated failures they become discouraged; and, having lost heart, all is lost. What such weary, way-worn souls want is to see the abundant provision made for their weakness and helplessness in the regenerating and sanctifying power of the Holy Spirit; and then, like Jacob, to wrestle with God in agonizing earnestness until the needed help comes. If we would get strength to live a holy, joyous, triumphant Christian life, we must make it the first business of our life to lay hold of God by faith, and earnest prayer, and pleading. In this busy, bustling age, how few, even of the best Christians, will take time to be holy, will take time to wait in their course until they have the consciousness that in every step they take they are walking with God! God is ready at every moment to help and keep those who trust Him: "The eyes of the Lord run to and fro throughout the whole earth to show Himself strong in behalf of them whose heart is perfect toward Him" (2 Chron. xvi. 9). But we require to be ready to receive God's help, else we will miss it. We must, moment by moment, be in a receptive attitude. Our hearts, as it were, must lie open to the touch of God. It is as if a king were passing through the country distributing gifts wherever he found an open door. How careful every one who loved the king and appreciated his gifts would be to keep the door open every moment! That open door is the proof that the king is loved in that house, and that his promise of blessing is believed. Hence Jesus says, "Behold I stand at the door and knock; if any man hear My voice and open the door, I will come in to him, and will sup with him, and he with Me" (Rev. iii. 20).

Here, then, we have a most important stage in the Divine life, THE OPEN DOOR—the heart moment by moment expecting the presence of the King, and continuing in such a state of love and purity as to be ready to welcome the King any moment, every moment. That is what is meant by "walking with God," by "walking in the light." "If we walk in the light, as He is in the light, we have fellowship one with another"—that is, we with God—"and the blood of Jesus Christ, His Son, goes on cleansing us from all sin" (1 John i. 7). Enoch was able thus to live. He walked with God; and "he had this testimony"—the witness in himself—"that he pleased God" (Heb. xi. 5). Now this is a possible experience for us all. You are not to excuse yourself by saying, "It is too high; I cannot attain to it." You can attain to it. Cannot you open the door while the king is passing? One would think the difficulty would be *not* to open the door. No one lacks the power to open the door of the heart to the waiting Saviour, if he has the will to do it. You have power to open it, and you have power to shut it.

Now this is the grand secret of the higher life of holiness, and peace, and power. It is seeing the King in His beauty, and welcoming Him to the heart. This is what Jesus means when He says, " Abide in Me, and I in you . . . He that abideth in Me and I in him, the same bringeth forth much fruit ; for without Me ye can do nothing " (John xv. 4, 5). Without Christ, nothing ; abiding in Christ, much fruit—" fruit unto holiness." Christ dwelling in our hearts by His Spirit, is our grand security, and the only source of fruitfulness and progress in holiness.

Christ dwells in the believer for rest, for keeping, for cleansing, for filling,—that is, for power. Resting, Keeping, Cleansing, Filling—we all want these four. First, REST. Soul-rest can be obtained at first only by coming to Christ. He is our Righteousness. His righteousness covers up our sinfulness, and the sentence of death is removed. We thus have peace in view of our past sins : " By Him all that believe are justified from all things from which ye could not be justified by the law of Moses " (Acts xiii. 39). " He has made peace for us through the blood of His cross " (Col. i. 20) ; and, being justified by faith, we have peace with God.

We are not to suppose, however, that we have received all that Christ has in store for us, when the sentence of condemnation has been removed. WE NEED KEEPING. And how refreshing it is to read, " The Lord is thy Keeper" (Psalm cxxi. 5). And again, " He is able to keep you from falling, and to present you faultless before the presence of His glory " (Jude 24). WE ALSO NEED CLEANSING. As the blood of Jesus Christ cleanseth from all past sin, so the heart is cleansed "by the washing of regeneration, and renewing of the Holy Ghost" (Titus iii. 5). And the heart that is thus cleansed and sanctified is FILLED —" filled with all the fulness of God" (Eph. iii. 19). " Of His fulness have we received" (John i. 16). But to be thus filled is to be clothed with power, power over sin, and power in service : "Ye shall receive the power of the Holy Ghost coming upon you, and ye shall be witnesses unto Me " (Acts i. 8). Therefore, by union to Christ, the trusting soul receives pardon, peace, protection, purity, power.

The Scriptural standard of Holiness is very high. Believers are enjoined to "be diligent, that they may be found of Him in peace, without spot, and blameless " (2 Peter iii. 14). This high standard of personal holiness and integrity is not a mere casual statement found in a single text. It pervades the whole teaching of Christ and the apostles. The Lord Jesus urges His followers to be holy as He is holy. The Apostle John affirms that "when He shall appear we shall be like Him ; and he that hath this hope in him purifieth himself, even as He is pure " (1 John iii. 3). The same high standard of personal piety and personal purity is insisted on by James : " Pure religion and undefiled before God the Father is this, To visit the fatherless and widows in their affliction, and to keep himself unspotted from the world " (James i. 27). It is clear, therefore, that there is to be no lowering of the standard of personal holiness for those who have received pardon for their past sins.

Now the natural inquiry of the earnest, anxious soul

is, Is this high standard of holiness possible? And the answer must be, God makes no impossible demands of His people. Instead of despairing of such high attainments the reverent, trustful soul will joyfully mount up on the wings of faith and love, and triumphantly exclaim, "I can do all things through Christ which strengtheneth me"; "Now thanks be unto God, who always causeth us to triumph in Christ" (2 Cor. ii. 14).

It is a source of constant weakness to most Christians that they assume as an axiomatic truth that while men are in the world they must necessarily be spotted by the world. Is God less than Almighty, that He cannot keep His people from falling? Cannot He who enabled Caleb and Joshua to follow Him wholly give strength to His trusting children to follow Him wholly now? Cannot the God who preserved Daniel at the corrupt court of Babylon preserve His children now amid all the corruptions of modern society? Is He not the unchanging, as well as the Almighty God?

Why, then, do we see around us so many lives spotted by the world? Surely it is because Christians do not realize their high privilege of being kept by God—kept in the hour of temptation, kept from falling. Men set out in the morning of their Christian life strong, and pure, and resolute for Christ. One subject engrosses their attention. It is "Jesus only." In their retirement HE fills their thoughts. Among their friends HE is the theme of conversation. He has so filled them with His fulness that the world and wickedness are wholly shut out. They think of Christ. They talk of Christ and His salvation. Their hearts overflow with love for their fellow-men, and an intense longing for their salvation. Under the full tide of this blessed experience they marvel that all men are not like themselves. They easily keep themselves unspotted from the world. Formerly it was a constant struggle, with repeated failures; now sin has no power over them. They pass through the corruptions of social life, as the sunbeam passes through the mountain mist, unhurt, and without losing any of their warmth, and purity, and brightness. They carry the brightness of heaven in their faces; and, if circumstances constrain them to weep with those who weep, there will be gleams of sunshine even in their tears:

"Like sunshine, broken in the rill,
Though turned aside, 'tis sunshine still."

Why, it may be asked, should such lives ever become spotted by the world? There is no reason why they should. The question we asked ourselves, when filled with such blessed experiences, was, How can such a life ever become spotted, and stained, and commonplace? We felt the power of Christ resting upon us. We felt the comforting presence of the Holy Spirit dwelling within us. We went forth joyously to duty like a strong man to run a race. We expected victory over temptation, and victory was ours. The shield of faith turned aside every fiery dart of the foe; and the evil one lay vanquished at our feet. The strong man was slain by a stronger than he. These are possible experiences, for they are actual experiences.

But why are these experiences so rare, and why are they so seldom permanent? Just because we keep them to ourselves, and do not seek to bless and comfort others by them. God gives His good gifts to men to be used; and if they are not used, they are withdrawn. When the gift of tongues was bestowed upon the apostles at Pentecost they immediately declared to the people of every tongue the wonderful works of God. If they had not done so, they would have lost the gift. There must be no waste in God's government. Perhaps we may see here the explanation of the saddening fact that there are so many dumb Christians in the Church—so many who never speak the language of Canaan. In times past they folded their talent in a napkin instead of using it. Here natural law and spiritual law is the same. If you bind your arm by your side, and never use it, it will soon become weak and shrivelled. If the eye is never allowed to see the light, the power of vision will be lost. In like manner, if spiritual gifts are not used, they will be withdrawn. Of the slothful servant Christ said, "Take the talent from him." Christian life must be active. Only thus can it be kept pure in the midst of surrounding evil. The water of the ocean is kept pure by being in constant motion. Stillness would mean stagnation. The great Gulf Stream, taking its rise in the Gulf of Mexico, ploughs its way across the broad Atlantic, making a course for itself for hundreds of miles without mingling with the opposing waters. Its onward progress preserves it from commingling with the water through which it passes. Now this same law holds good in the Christian life. If you would be preserved from spot and stain while in the world, you must be actively engaged in the endeavour to make the world brighter and better

You must carry Christ with you wherever you go; and be found like Him, ever going about doing good.

True religion is positive and · active. In this it differs from mere morality. Morality is largely negative; and mere negative goodness will not preserve a man from being contaminated by the evil that surrounds him. The life of the Lord Jesus must be our pattern. He came into our world of sin, and freely mingled with the sinning multitude, but always with the object of lifting men up into a higher and a nobler life. Hence the world's spots never soiled His garments. It is a remarkable fact that sin never stains a man, or soils his garments, so long as he regards sin as his foe against whom he fights. Sin harms those only who regard it as a friend—as that which in some way ministers to their pleasure, and adds to the sum of their happiness. In Eden our first parents were secure against temptation so long as they regarded sin as an enemy, who would deal out death to them. It was only when they believed the whispered lie of the devil, that the forbidden fruit would increase their happiness; that disobedience would bring a larger knowledge and a fuller life,—in other words, that sin would be a friend bringing life, and not an enemy bringing death, —that they yielded to the seductive tempter. It depends altogether upon our attitude towards evil, whether we will overcome it, or be overcome by it.

See how the religion of Jesus differs from the common opinions of men. Men declare it impossible to pass through this world without being stained by its spots—its follies and its sins. Religion declares they must do it. She refuses to lower her standard of holiness to accommodate the weakness of any one. The demands of religion would indeed be impossible apart from the promises of the Bible and the help of the Holy Spirit. In declaring the demands of religion to be ·impossible, men neglect to take God into account. God not only gives pardon for the past, but power for the present. Moment by moment He helps and keeps those who live in fellowship with Him. Therefore, with God above us, controlling all events; with God around us, making all things work together for our good; with God within us,' by His Spirit, giving us power to resist and strength to endure, we may, we ought, to pass through the world without spot and blameless. Except our religion has this power in it to keep us in the hour of temptation, then it is not true; for there is nothing more certain than that it promises this power.

The human life of Jesus must ever be regarded as the true type of Christian manhood. To be a Christian is not simply to assent to certain doctrines, but to receive Christ, to be truly united to Him, and to live as He lived. But what was Christ's life? It was a life of constant fellowship with God and constant Christian activity. He consecrated His life to the service of men. The way to keep the life pure is not to be always guarding it, and standing aloof from surrounding evil. The life must be kept pure as the running stream is kept pure, by flowing on and bringing refreshing water to the thirsty. A flowing stream keeps itself pure. It is only a stagnant pool that requires to be closely guarded. So it is with human lives. The vacant life of selfish ease and inactivity becomes putrid. It has no power of resistance. It was to the empty house that the devils in the parable came back to hold still higher revel.

What we want, therefore, to make us strong, and pure, and holy is so to abide in Christ by a constant, ever-acting faith, and to have Christ so abiding in us by His Spirit, and to have the power of Christ so resting upon us, that we shall go forth, like Him, pushing back evil and conquering it by the power of our personal holiness. We are not to retire from the world, like the hermit and the monk, in order to escape from its pollution. We are not, Pharisee-like, to shrink back from the sinful multitude, lest we should defile our garments. We are to go up close to the sinning world, and feel for its wickedness, and pity its condition, and deny ourselves in order to help and to save it. The pathway to perfection must be sought along the pathway of service. Doctors and nurses are the most secure against infectious diseases. And just so those who minister most to the needs of a sick and sinning world are the safest against its contagion.

The religion which Jesus came to reveal, and which He is willing to bestow on all who truly seek Him, is such that the man of business can take it with him during business hours, and feel its power; the workman can take it into the workshop, and find it restraining passion and controlling temper; the mother and the maid will find in it a soothing balm amid all the worry and trials of domestic duties; and the young will find it lightening every duty, sweetening every enjoyment, sanctifying every pleasure, and gilding life with glory and with beauty.

XXI.

CHRISTIAN COURAGE AND CONSECRATION.

"Add to your faith courage."—2 PETER i. 5.

THIS is an inviting theme—CHRISTIAN COURAGE AND CONSECRATION—the Courage of Faith and the Consecration of Faith. I take them both together, because in our practical experience in the Christian life we cannot separate them. We cannot have Christian Courage without Christian Consecration.

Christian Courage is absolutely necessary both to our own comfort and happiness, and also to our usefulness in the world. A timid person is always living in an atmosphere of discomfort. Fear, in a large measure, takes the place of faith, and perfect happiness is impossible. This is true both in the natural life and in the spiritual life.

The Apostle Peter, in our text, gives COURAGE the first place among the Christian graces : "Add to your faith virtue." Virtue here means courage. The original word is used to designate bravery in a soldier. We are not to suppose, however, that we have no faith, although we may lack that courage and daring which make the dauntless soldier. The language of the Apostle implies that there may be faith where heroic courage is lacking; for he exhorts us to add courage to our faith, showing that faith may exist before courage is added to it. However, we ought not to rest satisfied with our attainments in the Christian life until faith takes on the form of courage, and every doubt and fear is banished from our minds. Until this state is attained we should hear the words of the Master ringing in our ears, " Why are ye so fearful, O ye of little faith ?"

In every age God has found it necessary to urge His people to be courageous. When Joshua was appointed to succeed Moses, and to lead the children of Israel into the promised land, God said to Him, " Be strong and of good courage; be not dismayed, neither be afraid, for the Lord thy God is with thee whithersoever thou goest." These words, spoken in the first instance to Joshua, are for all time.

In a very special sense is the history of the Children of Israel—in bondage, in the Exodus, in the wilderness wanderings, in subduing their enemies, and settling down in rest and quiet in the land of Canaan— the history of individual Christians. And not only so, but I believe that the story of their life and wanderings was intended by God to give us in this pictorial way a vivid conception of our weakness when distrustful and disobedient, and our wonderful power when by faith we abide in Him. In the light of the New Testament and of our own Christian Experience the story of Joshua will be a comfort and guide to every earnest soul seeking to enter into the Rest of Faith.

The Children of Israel have been led out of Egypt and across the Red Sea with a mighty hand and a strong arm, and their enemies have been destroyed before their eyes. They have wandered for forty years in the wilderness, sinning and repenting—a picture of the life of too many Christians. All who came out of Egypt have died in the wilderness, except Caleb and Joshua; for they only had followed the Lord wholly. Moses, the leader and mouthpiece of God to the people, has been taken home to his rest and reward. Joshua is now appointed by God, and is formally ordained to his office by Moses by the laying on of hands, that he may lead the people into the promised possession. The land, however, is inhabited by enemies numerous and formidable. They must fight their way. Life, even in Canaan, for a time, will be struggle, and difficulty, and conflict. Therefore, at this particular juncture in their history, what they specially want is Courage,—Courage and Faith,—Courage to go fearlessly forward till every enemy is subdued; Faith to believe that they have really entered into the promised land although they have struggle and conflict. Hitherto their hearts were not steadfast, and because they feared they failed.

The first element of success in any undertaking is courage, and confidence, and hopefulness; and when, as Christians, we are engaged in fighting the Lord's battles, and doing the Lord's work, and struggling against doubt, and difficulty, and temptation, what we want most is the Courage of Faith—that courage and confidence which unwavering faith in God always supplies. Too many, like Elisha's servant, exclaim in the presence of difficulty or danger, "Alas! master, what shall we do?" They do not recognize the presence of God, and His power to keep those who trust in Him. They want to have their eyes opened, that they may see "the mountain full of horses and chariots of fire" round about them. They want to hear the voice of God saying to them, as He said to Joshua, "I will not fail thee, nor forsake thee; be strong and of good courage."

It is true now, as in the time of Joshua, "There remaineth yet very much land to be possessed." We look around, and we see the world lying in the wicked one. We look within, and see much not yet completely subdued to Christ. Here we have a double call to effort. The world around us and the world within us both need subduing to Christ. And the world within has the first call upon us. We look within and study our inner life,—our loves and longings, our aims and aspirations, our hopes and fears, our tastes and tempers,—and we see so much that is not Christlike, so much that falls short of the model life left us by the Master, that we are discouraged. We fear that we shall never attain to that holiness of heart and life, that self-denial and self-sacrifice, that sweet submission to God's holy will, that consciousness of acceptance with God, that felt sense of His comforting presence with us, which we are taught to hope for and expect, and we are discouraged. But are we to draw back in despair and say, " Such things are too high for me, I cannot attain to them "? No; assuredly not. We are rather to rally at the call of the Master, and hear Him say, " Why are ye so fearful ? How is it that ye have no faith ?" " Fear not, for I am with thee ; I will never leave thee nor forsake thee." " Be strong, and of a good courage."

But the inquiry naturally arises, How can the weak be strong? How can those that are timid and fearful command courage? However, God never gives a command to do, without a promise to help. He says, "Be strong; be not fearful." Timid and trembling, you reply, "Ah, Lord, but I am so weak." He knows your weakness, and provides for it. He says, "I will be with thee; yea, I will help thee; I will hold thee by thy right hand, and thou shalt not be moved." It is as if He had said, "Your own strength, whether great or small, really counts for nothing when added to infinite strength." This, then, is God's message to the fearful, "Be strong by believing in the constant presence and power of a loving personal God, who takes a tender interest in every one who seeks to do His will." Your courage must always be the Courage of Faith—courage inspired by the belief that God is with you to help and to deliver.

It was such faith in God that gave Elisha such calm confidence when his servant was filled with dismay: "Fear not; for they that be with us are more than they that be with them." The disciples were not afraid of the storm, and the tempest, and the raging billows while the Master was awake. But now He is asleep. He is with them, but He is asleep; and His presence gives them no comfort. Because He is asleep they have no faith in His power to help them. How often is this the case with many of us! The Master is with us, but He is asleep. To us He is asleep. We do not realize His presence. We have not the same joy and peace that we once had. We fear that He has ceased to care for us, and we are troubled. We long to hear His voice, speaking to the waves of trouble that destroy our peace and threaten our safety. But He is asleep. He allows the wind to blow, and the storm to howl, and the waves to dash against us; and we think He is angry with us, and cares not for our comfort. But "Why are ye so fearful, O ye of little faith?" The Master is still with you—with you in the storm and tempest as really, more really, than in the calm and sunshine. He says to every tempted and tried one, as He said to Paul, "My grace is sufficient for thee; My strength is made perfect in weakness." The Apostle was terribly harassed by "the thorn in the flesh, the messenger of Satan." He earnestly besought the Lord thrice that it might depart from him. However, the "thorn" was not removed. Shall we infer, therefore, that the Lord had ceased to care for His sorely-tried servant? Shall we infer that God does not hear and answer prayer? No; by no means. God proved His love by giving him strength to endure his affliction. *His prayer *was* answered; not indeed in the way which he expected, by removing the trial, but in a better way, by giving him grace to submit to it, and strength to endure it.

And so God deals with His people now. He may allow you to be tossed upon a very sea of troubles. He may allow you to grope your pathless way in the wilderness of doubt and temptation. He may allow the dark clouds of uncertainty and sadness to obscure your sun for a time. He may allow you to be stripped bare, and to be left desolate and alone, till you are constrained to cry out in the agony of your soul, "Oh, my leanness! my leanness!" But it is all in love.

It is because He wishes you to feel your own helplessness and emptiness, and your great need of Him. And when, in the midst of your overwhelming trouble, He comes to you in all His sustaining and comforting power, you will be able to say with Paul, "Most gladly, therefore, will I rather glory in my infirmities, that the power of Christ may rest upon me . . . for when I am weak, then am I strong."

Weak in ourselves, and strong in the Lord—that is the law of the Christian life. The first step towards a happy, triumphant Christian life is to realize our own helplessness. "Without Me," said Jesus, "ye can do nothing." What, Lord, nothing? No, absolutely nothing; I must be all. If you would be strong against temptation, strong under trial, and strong for service, you must be emptied of self and self-confidence, and be full of Me. This is Christ's teaching, and it is the object of His training. Only by the power of Christ resting upon us can the weak become strong. And only by recognizing our own weakness can the power of Christ rest upon us. We must feel our need, and ask Him for help before we receive it. He will not thrust His favours into unwilling hands. Therefore, to obtain power and courage, we must cling to Jesus by a constant ever-acting faith.

But having once obtained sustaining and comforting power, we can preserve it only by a holy, consecrated life—a life lived in perfect submission to the will of God in all things. We must give ourselves to the Lord wholly and unreservedly, and be ready to say, "I am the Lord's"; "Here I am, Lord Jesus; take me as I am; make me pure and holy. Lead me in the way that Thou wouldest have me go. Use me for Thy glory. I ask for nothing but power to do Thy will, and to enjoy Thy presence and favour." Nothing but faith, and consecration, and conscious fellowship with Christ can drive away fear. Never look within to thy fears; never look around to thy foes; never look ahead to trials that may never come; look to Jesus, and to Jesus only. He is the Author and Perfecter of our faith. He only is our strength; He only is our comfort; He only is our security. Look to Him in every time of trial, and doubt, and fear. Hear Him say, amid the surging billows, " Why are ye so fearful ? Know you not that I am with you ? Your frail barque cannot be engulfed in the sea with your Lord on board." Remember that your safety does not depend upon your feelings or your fears, but upon the fact that Christ is your defence. He has taken you by the hand, and says to you, "As thy day so shall thy strength be. The eternal God is thy refuge, and underneath are the everlasting arms."

Nothing so demoralizes the forces of the soul as fear. The man who is fearful and discouraged can never play the part of the hero. He cannot exhibit any noble qualities either in character or in service. Nothing promotes fear like a sense of loneliness. In spiritual struggles we are utterly alone, except we cling to Christ, and are conscious of His presence. No earthly friend can take you by the hand as you pass through the weary wilderness of doubt. No earthly friend can stand by you and help you to bear the burden of unforgiven sin. No earthly friend can shield you from the fiery darts of temptation, hurled into your unsuspecting heart by your arch-enemy, the devil. And, if you do not realize the presence of Christ with you, you will be filled with a terrible feeling of loneliness and desolation, and the feeling of loneliness will make you fearful. Faith alone can overcome fear; for it is only by faith that you can realize the unseen presence of your Lord. " This is the victory that overcometh the world, even our faith."

The child who has always stood by his father's side, and has never seen him flinch in the hour of danger, imbibes his spirit, and receives courage from him. The fact that his father is by his side makes him feel safe and strong. And just so, as we consciously stand by the side of Christ, and realize that He is our defence, we can bid defiance to every foe.

It was this simple heroic faith that nerved the heroes of the olden time—that gave power and daring to Samson and Samuel, David and Daniel, Elijah and Elisha. It is this unwavering faith in the constant presence of Christ, by His Spirit, that has won so many martyrs' crowns, and that now enables the children of God to carry sunshine in their faces, and to do and to dare for God and the right.

Christian courage is not the result of the long training of the iron nerve, but the upward glance of the trusting eye. The patriarchs of old endured as seeing Him who is invisible. Let us remember, therefore, that if we are feeble and fearful, it is because we see too little and too much—too little of the presence of God, and, like Elisha's servant, too many of the horses and chariots of the enemy. Hence it is that, like him, we have so often to exclaim, "Alas! my master, how shall we do?" In every time of anxiety and trouble may the Lord open our eyes that we may see the mountains around full of the hosts of God encamping round about us.

XXII.

THE JOY OF SELF-SACRIFICE.

" Looking unto Jesus, the Author and Perfecter of our faith, who for the joy set before Him endured the cross."—HEB. xii. 2.

OUR subject, THE JOY OF SELF-SACRIFICE, may possibly fall upon the ear of many, as some strange sound. The combination seems strange. Joy we understand. Self-sacrifice we understand. But, to find the one in the other, *that* is the wonderful thing. But we have it here. It was seen in the life of Christ, " who for the joy set before Him endured the cross." Here is self-sacrifice of the noblest and intensest type ; and there was joy in it.

What a wonderful life the life of Jesus was ! There is no point in human experience but what it touched. In that life of self-sacrifice He has shown us how to bear ourselves in the sorrows and trials of life, as well as in its joys and triumphs. The lesson we have taught in the passage before us is, that self-sacrifice may be borne with joy.

There are various forms of self-sacrifice, and I will endeavour to show that we may have joy in them all.

First, and nearest to us, is the duty of sacrificing our lower self to our higher self—passion to principle—the craving of the animal nature to the longings of the spiritual nature. A man rises or falls in the scale of existence according as the one or the other is allowed to predominate. Any man of principle will be ready to acknowledge that it is right to control the lower passions of his nature; and if he be an earnest man, and has not wholly lost self-respect, he will use every endeavour to do so. But, in making the endeavour, he is confronted with a serious difficulty. It is a struggle and a warfare. Like Paul, he finds a law in his members— in his lower nature—warring against the law of his mind, and bringing him into captivity to the law of sin in his members. He is in an agony of earnestness to deliver himself from his bondage, and to break the chains with which he is bound to sinful habit. He feels that he must sacrifice passion and appetite to the demands of his higher nature. All men have to engage in this struggle. Many overcome; and many others go to the wall—the greater in them being beaten and overcome by the less.

But why were they beaten? That is the question of practical interest. Why did the lower passions triumph over the higher principles? Just because they had never learned to make the sacrifice with joy. They gave up their sinful habits, but with reluctance. They loved their low pleasures, even after they had temporarily forsaken them. Their conduct resembles that of Lot's wife. Touched by the visit of the angelic messengers, and terrified by the tidings of the approaching doom of Sodom, she allows herself to be borne away by her husband and daughters. But, alas! her heart is left behind her. The clay body is borne away by the pressure of circumstances; but all that constituted the woman—the heart, the affections, the will—are still in the doomed city. The backward look was a look of longing desire for the continuance of sinful pleasures. Her affections and desires still kept clinging to the vices of Sodom. And because she will not make the sacrifice with joy, she must ignominiously perish.

Now a man has not conquered evil habit by merely forsaking it. It is his master until he learns to hate it, and treats it as his enemy—until, with exultant tread, he tramples it under his foot and rejoices in his victory. He must not only make the sacrifice, he must do it with joy.

But there is a second form of self-sacrifice—sacrificing self for the good of others. This form of self-sacrifice is perhaps more difficult than the other; and many are so selfish as not to entertain it at all, much less to do it with joy. It may be accepted as certain that no man will cheerfully sacrifice self for the good of others, until he has made the first sacrifice of which we have spoken, until he has sacrificed the passions of his lower nature, and has overcome them. The continuous indulgence of any evil habit tends to shut a man up within himself. He becomes selfish, and gradually loses his regard for the comfort and welfare of his fellow-men. He must first overcome the habits of self-gratification before he can make sacrifices for others. The great evil of indulging in any habit, even those that many consider excusable, is that the person gradually becomes selfish, and comes to think less of the comfort of others than of his own gratification. When a man finds this feeling creeping over him, let him know that he is on the downward track. The power of appetite is becoming stronger than the power of love—the lower elements of his nature are overcoming and crushing the higher. If he is a wise man, he will make the sacrifice, and utterly abandon the habit that is dragging him down. And let him make the sacrifice with joy. Let him have a feeling of exultation that the nobler elements of his nature are rising in their might to subdue selfishness and crush the cravings of appetite. For, just in proportion as he can do this, is he becoming ennobled and fitted for higher pleasures and intenser joys.

There is, however, a higher form of self-sacrifice still—the entire surrender of the will—giving up our will to God's will in everything. You have gone through the first and the second stage. You have sacrificed your lower self to your higher self. You can also make sacrifices for others without grudging. But now comes the great test and trial of life. You are asked to place everything in God's hands, to have no anxious care for anything but to do His will. If He sees it to be best for you to bear a heavy cross, then, like Jesus, you are asked to endure the cross for the joy set before you. We are apt, in thought, to separate the joy and the cross. However, God's order is, not the cross alone, but the cross with the joy that invariably follows patient cross-bearing. The joy will surely come to all who patiently do the will of God. But remember, that so long as you bear your cross *as a burden*, you will have to bear it. If God loves you, He is training you and teaching you to be like Jesus. Jesus Himself had to pass through these three stages. In the record of the temptation in the wilderness we see Him overcoming and sacrificing the lower cravings of His human nature to principle and to duty. He will not use His Divine power to satisfy His hunger until God's appointed time. During the whole of His earthly life we see Him sacrificing self and ease for the good of others. And during the agony in the Garden of Gethsemane we see Him yielding up His will entirely and unreservedly to the will of the Father. See Him in His agony in Gethsemane! How real it is, and how intense! See the great drops standing out upon His brow, coursing down His cheeks, and falling down to the ground! But what is His prayer? for He is crying out to God. Hear it: "Father, if it be possible, let this cup pass from Me!" Ah! it is a sore trial, and His human sensibilities cry out under it. Like ourselves, for a time He is bearing His cross as a burden. He is bearing it; but He is crying to be delivered from it. And as long as He is in this mood He must bear it. But presently He overcomes, and is able to yield up all to God. Now His cry is, not "Father, remove the cup of sorrow," but "Father, glorify Thy Son." Previously the sight of the cross filled Him with intense agony; now the cross is gladly embraced. He, as it were, rushes to it as His chief joy, longing for the hour: "Father, the hour is come; glorify Thy Son." Jesus was to be glorified through the cross, and so must we. If we would be filled with all the fulness of God, we must learn to bear our burdens and meet our trials, not only with submission, but with joy. Then our cross will become transfigured, and become our crown. Our sorrows, and trials, and duties may all become transfigured to us, and become a joy.

THE JOY OF SELF-SACRIFICE.

Now, how very different from this is the experience of most Christians. Not many, I suspect, find it easy to make sacrifices with joy. They practise self-denial rather as a disagreeable necessity. To such Christians, if they are thoroughly earnest and conscientious, life is a perpetual martyrdom. An earnest person striving to do right, once said of some particular work, " I know it is my duty, because I hate it so." Such a state of mind clearly proves that the heart is not in sympathy with the mind of God. We should never rest satisfied with our attainments in the Divine life until we can say of every duty, "I know it is my duty, because I love it so." God never requires anything of His children but what is for their highest good. And if we would only acquire the habit of accepting our trials, and sorrows, and disappointments, as God's good gifts to us, sent to make us purer, and nobler, and richer, and thank God for them, we would soon find that all our trials and troubles would be removed.

God, in training us for His service, must bring us into perfect sympathy with His will; and our trials must remain until we become perfectly submissive, so that we can do His will with delight. No man can hold fellowship with God, either in this life or in the future life, except he is in perfect sympathy with God. We must be taught to prefer God's will to our own will. Until we come into this state we are virtually in rebellion against God; and so long as our will is opposed to God's will, there can be no heaven for us, either present or future. But whenever we yield ourselves up to God in willing self-surrender, we have heaven begun on earth.

As an illustration of how joy may be found in self-sacrifice, take the case of a business man who has had the misfortune to fail in his business. He failed through circumstances over which he had no control. He is an earnest, upright Christian man, just such a man as might expect the blessing of Heaven. And when he goes down with a crash the sneering sceptic points to him and says, "Where now is his God in whom he trusted ; and what kind of a God is He to let His faithful servant be ruined by a mere accident ? Surely it is a vain thing to serve the Lord !" But, is he ruined ? Ah no! His faith does not falter. He does not murmur or repine. He not only yields up all to God ; he also yields up all to his creditors, and keeps nothing back. They accept a composition, and are satisfied. The law also is satisfied, and has .no further claim upon him. He has nothing ; but he is free. He starts anew. He has lost all but honour and integrity, and faith in God. Ah yes! but that is good capital to start with— INTEGRITY AND FAITH IN GOD. It does not count much indeed at the bankers' on earth ; but in the bank of heaven it is more than mountains of gold. If man will not give him credit, God will. And now he is "like a tree planted by the rivers of water, and whatsoever he doeth shall prosper."

Wealth returns to him, and men are astonished to see how frugal he is. They say, "Why does he walk to business, when he can easily afford a carriage ? " They think that he is afraid of another crash, and is laying up a store against the evil day. But no ; he has a far nobler motive, enabling him to make all his sacrifices with joy. Presently the day arrives for revealing the secret. He calls his creditors; seeks out the widow of one that is dead, and pays her everything he owed in full, principal and interest. The sharp man of the world says, "What a fool; he did not need to pay a penny of it!" But what does Heaven say? Heaven says: "Well done, good and faithful servant; enter thou into the joy of thy Lord." And he enters into joy. His heart is filled to overflowing with joy unspeakable and full of glory. He never experienced any joy to be compared to the joy of self-sacrifice. And now we see the purpose of God in permitting His servant to pass through such trial and loss. In him God was able to exhibit to the world the power and blessedness of a religious life, and to show that there was no joy like the joy of doing good.

But do you ask, Can the Christian rise into such a high and blissful state that self-sacrifice and trial will not give him pain? Certainly the element of pain enters into all losses, and trials, and sacrifices. But to the trustful heart, that always accepts God's will with joy, the pain is instantly swallowed up in the joy. Here is a child that has lost a toy. Its feelings are hurt. The pain is acute. But you place in the child's hands something far more beautiful than the lost toy; and what a change! All in a moment the pain is swallowed up in the joy. Such is precisely the experience of all who have faith enough, in the midst of trial, to believe that God is preparing them, by means of trial and suffering, to receive richer blessings than ever they enjoyed before. There will be pain in the sacrifice demanded; but the moment we cheerfully take up the burden which our loving Father sees good to lay upon us, then we shall be so filled with His love, and enjoy such a comforting sense of His presence, that the pain will be wholly swallowed up.

Such was the experience of the early disciples. Jesus, their only comfort and joy, was taken away. There was, for the time, the agonizing pain that accompanies every bereavement. However, in a short time their sorrow was swallowed up in joy. He rises from the dead, and appears to them in His wondrous glory. Again He is taken away to heaven; and again there is momentary loss. But in a few days He comes to them by His Spirit, and they are clothed with power and filled with joy—such power and joy as they had never dreamed of before.

Here, then, is a blessed experience certainly attainable by ordinary men; and the grand, practical question which concerns us all is, How can we make it ours? The key to the mystery of converting pain to joy is found in our relation to God, and our faith in His fatherly love and care. See what sacrifices a mother makes for the child that is dearer to her than her own life. What would be pain, and toil, and drudgery to another, is the joy of her life. Therefore we see that the way to find joy in self-sacrifice is to love those supremely for whom the sacrifice is made. If we have more regard for the higher principles of our nature than for the lower passions, we can sacrifice the lower to the higher with joy. If we have a higher regard for the good and comfort of others than we have for mere selfish ease, we can sacrifice ease without any regret in order to help and bless others. And if we love God supremely, and really prefer His will to our own, the surrender of our will in everything can be made with joy. Love, therefore, is the key to the mystery. And let it be remembered that this love can be kindled only by beholding Christ and His cross— by looking unto Jesus.

Here is a man who thinks very little of himself, who has very little self-respect, who has a very low estimate of the value of human nature. He says, "Let us eat and drink, for to-morrow we die." But let that man come to understand the high value set upon our human nature by the Lord Jesus, as seen in His Incarnation, and in His efforts to reclaim and save a fallen race. He will then be constrained to say, "If Christ so loved me, and did and suffered so much to redeem and save me, then surely there must be something noble and Godlike in me." And, if he be not wholly lost to self-respect, he will resolutely set to work to crush low passions and evil appetites. The fact of Christ setting such a high value upon humanity will help him to respect himself.

So, too, the sight of Christ making such sacrifices for others will enable us to set a higher value upon our fellow-men; so that to make sacrifices for their welfare and salvation will become easy.

So, also, when we see the heart of God revealed in the life and love of Christ, it becomes easy to love Him, and easy to do His will with joy. Thus we see that a man's own soul, his fellow-men, and his God, are all transfigured to him by beholding Christ and His cross. There can be no true consecration of our lives to our fellow-men and to God in any other way. Our motto must always be: "LOOKING UNTO JESUS."

We must fix our eyes upon our Saviour, and never take them off until His image is imprinted upon them. Then we shall see Him in all our duties. Just as when you look at any object through coloured glasses. The colour of the object seems to have changed to the colour of the glass. In the same manner any disagreeable duty, when looked at through Christ, in the light of His marvellous love to us, will have changed its hue, so that we can thereafter contemplate it with pleasure and joy.

Tell me how it was that the martyrs in every age could go up to the burning pile with the song of triumph on their lips, embracing the stake and rejoicing in the midst of the flames. Was it not because they looked at the flames and the stake through Jesus, and they were transfigured? We, too, may have every disagreeable duty transfigured. In your efforts to help others, try to realize that you are doing it for Christ, and not merely for them. Hear from His own lips the words of encouragement, "Inasmuch as ye have done it unto one of the least of these My brethren ye have done it unto Me."

This is the grand secret of a happy life. If you hold the secret you may always have joy in your sacrifices. Your heaviest crosses will become transfigured, and become your highest joys. The life of Jesus is our pattern-life. First the cross, endured not only patiently, but joyously. Then the crown, and the song of victory, and the "Well done, good and faithful servant, enter thou into the joy of thy Lord."

XXIII.

DIVINE ELECTION AND HUMAN FREEDOM.

"According as He hath chosen us in Him before the foundation of the world, that we should be holy and without blame before Him in love."—EPH. i. 4.

"God hath from the beginning chosen you to salvation, through sanctification of the Spirit and belief of the truth."—2 THESS. ii. 13.

THE doctrine of Election is very embarrassing to many thoughtful Christians. It is a subject, therefore, that cannot be omitted in dealing with doctrinal difficulties. The doctrine is clearly taught in Scripture; and, when properly understood, is a most precious and comforting doctrine. There is nothing in the doctrine itself to cause anxiety and embarrassment. It has, however, been so misrepresented, and such distorted views have been given of it, that one ceases to wonder that many approach it with an instinctive shrinking and repugnance. Many mentally associate it with the idea of reprobation, making it to mean *God refusing*, instead of *God choosing*. Others so caricature it as to confound it with the formula of Fatalism: "If I am elected, I shall be saved, do what I will; and if I am not elected, I cannot be saved, strive as I may." In this way the doctrine of Election has been made to bear many burdens, which it never was intended to bear.

Again, there are earnest, anxious, seeking souls, who puzzle and perplex themselves in the first stages of their religious experience, in the endeavour to ascertain whether or not they are included in God's purpose of love. However, at this stage they cannot possibly find out God's secret purposes : "The secret things belong to God ; but those things which are revealed belong to us, and to our children for ever" (Deut. xxix. 29).

God has two classes of purposes—secret purposes and revealed purposes. His secret purposes are not for us to know; and by seeking to pry into God's secrets we only perplex and harass ourselves to no purpose. All of God's purposes which are necessary for our comfort and direction in seeking salvation are revealed in the promises. Every promise of Scripture is a purpose revealed. With these only have seeking souls to do. God purposed to save all who come to Jesus. This purpose is embodied in the promise of our Lord: "Him that cometh unto Me I will in no wise cast out" (John vi. 37). God purposed to give His Holy Spirit to regenerate and sanctify all who sincerely seek Him. This purpose is revealed in the promise: "If ye then, being evil, know how to give good gifts unto your children ; how much more shall your heavenly Father give the Holy Spirit to them that ask Him" (Luke xi. 13). God purposed to hear and answer the prayerful longings of the human heart that draws near to Him in faith. Hence we have the promise : " Whatsoever things ye desire when ye pray, believe that ye receive them, and ye shall have them" (Mark xi. 24). Anxious souls, seeking rest, have to deal with the promises, and have nothing to do with the secret purposes of God. We can make our calling and election sure to ourselves only by accepting Christ and by experiencing the regenerating and sanctifying power of the Holy Spirit. When the love of God is shed abroad in our hearts by the Holy Ghost, given unto us, we then obtain a hope that maketh not ashamed (Rom. v. 5). This hope, however, is the result of experience; and it cannot be arrived at until we have personally accepted Christ, and have felt the power of the Gospel.

While those who have not found peace and joy through believing in Jesus have nothing to do with the doctrine of Election, it is nevertheless a most comforting and strengthening doctrine to true believers. It is much more comforting for me to know that Christ has chosen me, than to know simply that I have chosen Him: " Ye have not chosen Me, but I have chosen you, and ordained you, that ye should go and bring forth fruit, and that your fruit should remain." (John xv. 16). There are times in our experience when we are depressed, when our faith becomes feeble, and our love grows cold. We feel as if we were letting go our hold of God. The only true source of comfort under such circumstances is the assurance that God has laid hold of us—that we are His called and chosen ones. By clinging to the promises we find comfort and strength: "I the Lord thy God will hold thy right hand, saying unto thee, Fear not; I will help thee." The promises are ours; and, leaning upon them, we become hopeful and strong. The eternal purpose is God's secret, and the curious will find in it only perplexity and discouragement.

In the plan of salvation there is the Divine side and the human side. God saves no man against his will. He is willing to receive all who come; but they must come. All that believe " are justified from all things ; " but they must believe. He gives the Holy Spirit to them that ask ; but they must ask. We are to work out our own salvation, while God works in us both to will and to do—both to make us willing and to give us power to lead a holy life.

In the age of theological controversy these two truths were pitted against each other, instead of making one the complement of the other in accordance with the teaching of Scripture. One party magnified the Divine side, giving perhaps undue prominence to God choosing and calling, without dwelling sufficiently upon man's part in repenting and believing. Their opponents, on the other hand, went to the opposite extreme, ignoring in a large measure the Divine call and the striving of the Holy Spirit, claiming for man the ability to turn to God and to lead a holy life. After the dust of controversy cleared away it was seen that the truth lay between these two extremes. Each party held a part of the truth, but not all of it, as set forth in Scripture.

In the complete scheme of salvation, as taught by the Apostle Paul in the texts we have chosen, there are five distinct steps, all of which are essential; and which, when taken together, constitute the way of salvation.

First, CHOSEN BY GOD—" God hath from the beginning chosen you to salvation ; " " according as He hath chosen us in Him before the foundation of the world." Here God is represented as choosing, electing. God's eternal purpose is a purpose of love in choosing us to salvation, and in providing the necessary means to secure it. Election, therefore, is the first link in the chain, but not all of it.

Secondly, We are said to be CHOSEN IN CHRIST— "According as He hath chosen us in Him." A most essential part of the plan of salvation is Christ's redemptive work. We are not chosen independent of Christ, but IN HIM. Those whom God hath chosen eventually become united to Christ by a living faith.

Thirdly, Attention is directed to THE WORK OF THE SPIRIT. "God hath from the beginning chosen you to salvation THROUGH SANCTIFICATION OF THE SPIRIT." This is the third link in the chain; and it cannot be dispensed with. No man is elected to be saved, do what he will. We are chosen "through sanctification of the Spirit." Man must have a new life. The Spirit of God gave life at first; and He only can give new life. If any man be in Christ Jesus, he is a new creature. He is created anew in Christ Jesus.

Fourthly, Another essential link in the chain is FAITH. We are chosen through sanctification of the Spirit *and belief of the truth.* Only those who believe the truth,—the truth about sin, as forfeiting life and the favour of God,—the truth about Christ, as the Redeemer, and Mediator, and Way to the Father,—are the chosen and called of God. God chooses no man to salvation apart from believing the truth. And he who believes the truth and accepts Christ as Saviour and Lord, may know that he is chosen of God, and redeemed by Christ.

Fifthly, the final link in the chain, to which all the

rest lead up, is HOLINESS—" Chosen that we should be holy and without blame before Him in love." Election, Redemption, Regeneration, Faith,—all have their consummation in a holy Christlike life. Holiness is the ripe fruit of the completed plan of salvation. God selects, or chooses the plant. It is planted or ingrafted into Christ, rooted and grounded in love. The Holy Spirit, as the life's sap, conveys the life of Christ into the plant. Faith keeps clinging to Christ, thus preserving the union between the soul and its Saviour. Then follows the grand result—" fruit unto holiness, and the end everlasting life."

These five links are all essential to the completed chain; and they will be found to be inseparably connected with each other. Those who are chosen by God Christ redeems, the Holy Spirit regenerates, and they believe the truth, and lead a holy life lived in love to God. If, therefore, we can lay our hand upon any one of these links in our own experience, we can thereby assure ourselves of all the rest. Taking those links that reach down to us in our own personal experience, we can follow them upwards until we reach the topmost link—the electing love of God. He who is conscious of living a holy life in fellowship with God, dwelling in love, and overcoming the world, has the evidence within himself that he is chosen of God. Or, if by a living, ever-acting faith he clings to Christ as his Saviour, and realizes, like Paul, that the power of Christ is resting upon him, he may in this manner prove his election. Or, again, if he has felt the life-giving touch of the Holy Spirit new-creating him, changing his loves and desires, and bringing His will into sympathy with God's will, so that he loves what God loves, he may thus know and prove his election of God. Hence it follows that he who would make his calling and election sure, or, in other words, obtain the assurance that he is one of God's chosen ones, must begin with his own experience, and from it mount up to God's electing love. It also follows that those only who have a Christian experience can possibly know of their election. The doctrine of Election, therefore, cannot be profitably studied until we have accepted Christ as our Saviour and are being conformed to His image. The tree is known by its fruits ; and so are the called and chosen of God.

A wild caricature of the doctrine of Election and Foreordination has endowed God with the attributes of an unfeeling, selfish autocrat, who puts engines of irresistible force all along the path of life, and lays down a track for man which he must helplessly follow. Those who deny the freedom of the human will make God pre-ordain the issues of life apart altogether from the life itself. This God never does. He has left the will of man perfectly free to choose the good or the evil. Otherwise man would not be responsible for his acts. God does not make it impossible for those who are eventually saved to go astray, if they choose to do so. Nor does He make it impossible for those who are eventually lost to do right. Each man starts in life conscious that his will is perfectly free. He is free to choose the upward or the downward path. It is only when he has deliberately and persistently followed the downward path for a lengthened period that his will becomes enslaved by the power of sinful habit.

He was free to go down; but he is not free to return. He is weighted by the power of habit, and his will is weakened by constant yielding to bodily appetite. Freedom is God's good gift; and it is only when man abuses his freedom that he becomes enslaved.

When that distinguished botanist, Professor Agassiz, was travelling amid the snows and glaciers of the Alps, he looked down a deep crevasse, and espied what he took to be some rare plants. He determined to make the descent. His guides arranged the windlass, carefully calculating their own weight and the weight of the Professor and his bucket, and provided leverage according to their respective weights. He descended several hundred feet in safety, secured the plants, and gave the signal to be taken up. To the horror of all, the party at the top were unable to bring up the bucket and its precious freight, until assistance arrived some hours after. How was this? Their calculations were correct so far as they had gone; but they had neglected to take into account the weight of the rope. He was free to go down, but the weight of the rope made him powerless to return. Now, sinful habit is such a rope. Men feel perfectly free to pursue the downward course; and they imagine that they will be perfectly free to retrace their steps at any moment they choose. But, having neglected to take into account the power of sinful habit,—the weight of the rope—to their horror and dismay they find themselves held fast in the shackles of vice.

This is an illustration of an undoubted fact, namely, that the will of man, originally free, becomes enslaved by a persistent course of sin. Man is now helpless.

He cannot save himself; he can only struggle. And except help comes to him from above he must be for ever lost. He is a bond-slave to sinful habit—the hardest of all task-masters. Under these circumstances there is but one voice that can bring comfort and hope : " If the Son shall make you free, ye shall be free indeed." It is true, therefore, that the human will is free ; and it is also true that it may become enslaved. Both facts are known in human experience.

Man's inability, however, does not destroy his freedom. The will is still free in its choice. It is as free in choosing the wrong as it would be in choosing the right. It is this perfect freedom of choice that makes man entirely responsible for his acts. His inability only proclaims his need of Divine help—his need of the quickening and helping power of the Holy Spirit. God in His great love has made abundant provision for man's needs, and He expects struggling mortals to avail themselves of that provision. In the finished work of Christ He has provided for " the remission of sins that are past." In the gift of the Spirit, promised to all who ask, He has provided for the renewal of the heart and will, and for power over sin, bringing the trusting soul into fellowship with Christ, thereby making a holy life possible. God does not elect any man to eternal life apart from union to Christ and holiness of heart and life. Those who have been chosen and redeemed become united to Christ by faith and the indwelling of the Holy Spirit, and eventually become conformed to His image : " Whom He did foreknow, He also foreordained to be conformed to the image of His Son " (Rom. viii. 29).

Thus it is seen that the five links in the chain—Election, Redemption, Regeneration, Faith, Holiness—are all linked together; so that he who possesses one virtually possesses all. Therefore God does not choose men to salvation irrespective of faith in Christ and a holy life. His original plan and purpose include all the means necessary to the end in view. The saved are not simply elected; they are "called, and chosen, and faithful" (Rev. xvii. 14). And it is quite as necessary that they should be faithful, as that they should be chosen and called.

A true theology will not lose sight of either the Divine side or the human side in the plan of salvation. As in the Saviour Himself, so also in Salvation there is the mysterious union of the human and Divine. The grand error into which superficial theologians fall is taking a part of the plan of salvation, as if that part were the whole. And part truths are often found to be the most dangerous errors. It is this partial and imperfect knowledge of Bible truth that causes people to have difficulty about God's electing love. If the scheme of redemption be viewed as a whole, at the same time having regard to the proper balance of all the parts, it will be seen to be, not only wise and benevolent, but in every way worthy of the all-wise and ever-loving God.

God's electing love does not in any way interfere with man's free agency and choice. He who freely chooses God, and accepts Christ as Saviour and Redeemer, and feels the life-giving touch of the Divine Spirit, will never have any doubts or questionings as to whether he is chosen by God or not. "He that believeth on the Son of God hath the witness in himself." "The Spirit Himself beareth witness with our spirit that we are the children of God." And just so soon as our hearts have learned to go out to God in filial love and confidence, we will be ready gladly and gratefully to take up the words of the beloved disciple and exclaim, "We love Him, because He first loved us."

XXIV.

INSPIRATION AND REVELATION.

"No prophecy ever came by the will of man; but men spake from God, being moved by the Holy Ghost."—2 PETER i. 21.

IN this age of doubt and denial it is well to have clear views with regard to the Authority and Inspiration of the Scriptures. We want not only to believe that the Scriptures are the Word of God, but also to be able to give a reason for our belief. The spirit of Rationalism is abroad in the world, which demands that all our beliefs shall be brought to the touchstone of reason. Although this spirit has no sympathy with the revealed Word of God, yet its influence may be overruled for good. If it arouses Christian men to make themselves familiar with the proofs of Revelation and Inspiration, it will serve a good purpose in lifting blind faith up into the region of intelligent belief. Where positive knowledge is possible it is more comforting than simple faith, because it is secure from attack. To be strong for service, and strong against temptation, we want, not faith merely, but the full assurance of faith—a faith that never wavers and knows no doubt.

In order to be able to take the comfort from the promises of God's Word which they are intended to give, we must be able to say of each promise—" It is true ; God says it." However much it may seem to differ from our own feelings, or from reason, or from what we might naturally expect, we ought to be able to rise above every doubt and fear and make the promise our own. If not, we cannot be happy, joyous, triumphant Christians. It is only when the word of Christ dwells in us richly in all wisdom that the peace of God can rule in our hearts, and we can successfully turn aside the fiery darts of the wicked one. The Word of God is declared to be the Sword of the Spirit. In the hour of trial and temptation the Holy Spirit brings to the mind with sweetness and power the particular promise suited to the need of that moment, and thus the tried and troubled heart is strengthened and comforted. It is, therefore, of prime importance that we should know that the promises of Scripture are in very deed and in truth the words of the living God.

Therefore there are two points that will demand attention. First, The Fact of Inspiration. Second, What is meant by Inspiration ?

The Divine authority of the Scriptures is due to the fact that they are not simply the writings of men— the product of human wisdom merely ; but the Word of God. And they are the Word of God, because " holy men of old spake as they were moved by the Holy Ghost." Hence the Apostle Paul declares that " All Scripture is given by inspiration of God, and is profitable for doctrine, for reproof, for correction, for instruction in righteousness, that the man of God may be thoroughly furnished unto every good work" (2 Tim.

iii. 16). It is here declared that all Scripture is "God-breathed," θεόπνευστος. All the writers of the Bible declare that what they wrote they received as a revelation from God. The prophets of the old dispensation did not speak in their own name. They prefaced their utterances by "Thus saith the Lord."

An easy and decisive proof of the Inspiration of the New Testament is found in the fact that Christ promised the disciples the gift of the Holy Ghost, and that He would guide them into all truth, and bring all things to their remembrance whatsoever He had spoken to them. As a matter of fact, they did receive the gift of the Spirit on the day of Pentecost, and also the gift of tongues. They were, therefore, guided and inspired in what they spoke and wrote. We never find them claiming their superior wisdom and power as their own. If they had made any such claim they would have lost their gifts. The Apostle John declares that God signified to him by His angel the Revelation which he wrote. He was simply God's mouth-piece. The Apostle Paul thanks God that the Thessalonian converts received his message, "Not as the word of men, but, as it is in truth, the Word of God" (1 Thess. ii. 13). Moreover, he pronounces an anathema even on an angel from heaven who would preach any other gospel than that which he taught (Gal. i. 8). Here, then, we have a short and easy method of proving the Inspiration of the New Testament. Christ promised the Apostles the guidance of the Holy Spirit. The Apostles invariably claim to have received their message from God. The fact that in making this claim they retained their power and gifts is proof positive that the claim was genuine. If they were false teachers, making false pretensions to Divine gifts, they would have lost their power.

A short and decisive method of proving the Inspiration and Authority of the Old Testament Scriptures is found in the fact that Christ and the Apostles quote them as the Word of God. This at once stamps them with Divine approval. Christ Himself affirms that David by the Spirit called the Messiah Lord. (Matt. xxii. 43.) He thereby recognized David as an inspired writer. The Apostle, in writing to the Hebrews, quotes the words of David in the 95th Psalm as the words of the Holy Ghost: "As the Holy Ghost saith, To-day if ye will hear His voice, harden not your hearts" (Heb. iii. 7). He also quotes the words of the prophet Jeremiah (xxxi. 33) as the words of the Holy Ghost (Heb. x. 15, 16). The Apostle Paul, in addressing the Jews at Rome, makes the same claim for the prophet Isaiah: "Well spake the Holy Ghost by Isaiah the prophet unto our fathers" (Acts xxviii. 25). It is clear, therefore, that Christ and the Apostles believed and taught that what the Old Testament writers said, was said by the Holy Ghost. The testimony of the Apostles, according to Christ's own authority, is placed on a par with His own testimony. Of their utterances He said, "It is not ye that speak, but the Spirit of your Father that speaketh in you" (Matt. x. 20). "He that heareth you, heareth Me" (Luke x. 16). From the day of Pentecost they were the infallible organs of God for the communication of Divine truth; and on all matters of fact and of doctrine their teaching must be accepted as a true revelation of the will of God. Therefore their testimony to the Inspiration of the Old Testament Scriptures is conclusive. But they affirm that "all Scripture is given by inspiration of God;" that "no prophecy of the Scripture is of any private *communication;* for the prophecy came not in old time by the will of man ; but holy men of God spake as they were moved (borne along) by the Holy Ghost."

The Jews divided the Old Testament Scriptures into the Law, the Prophets, and the Psalms. These divisions included the whole Old Testament as found in our Protestant Bibles. Christ and the Apostles repeatedly refer to these divisions, and quote them as having Divine authority. Whatever was written in "The Law and the Prophets," or in "The Book of Psalms," is thereby stamped with the imprimatur of God.

Christ never quoted or approved any of the Apocryphal books found in Roman Catholic Bibles ; and for this reason Protestants do not receive them as having any more than human authority. They were never included in the Jewish canon of sacred writings, and were not written in Hebrew. Then, again, they contain many puerilities, and are wanting in that majesty and sublimity that characterize the other Scriptures. But the entire Old Testament Scriptures, including the historical books, are infallibly the Word of God. Historical facts, and even minor incidents, are quoted with the same confidence as the commandments and prophecies, showing that Inspiration extended to all parts of the sacred canon. Even the book of Jonah, that great stumbling-block to Rationalists, is quoted by Christ Himself: "As Jonah was three days and three nights in the whale's belly ; so shall the Son of Man be three days and three nights in the heart of the earth" (Matt. xii. 40).

For all who accept the divinity of Christ, no further arguments or proofs are necessary to establish the Inspiration of the Scriptures. Yet it may be noted that the prophetic books prove themselves to be Divine. The argument from fulfilled prophecy is irresistible; and many of the prophetic utterances of the Old Testament have had a most minute and literal fulfilment. No mere man, for example, could predict the fall of Jerusalem, the dispersion of the Jews, and the death of Christ with so many attendant incidents, all of which have been literally fulfilled. Frederick the Great of Prussia once asked his chaplain to give him a short proof of the Inspiration of the Scriptures. His brief and satisfactory answer was: "The Jews, your Majesty." If there is a single passage in the Bible that is plainly prophetic, and which has been literally fulfilled, it is a conclusive proof of the Divine origin of the Book. Modern Infidelity does not even attempt to show that the prophecies respecting the Jews have not been fulfilled. Rationalists dare not face the question of the Jews. A very large proportion of the prophecies having been already fulfilled, both as to time and to circumstances, even Rationalists are compelled to admit that the Word of God is in the Bible, although they decline to go so far as to admit that the whole Bible is the Word of God. They wish to apply their own reason to the different parts of the Bible, reserving to themselves the right of rejecting such portions as they are not compelled to receive.

Hence the necessity arises of showing the entire

Unity of the Bible—that the sixty-six books are really one book—that although written by fifty different hands, the Bible is the product of one mind, that is, the mind of the Spirit. It is a progressive revelation. Its grand aim throughout is to reveal God and make known His will. The whole Old Testament is preparatory and prophetic of Christ. The New Testament records the fulfilment of the Old, and further and more clearly reveals God in Christ. The writers are many; their education and surroundings are very varied; yet throughout the whole Bible there is a unity of purpose and an agreement in doctrinal statements, which cannot be accounted for except by acknowledging that the writers were guided and inspired by the same Spirit.

But there is a further proof that the Bible is the Word of God. It exactly suits man's needs. The only satisfactory proof of the real value of a medicine is its healing efficacy. Now, the Bible is the only true remedy that fully meets man's needs. It warns man against sin, and provides a remedy for it. It never poisons. Its effects are always remedial and reformatory. Everything that the Bible enjoins will bear full and permanent translation into life. It suits not only one age, but every age. It has proved itself to be the stability of nations, and the preserver of society. Those nations and peoples that have not possessed the Bible have crumbled, or are fast crumbling, to the dust; while those that live according to its precepts are stable and enduring. This proves it to be a book of Divine origin. The like cannot be said of any other book. There is not a single precept in the whole Bible but what has an elevating influence not to be found in the writings of men. Take away from our libraries and our homes the Bible, and all the books that have been written under the influence of Bible truth, and what would there be left of pure and elevating literature? And what would the effect be upon society? Were it not for Bible truth, and its condemnation of crime and impiety, and the penalties attached to a life of sin, both in this world and in the world to come, what would be the state of society and the world to-day? Take away our Bible Societies, and Missionary Societies, and Religious Tract Societies, and all benevolent and philanthropic societies supported by Christian men; take away our Churches, and Sunday Schools, and all Bible teaching, and in a marvellously short time the whole population would come down to the low level of those who are found in the slums of our large cities. There is no agency in this world that can preserve society from corruption, and lift up the fallen, and elevate and ennoble all who embrace it, except Bible truth brought home to the hearts and consciences of men by the power of the Holy Spirit. The nation owes its conscience and love of right to the Bible. In all ages the Bible has been the spring of purity and honesty and brotherly love. Where else can we find such high-toned morality as in the Ten Commandments and the Sermon on the Mount? Where else do we meet with any precept approaching to the Golden Rule: "Do to others as ye would that they should do to you"? There is no such teaching to be found anywhere, either in ancient or modern literature. Thus it is clearly seen that the proofs are multitudinous that the Bible is a Divine Book.

We have still to add a word as to the nature of Inspiration. We do not hold that every word of Revelation is necessarily dictated by the Spirit of God, and that the writers were not allowed in any case to use their own language. They were not mere machines. Their personal knowledge of events was not superseded, but used. Their own minds were allowed free exercise, but were so quickened and guided that they were able to communicate God's will to men, just as He wished to have it communicated. Hence we find Isaiah, and John, and Paul, each using a style and mode of expression distinctively his own, yet all the while uttering and recording just what God intended should be recorded for the instruction of His people in all ages. While holding to Plenary Inspiration, that is, that the whole Word of God is fully inspired, it must be admitted that the several writers were allowed to exercise their own powers and to employ their own language. For in no other way can we account for the fact that each writer has a style of his own. The true idea of Inspiration is that God so superintended the writing, and so guided the writers, that they all recorded whatever God wished them to record, being inwardly moved by the Holy Spirit.

It is usual to regard Inspiration as having different degrees. In the historical parts of the Bible, such as the Chronicles of the Kings and their wars, and the Acts of the Apostles, we have the Inspiration of Superintendence. That is, God so superintended and guided the writers that they did not fall into error, and were able to select what God wished to be preserved and handed down in the Church. He allowed them to use their own faculties freely, and their own language; but they were guided as to what they were to record by the Spirit of God.

In the Psalms and devotional parts of Scripture we have the Inspiration of Elevation. We are not to suppose that the prayers of David, and Asaph, and others, and their ascriptions of praise to God, were verbally dictated to them. The prayers and praises were in a very real sense their own; and yet their minds were so elevated by the constant presence of the Spirit of God, that the words they used in giving expression to their desires were such as to be suitable for all time.

In the prophetic parts of Scripture we have necessarily a higher degree of Inspiration. The subject-matter could not possibly be known to the writer. It must have been communicated directly by God. Daniel, for example, tells us that he records a revelation which he himself did not understand. It was given to him as really and as fully as Nebuchadnezzar's forgotten dream. When we affirm, therefore, that the whole Bible is fully inspired, we do not mean that every word in the Bible was dictated by God. Certain portions must have been given in this way; but in other portions the writers were permitted the free use of their own faculties and knowledge. However, such portions of Scripture are not less infallibly true; for the writers of the whole Bible were so superintended and guided by the Holy Spirit that they recorded just what God saw fit to have recorded. Therefore, the true theory of Inspiration is in every way consonant with Reason. If it were affirmed that every word in the

Bible were dictated by God, and that the writers were no more than passive machines, it might well be deemed unreasonable. It is such extreme views of Inspiration that have provided a field for the Rationalist and unbeliever.

XXV.

THE SPIRITUAL FACULTY IN MAN.

"The natural man receiveth not the things of the Spirit of God, for they are foolishness unto him; neither can he know them, because they are spiritually discerned. But he that is spiritual discerneth all things, yet he himself is discerned of no man."—I COR. ii. 14, 15.

THE Apostle in this passage clearly sets forth the importance of spiritual discernment. It is everywhere taught in Scripture that "the things of the Spirit"—"the deep things of God"—great spiritual truths—can be discerned only by spiritual men, those who are taught by the Spirit of God: "Ye have an anointing from the Holy One, and ye know all things."

This truth meets two mistakes very common among men and very plausible to many. First, That all Christian truth can be tested by the Intellect; and, secondly, That all Christian duty is performed by merely keeping the commandments. In opposition to these errors the Apostle urges the necessity of securing and maintaining a spiritual relation to God—not simply an intellectual relation, or a legal relation. Truth and Duty—"the things of the Spirit"—are spiritually discerned.

The Corinthian Church, influenced by a worldly, speculative spirit, had demanded of the apostle that he should conform more to the methods of other teachers. They had recourse to philosophical speculations; and the converts at Corinth began to say, "Give us some philosophy. We want to hear some new speculations some new theories, something to excite thought and discussion." The Apostle replied by showing how valueless human philosophy and speculation were, when applied to the mystery of God, and Life, and the Spiritual World.

The world by its wisdom knew not God. For four thousand years human philosophy had failed in its search to know God—to find out the Almighty unto perfection. This is given as a clear proof of how little value there is in speculative philosophy as a means of arriving at spiritual truth. The Apostle further declares that God has not chosen the world's philosophers. "Not many wise men after the flesh are called." The argument is: The world by its wisdom had failed to discover the highest truth; God, the All-wise, had rejected human wisdom—speculative philosophy; therefore, "I came not unto you with excellency of speech or of wisdom, declaring unto you the testimony of God. My speech and my preaching were not with persuasive words of man's wisdom, but in demonstration of the Spirit and of power; that your faith should not stand in the wisdom of men, but in the power of God."

Here the argument takes a turn. He claims to have a higher philosophy than the speculations of philosophers. We have a philosophy—a Divine philosophy, given by God to those who are able to receive it. " Wisdom, however, we do speak among them that are mature; yet a wisdom not of this world, nor of the rulers of this world, which are coming to nought; but we speak God's wisdom in a mystery, the wisdom that hath been hidden, which God foreordained before the worlds unto our glory." By God's wisdom is here meant, God's scheme of Creation and Redemption. It is not simply the preaching of Christ crucified; but God's entire purpose and plan in creating man, and in redeeming him and securing his salvation. Those profound questions that so intimately concern man, and which give him so much anxiety, the Divine philosophy answers. Such questions, for example, as: The Origin of Man; His relation to the Supreme Being; How to secure the highest happiness; What is there after death? Can God forgive deliberate sin? The God-given philosophy deals with these profound questions with a clearness and a certainty not even approached by human speculation. We speak wisdom among them that are mature and initiated into these great mysteries. What eye hath not seen; what ear hath not heard; what hath not entered into the heart of man; what God hath prepared for them that love Him: of these things we speak; for to us God hath revealed them by His Spirit.

In Christianity, therefore, there is a Divine philosophy; a true philosophy dealing with the greatest facts in the universe—Sin and Salvation. And the key to the whole scheme of Redemption is CHRIST AND HIM CRUCIFIED. Hence the one grand aim of the Apostle was to put into men's hands the key to this Divine philosophy: "I determined not to know anything among you, save Jesus Christ and Him crucified."

The first thing for them to do was to accept the personal Christ and His finished work, and after that they would be in a position to discuss doctrine with profit. The great danger of Rationalism is that it refuses to comply with God's order. This order is, first, *a heart-hold of Christ*, which is accompanied by the spirit of wisdom and inward illumination; for the Holy Spirit enlightens as well as sanctifies. Afterwards the profounder doctrines of Christianity may be studied intelligently, and are easily apprehended.

We have five natural Senses—Taste, Touch, Sight, Hearing, Smell. By these we obtain knowledge of natural objects. We have the Moral Sense, or Conscience, which approves or disapproves of our actions, giving us a knowledge of right and wrong. We have also the Spiritual Sense, or Faith-faculty, which realizes the presence of God and discerns spiritual truth. These are all given to man by God Himself—the natural senses and the moral sense in our natural birth, the spiritual sense in the New Birth. The New Birth gives us a new power of seeing spiritual truth. No man can see the Kingdom of God, or understand its mysteries, until he is born of the Spirit. Mere intellectual eminence counts for nothing in the spiritual sphere. The natural man cannot possibly know the things of the Spirit, because they are spiritually discerned. It would be as reasonable to expect a deaf man to hear with his eyes, as to expect a natural man to understand spiritual experience by means of the intellect alone. The thing is utterly impossible.

Everything that can minister to man's true welfare and happiness finds some faculty in man to lay hold of it. Food is needful for man's support and comfort. Hence the human body is provided with a stomach and powers of digestion and assimilation. Air is necessary, and it has its appropriate organ in the lungs. Light has its organ in the eye. Harmony and sound in the ear. Knowledge is received by the intellect. For friends we have the power of loving. So for spiritual truth and experience there is the spiritual faculty. Everything that ministers to man comes to him through its appropriate organ, and in no other way.

It is a fact abundantly attested by human experience that these several faculties must be used and cultivated, else they will lose their power—they will practically perish. If the eye be deprived of light, in time it loses the power of seeing. The ear that never hears musical sounds loses the sense of harmony. So the spiritual faculty must be brought into relation with God and spiritual truth, else it will lose its power. Of such a person it is said, "having eyes he sees not." He becomes dead to spiritual things. As the body will languish and die except it receive its appropriate food, so will the spiritual faculty in man. The spiritual man—that is, one who has received the Spirit,—and he alone, can take in the deep things of God. Spiritual truth, which seems to the intellect to be "foolishness," is readily received by the faith-faculty. . Revealed truth must be received before its beauty can be seen and its power felt. Like a painting or a beautiful scene; critical analysis destroys it. Gospel truth is not a science to be proved, but a revelation from God to be received. By receiving it we discover its power. It appeals to that part of our nature which God made to receive it.

We are apt to lose sight of this faith-faculty as a distinct organ, from the fact that it works in conjunction with other faculties and powers. It is more than love, and trust, and belief—these being its outcome. It is because we possess this faculty that we are able to love and trust and lay hold upon God. It is in some real sense oneness with Christ, by His Spirit dwelling in us. The faculty, if it exists at all before the New Birth takes place, is dormant, inoperative. Christ declared to Nicodemus that a man, to see the Kingdom of God, must be born again. And there is nothing more certain than that human experience confirms the teaching of the Master.

It is a fact that Christ constantly addressed Himself to this faculty: "According to your faith be it unto you." "Believest thou that I am able to do this?" He always waited for the inward eye to open: "Behold, I stand at the door and knock; if any hear My voice and open the door, I will come in unto him, and will sup with him, and he with Me." His teaching and miracles were all intended to awaken faith, and thus to open the eye of the soul. Where there was no faith He did no mighty works. The unsympathetic crowd, who merely gazed at Him with the bodily eye, and the critical Scribes who measured His teaching by intellectual standards, never felt the power of His teaching. He revealed the power of spiritual truth and the joy of spiritual fellowship to those only who opened their hearts to Him. Only through love and trust can Christ reveal Himself.

As spiritual truth can be discerned only by spiritual men, so their mode of discernment is a mystery to the mere natural man : " He that is spiritual discerneth all things, yet he himself is discerned by no man." Hence it follows that only spiritual men are qualified to judge of spiritual things. The Apostle even goes so far as to limit the judging of human conduct to spiritual men : " Brethren, if a man be overtaken in a fault, ye which are spiritual restore such a one in the spirit of meekness."

Man has a threefold nature. He is composed of body, soul, and spirit. And he necessarily possesses a corresponding threefold life: natural, or animal life; intellectual, or soul life; and spiritual life. All life requires sustenance ; and each order of life must have its appropriate food. The intellect cannot be nourished and strengthened by mere bodily food ; nor can the spiritual nature of man be sustained by intellectual food. The spiritual part of man must have its appropriate food. It must feed upon God and spiritual truth by holding fellowship with the Divine Spirit. Man is so constituted that he has a natural craving for food ; and there is the hunger of the heart and spirit, as well as the hunger of the body and the intellect. And the spirit must have its appropriate food, else it cannot be at rest. The hunger of the heart cannot be overcome by ignoring it, any more than the hunger of the body. Once admit, what no thoughtful man can deny, that man has a threefold nature—body, soul, and spirit,—then it follows that these three departments of his nature must be fed ; that there must be appropriate food for each department ; and that he must have organs, or faculties, for receiving this food. The spiritual nature, therefore, must have a spiritual organ for receiving spiritual food.

Now, an important inquiry is—What shall be the kind and quality of food best adapted to the spiritual nature of man ? This can be ascertained only by Revelation and experience—by testimony and by trial. The rule laid down by God is : "Taste and see that God is good." We take food and medicine on testimony ; and prove its value by experience. We cannot know its worth in any other way. We do not reject our doctor's prescription by a critical intellectual analysis. We do not make a microscopical examination of the several ingredients, and satisfy the intellect by discovering how each particular ingredient will meet some particular want in our system, before we take the prescribed remedy. No ; we trust the physician and prove his skill by experience. We act in precisely the same way in reference to food for the body. We trust the baker and the cook. So if our spiritual nature is to be fed we must trust God, and prove the power of prayer and spiritual truth by experience. What a marvellous thing that men can trust their cook, their baker, their chemist, and their doctor, and yet hesitate to trust God ! What low ideas they must have of the loving Father !

Christ did not come into the world with such convincing credentials as to compel men to believe in Him. He had credentials enough to invite men to make trial of Him and His teaching. He would bind men to Himself, not by outward evidence, but by inward attachment, arising from a heart-felt experience of His power to save and bless. It is this side of our nature that is capable of touching God. Nothing but a heart-hold of Christ can satisfy the longings of our spiritual nature and give inward rest.

It is worthy of note that the Apostle claims for spiritual men supernatural knowledge—a spiritual discernment above the comprehension of natural men. Now, there are some interesting practical inquiries respecting this affirmation. To whom are these attainments possible? In what degree is this spiritual discernment possible? And by what means can we attain to it? Scripture clearly teaches that this gift of spiritual discernment is not confined to any favoured class or order in the Church. At Pentecost others than the Apostles received the baptism of power. However, it is certain that all believers in the early Church did not enjoy this gift; for Paul addresses some of them as "babes in Christ," whom he could not recognize as "spiritual." They were believers—they were "in Christ;" but they were but babes in spiritual discernment.

The first step towards spiritual discernment is the New Birth. Only they who are born of the Spirit can discern "the things of the Spirit." The question put to the converts at Ephesus by the Apostle Paul has special significance: "Have ye received the Holy Ghost since ye believed?" Only by the illuminating power of the Holy Spirit can spiritual truth be apprehended. The power of spiritual discernment is perfected by being filled with the Holy Spirit. The

Apostles were so filled; and, therefore, they became the infallible organs for communicating the will of God to men. It was because he was thus filled with the Spirit that Paul could claim to have "the mind of Christ."

What are the necessary qualifications on our part to arrive at this power of spiritual discernment? By what means can we obtain the comforting assurance that we have the mind of Christ? First, There must be a perfect readiness to prefer the mind of Christ to our own opinion, and to do His will cheerfully, gladly, so far as it is known to us. This state of mind is indispensable. Secondly, there must be an entire sinking of self and self-interest—a readiness to love what God loves—that Christlike spirit which always says, "Not my will, but Thine be done." Thirdly, There must be thorough familiarity with the Word of God, and constant communion with Him, so that the Spirit may guide us into all truth. Like David, we must cry, "Open Thou mine eyes that I may behold wondrous things out of Thy law." Fourthly, There must be earnest, believing prayer for spiritual illumination. "If any of you lack wisdom, let him ask of God, who giveth to all liberally, and upbraideth not; and it shall be given him" (James i. 5). Lastly, There must be sincere love to God and man. "He that dwelleth in love dwelleth in God, and God in him" (1 John iv. 16). Love is the law of Spiritual Light. If we surrender our whole heart, and will, and conduct to God, He will fill us with all the treasures of wisdom.

These attainments are not limited to apostolic times. They are for the consecrated ones in all ages. Those who have been quickened by the Spirit of God discern the presence of God. They are conscious of the presence of the Holy Spirit, and can discern what the natural man cannot perceive. Blind men will discern the presence of an object by the resistance of the atmosphere. Their sense of touch has been so cultivated that it is sensitive to an increase of atmospheric pressure. In like manner the spiritual sense may be so cultivated as to be ever sensitive to the presence of God. God is present everywhere. But as a man, if his eyes be put out, may move in the very presence of the sun, and yet see no light; so the natural man moves day by day in an atmosphere that is fuller of God than our atmosphere is of sunbeams at noonday, and yet discerns Him not.

It is only by constantly discerning Christ, as present by His Spirit, that we can obtain power of spiritual discernment, power in prayer, power over sin and temptation, and power in service. After the Apostles received the baptism of the Holy Spirit on the day of Pentecost they were new men. They were clothed with power. God's best gift to the believer is the baptism of power. By faith in the finished work of Christ and the quickening touch of the Holy Spirit we obtain pardon and peace. By being filled with the Holy Ghost we obtain purity, power, and spiritual illumination. We become temples of the Holy Spirit, and channels for conveying spiritual blessings to others.

Take the matter of prayer. It is essentially a spiritual exercise; and it is only by means of the spiritual faculty that the power of prayer can be known. Only he that is spiritual is qualified to judge of it. Prayer is a personal act between two persons. It is outside the sphere of abstract reasoning. One of the parties is Divine; and, therefore, mere human reason is not competent to decide on His modes of action. It is a matter, not of reason, but of revelation and experience. We are so constituted that we feel our need of Divine help. God assures us that if we ask, we shall receive. Others testify that God has heard and answered them. We ask and receive, and thus know in our own experience that God answers prayer. It is a matter entirely of revelation, testimony, and experience. These are the conditions of prayer. The natural man will not accept the conditions, and, therefore, must remain in ignorance. It is only the spiritual sense, or heart, which loves, trusts, confides, and feels after God, that can discern Him. An inward sense of communion with God is a spiritual thing. The natural man can know nothing of spiritual fellowship and spiritual power, for they are spiritually discerned. But he that is spiritual discerneth all things; yet he himself is discerned of no man.

XXVI.

THE MODEL PRAYER: SONSHIP.

"After this manner, therefore, pray ye: Our Father, which art in Heaven, Hallowed be Thy name."—MATT. vi. 9.

IN the discourse which preceded the giving of this Model Prayer the Lord Jesus exposed and condemned the traditional teaching of the Scribes and Pharisees. By their traditions they made void the Commandments of God, teaching for doctrines the commandments of men. Hence He enforced a higher code of morality, that would reach the heart as well as the outward life.

Then He proceeds to unveil the falseness and hollowness of their practical piety. The religious life of the Pharisees manifested itself under three outward forms: Prayer, Almsgiving, Fasting. The Pharisees prided themselves on having attained to the highest possible eminence in these three phases of practical piety. Prayer was intended to express their right relation to God; almsgiving their right relation to their neighbour; and fasting their right relation to themselves. Such modes of expressing our love to God and our neighbour are right enough in themselves; and Christ does not condemn prayer, or almsgiving, or fasting, but the unreal and ostentatious manner in which they observed these religious duties. They gave alms, not from genuine regard for the poor and a desire to promote their comfort, but to receive praise from men. This was their motive, and it is this self-glorying spirit that Christ condemns. With a haughty air a man may throw his paltry pence to the poor, and his manner may bring more hurt to their feelings than his money can bring comfort to the body. But the Christ would teach men to add to their gifts love and sympathy. He would have His followers draw near to the poor and the outcast, and take them by the hand, and help them by their sympathy as well as by their gifts. The Lord Jesus knew human nature perfectly, and He knew that it is a much greater act of self-denial for the deserving poor to receive relief publicly than for the rich to bestow it. True regard for their feelings, therefore, would not only assist them privately, but also contrive to give assistance in such a manner that they would scarcely be conscious that they were debtors to man. Suppose a Christian man or woman should discover an honest deserving person in real want, and should approach their poor neighbour in some such way as this : " We are all brethren in Christ Jesus. He has been pleased to give to me more than He has given to you of this world's goods. It is His will that we should love and help each other, and share in His good gifts." If we would approach our poorer brethren in this spirit, what an immense power it would give us among them for good ; and how it would convince them of the power and blessedness of religion. Alms, given in such a spirit, would be truly acceptable to God. The conduct of the cold, heartless Pharisee disgusted men, with his haughty air and formal rites; and, judging religion by its unworthy representatives, they turned away from it altogether.

However, I wish to direct attention more especially to Prayer, and particularly to what Christ has taught us about prayer. His disciples, like all young disciples, found great difficulty in knowing how to pray; and one of them said to Him, "Lord, teach us to pray, as John also taught his disciples." Anxious to assist them in a matter of such importance, He gave them a brief and comprehensive model prayer.

Before taking up the several petitions in this Model Prayer let us look at prayer in general.

The essence of prayer does not consist in the words used, or the attitude assumed, or the place in which prayer is offered. The Pharisees assumed the attitude of prayer. They frequented the synagogue—the house of prayer. They used the words of prayer. And yet in the eye of God their whole religious ceremony was a mere empty form. A reference to the injunction of the Apostle, "Pray without ceasing," ought to convince any one that true prayer does not consist in attitudes, or in the words used, or in the place where prayer is offered. It is impossible to pray without ceasing, if you must pray always on your knees; for then you could do nothing else all the day long. And you cannot always be in the house of prayer; nor can you go on using audible words from morning to night. The essence of prayer, therefore, does not consist in the use of set words, or in assuming certain attitudes, or in resorting to any particular place.

In what, then, does true prayer consist? Prayer

must always be a thing of the heart. Prayer is the outgoing of the heart to God in longing desire, in reverence, dependence, and confidence. This may take place at any moment, and in any place, and is not necessarily accompanied by audible words. Prayer, being the longing and yearning of the spiritual nature after God, cannot be understood by the unaided human reason. Hence there is always a danger of running to either of two extremes: a mere superstitious observance of prayer on one side, and the neglect of prayer altogether on the other. Weak, sentimental natures have a strong tendency towards a superstitious observance of outward forms of worship, under a secret conviction that certain words and attitudes and places have a kind of magical charm. On the other hand, strong, highly-intellectual natures, that can accept nothing that cannot be grasped by the intellect, are apt to rebel against the use of words in prayer altogether, and say, "What need is there of prayer, when God knows all I want and all I desire?" These are the two extremes—superstition on the one hand, and doubt on the other. The Scriptural view of prayer is the happy mean between these extremes. True prayer is a humble recognition of our dependence upon God for every needed blessing, and an expression of our confidence in Him as our Father and Friend.

No man is living in a right relation to God who does not feel dependent upon Him. Conscience tells us that we are dependent. The feeling of responsibility to a higher power which exists within every one, until blunted and stifled by persistent sin, tells us with no uncertain voice that we are not our own. The voice

THE MODEL PRAYER: SONSHIP.

within that says, "I ought," "I must," proclaims our dependence. Prayer helps us to feel this dependence —helps to bring us back to it, when by waywardness we have lost it.

The use of prayer, therefore, is not simply to move God and to awaken sympathy and compassion in Him by a recital of our needs, but rather to prepare us for the reception of blessing, which God is always ready to bestow, so soon as we are ready to receive it. God cannot give rest and satisfaction to a human heart that asserts its independence of Him. He must allow all such to be tossed about on the waves of trouble, until, weary and sick at heart, they come back to God feeling their need and crying out for help. The wanderer from God must have no rest until he returns to God and seeks shelter in his Father's house. Prayer promotes and deepens this feeling of dependence.

But prayer also implies confidence—an inward conviction that God will certainly bless those who seek Him. We want not only the feeling that we need God, but the confidence that God is ready and willing to meet that need. For this reason prayer should always have a promise to lean upon. In no other way can implicit confidence be secured. The promises of God are our warrant for confidence.

In this Model Prayer, which the Lord Jesus gave to His disciples, He seeks to inspire confidence by the very first word. God is to be addressed as " Father." He recognizes the fact that the feeling of dependence is not enough. There must be confidence as well. Dependence without confidence cannot give peace. It is like a man suspended over a precipice by a rope that he does not believe is strong enough to bear his weight. He is in agony every moment. The rope *may* be strong enough to bear him, but that does not give him any comfort so long as he does not believe it. To have comfort he must have cofidence in the rope. So if we would enjoy peace and rest we must do more than feel our need of God and cry to Him for help—we must put confidence in His Fatherly love and care, and never doubt His readiness to help and keep us every moment. Therefore, the question is not so much, " Do you believe in prayer ? " as, " Do you believe in the God of prayer ? " We must realize that we are having personal dealings with a personal God, who is both our Father and our Friend.

True prayer implies a personal relation of dependence and confidence. Hence we must be on our guard against a superstitious confidence in the mere mechanism of prayer, as if " saying prayers " had some kind of magical power. Even those Churches that use no set forms of prayer are not entirely free from danger on this point. Worshippers may content themselves with being prayed for, instead of placing themselves in such an attitude towards God that their hearts will go out in longing desire towards Him and in confident expectation of present blessing. In all true prayer there must be the sincere expression of the actual desires of the heart ; for otherwise it cannot be offered in faith. You cannot possibly believe that God will answer a prayer that is not sincere. And your uttered words are not prayer at all, if you do not believe that God will answer your cry. The answer may not come at the precise time you expect, or in the precise way you desire; but the answer will come, if the prayer is the sincere expression of the heart, and is for your real good, if it be offered up in faith, with humble submission to God's will. "Whatsoever things ye desire when ye pray, believe that ye receive them, and ye shall have them" (Mark xi. 24).

See how confidence and dependence run through the whole of this Model Prayer. The first three petitions express confidence; the remaining three dependence. In the first three, in addition to confidence, there is an undertone expressing a different state of mind, giving to them both variety and comprehensiveness. (1) Confidence with filial love and reverence, as *sons*: " Our Father, which art in heaven." (2) Confidence with submission, as *subjects*: "Thy kingdom come." (3) Confidence with self-surrender, as *servants*: "Thy will be done."

We are here taught, in the first place, that we are to draw near to God with the love and confidence of trusting children—" Our Father." In Christ we take the position of sons: "Ye are all children of God by faith in Christ Jesus;" "As many as received Him, to them gave He power to become the sons of God, even to them that believe on His name." By faith we are united to Christ; and in virtue of that union we are one with Him in sonship. By receiving Christ as our Saviour we become adopted sons—we are received into the family of God. But that is not all. Because we are sons God gives us His Spirit, new-creating us, making us born sons, enabling us to cry, "Abba, Father" (Gal. iv. 4). In a Hebrew household an adopted child was not permitted to address the head of the household by the name "Abba." That was the peculiar privilege of the born sons and daughters.

This twofold aspect of salvation must be borne in mind if we would form a clear conception of sonship. (1) *Christ's work for us*, which, the moment we accept Him as our Saviour, gives us the adoption of sons, bringing us into the family of God. (2) *Christ's work in us*, by His Spirit, which gives the consciousness of sonship, and with it the feeling of confidence. This inner consciousness of sonship is a matter of personal experience. He who has passed through this experience can say, "I know I am a child of God," while others may have to content themselves with saying, "I believe," or, "I hope."

When one is born there is life—the consciousness of life and the enjoyment of life. There is no doubt about it. There is no possibility of mistaking it. And just so when God sends forth the Spirit of His Son into our hearts, new-creating us, there is new life; and there will be the consciousness of that new life, and the enjoyment of it. Being an accomplished fact, it is a certainty in our experience. This experience is not simply a feeling, an emotion, a sentiment, but the thrill of life, permeating and transforming the whole man. It is much more than natural goodness and virtue. It is life more abundant. If, therefore, you have any difficulty in addressing God as Father, and in coming to Him in the confidence of prayer, it is because you want this life more abundant—the life of Christ in the heart.

It is of immense importance that we make no mistake here. We do not become sons of God in our natural birth, or by baptism, or by attendance on ordinances. We become sons of God when we personally accept Christ as our Saviour and Lord. We are born, "not of blood, nor of the will of the flesh, nor of the will of man, but of God" (John i. 13). That believers only are sons of God is evident: "Whosoever believeth that Jesus is the Christ is born of God" (1 John v. 1). That this birth is very real, and brings about a radical change, and introduces to an entirely new life, is evident from what the Apostle John affirms of it: "Whosoever is born of God doth not commit sin;" "Whosoever is born of God overcometh the world." When we are born of God, and enter upon sonship, we become "partakers of a Divine nature" (2 Peter i. 4). As our Divine Lord when He was born of a woman became a partaker of a human nature; so, when we are born of God, we become partakers of His nature. His seed—that which gives the new life, namely, the Holy Spirit—remains in us (1 John iii. 9). Not only does the quickening Spirit give new life in the act of regeneration; but He remains in the believer as a permanent life and power. "God is love; and he that dwelleth in love dwelleth in God, and God in him."

The Christian life, therefore, is a dwelling in God, and having God dwelling in us, by His Spirit (Rom. viii. 11); and "the Spirit beareth witness with our spirit that we are the children of God" (Rom. viii. 16). It is the Spirit, witnessing within, that assures us of our sonship; and thus only are we enabled to draw near to God with confidence as to a loving Father and Friend. If, therefore, we would enjoy the privilege of drawing

near to God with that confidence which the words
" Our Father" are intended to inspire, we must so live
in holiness and love and purity that the Holy Spirit
can take up His abode in us. We must walk with God.
We must walk in the light as He is in the light, and
then we shall have constant fellowship with Him; and
every moment our hearts may go out to Him in trustful
confidence, saying, " Our Father."

The last clause of this petition is evidently intended
to beget reverence : " Hallowed be Thy name." We
are not to approach God lightly, but with a serious,
earnest purpose. We are to remember that He is
greater than we, that we are unworthy of His favour
and mercy, and have no claim upon His bounty. We
are to hold His name sacred. And when we call ourselves by His name, we are to see that His name is
hallowed in us by a life worthy of His name.

Here, then, is a great privilege within the reach of all.
We *may* draw near to God in love and confidence.
Prayer is not a matter of constraint, but of lofty
privilege. In dealing with the careless and prayerless
around you, you are not to go to them and say, "You
must pray to God, or be for ever lost." That is true ;
but it is not the best way of putting the truth. If you
want to touch hearts, do not say, "You *must* pray ; "
but "You *may* pray." You may come to God and ask
Him to help and keep and comfort you. In your
doubt and uncertainty you may ask Him for guidance.
In your weakness and inability to live up to your own
ideal of right you may ask Him to help you. In every
danger and trial and temptation that beset your path
you may ask Him to keep you. In all your sorrows

and troubles and disappointments, you may ask Him to comfort you. This is the position of lofty privilege into which your sonship brings you—the privilege of coming to God as a Father and Friend, with the burden of sin, with the burden of trial, with the burden of sorrow, with the burden of anxiety. You may bring to Him every evil habit, every evil appetite and desire, and ask Him to take them all away. You have the privilege of saying, " Thou art my Father. I am Thy trusting child. Thou lovest me for Jesus' sake. And because Thou lovest me, do this for me, and make me wholly Thine."

This blessed privilege of sonship carries with it filial duties—love, obedience, respect. Love and obedience always go hand in hand. We must love His person, obey His commands, believe His promises, and trust His care. While we have filial confidence, we must also have humble dependence.

When God is declared to be "in heaven," it is not intended to represent Him as far off; but as the God of heaven, and, therefore, possessing all power to help and keep and comfort His people in every time of need. Such will God be to all who sincerely love and trust Him. They may enjoy every moment the consciousness of His comforting presence.

XXVII.

THE MODEL PRAYER: DEPENDENCE.

"Give us this day our daily bread; and forgive us our debts, as we also have forgiven our debtors. And bring us not into temptation; but deliver us from the Evil One."—MATT. vi. 11-13.

WE have already seen that the first three petitions of this Model Prayer are designed to call forth confidence in God,—confidence with filial love, as sons—confidence with submission, as subjects—confidence with self-surrender, as servants.

In the second division of the prayer we have several petitions intended to teach us our entire dependence on God, and our constant need of His help. In these petitions we are taught to approach God as suppliants and as sinners. We need daily bread, and we need daily pardon. And this prayer assures us that God is willing to bestow these needed blessings. He gives and He forgives.

God is here represented as the Giver of temporal blessings. This is an aspect of God's goodness that is too often overlooked. We are so accustomed to regard God as bestowing pardon that we are in danger of losing sight of the fact that He also bestows food.

The petition, "Give us this day our daily bread," refers not only to temporal food, but also to spiritual food. It includes the supply for the whole man. We need this supply daily; and we have the privilege of going to God daily for it. Man does not live by bread alone; and yet his daily food is a necessity of his existence. God is ready to provide for the wants of His trusting children, and He encourages us to ask for daily supplies.

We are to ask God for needed blessings; but we are not to be over-anxious about them. However great our needs, we are not to lose our confidence in God; for, if we have not confidence, our prayer ceases to be prayer. We are, therefore, to carry the confidence of the first three petitions into the dependence of the last three. Hence Jesus says, "Take no thought," that is, no anxious, worrying thought—"saying, What shall we eat? or, What shall we drink? or, Wherewithal shall we be clothed? Your heavenly Father knoweth that ye have need of all these things. But seek first the kingdom of God and His righteousness, and all these things shall be added unto you." Make it your first grand aim to have the kingdom of God set up in your hearts; see that you are entirely in sympathy with God and resigned to His will; then trust Him confidently for all needed temporal blessings.

Confidence in God is especially necessary, because with our imperfect knowledge we do not always know what is best for us. We want our desires granted now; but God may see that we are not prepared to receive the particular blessings we ask for, and so He will keep us waiting until we are ready to receive them with profit to ourselves. A child asks its mother for food. But the intelligent mother, knowing that too frequent eating tends to create a false appetite, which is most injurious to health, keeps the child waiting until the proper time. The child may fret and worry for a time ; but the mother is looking to the permanent health of her child, and, therefore, denies it present gratification. God deals with His children in the same way. And when He withholds from us present gratification, it is always for our permanent good. When God withholds or withdraws temporal blessings we may rest assured that He has a wise purpose in it. He is teaching us some useful lesson, and we ought to seek it out and be willing to profit by His discipline.

The grand qualification on our part for receiving from God either temporal or spiritual blessings is so to enter into His Spirit as to become like Him, so that we will be ready to do for Him and for our fellow-men what we ask Him to do for us. We must give as He gives, and forgive as He forgives. When we ask God to forgive us we must be able to say, "For we forgive men their trespasses." Thou, Lord, hast implanted in us Thine own spirit of forgiveness, so that we are ready to forgive others ; therefore, we feel assured of Thy forgiveness. The Lord Jesus faithfully warns us that if we do not forgive others, God cannot forgive us. For God to forgive a man who continues to cherish an unforgiving spirit would be to ruin him. It would be saying, " Peace, peace, when there is no peace." To cherish an unforgiving spirit is sin ; and a man who is living in sin cannot enjoy the assurance of God's forgiveness. We must come to God in such a spirit of charity towards all men that we can say, " Lord, we have forgiven from the heart all who have injured us.

We have by Thy help entered into Thy spirit. And now that we are one with Thee in love and sympathy with our fellow-men, do Thou blot out our transgressions, and restore to us the joy of our salvation."

The great principle laid down in this petition is that we must forgive if we would be forgiven. "If thou bring thy gift to the altar, and there rememberest that thy brother has aught against thee, leave there thy gift before the altar, and go thy way; first be reconciled to thy brother, and then come and offer thy gift." We cannot be reconciled to God until we are reconciled to our fellow-men. In the early Christian Church it was customary for the members of a family to ask each other's forgiveness before going to the Lord's Table. We should carry this spirit with us every day, and extend it to all men. No man can be at peace with himself or with God, who cherishes any grudge or ill-will against his neighbour. Life on earth must be such as to fit us for life in heaven. But in heaven all will be harmony, and love, and sweetest fellowship. Therefore, these graces must rule in us here. We must forgive others frankly and freely, if we expect God to forgive us. The whole design of the Gospel is to cultivate in us the spirit of meekness and gentleness, "forgiving one another, as God for Christ's sake has forgiven us."

It has been well said that "peace is love reposing." The soul can never enjoy perfect repose until it is dwelling in love. Love is the spring and source of all our comfort. "He that dwelleth in love dwelleth in God, and God in him."

In coming to God we are to come as suppliants

begging for bread, and as sinners crying for mercy. All prayer is an acknowledgment that we cannot do without God. "Give us this day our daily bread" is an acknowledgment that we are indebted to God for all daily food and for all temporal and spiritual blessings. It is a prayer of contentment and trust. Enough for to-day, I will trust for to-morrow. It is also a prayer of heavenly longing—a desire to be fed with bread from heaven. We pray for soul-food as well as for bodily food.

But we need more than food. We need cleansing. We require to be washed in the blood of the Lamb. Hence we cry, "Forgive us our debts." Here is the prayer of penitence—the cry of a soul burdened with the load of sin and longing to be free. The prayer of faith will always find expression in penitence. Only presumption will go to God and ask for nothing. The proud Pharisee thanked God that he was not as other men. He asked for nothing, and got nothing. The publican humbly confessed his sins, and found forgiveness. All who come humbly to God, feeling their need, may be confident of blessing.

So far God has been represented as a great and generous Giver—as giving food, and as giving pardon. He is further represented as our Leader and Keeper. "Lead us not into temptation; but deliver us from evil." These two aspects of God's daily care are included in the one expressive word Shepherd. A shepherd leads and keeps. Here, then, we have two beautiful and comforting thoughts: The Lord is my Leader—The Lord is my Keeper.

The petition, "Lead us not into temptation," presents

some difficulty, as it might seem to imply that God may actually lead His people into temptation.' That this is not the meaning of the words is evident from other passages of Scripture : " Let no man say, when he is tempted, I am tempted of God ; for God cannot be tempted with evil, neither tempteth He any man " (James i. 13). Temptation in Scripture is frequently used in the sense of trial, as when it is said, " God did tempt Abraham." He simply brought His servant into circumstances that severely tried and tested his faith. This trying and testing is a necessity in the life of faith. Abraham stood the test, and became the father of the faithful. Adam and Eve in a state of innocence were tested and tried. The angels in heaven were tried. Some stood the trial, and were confirmed in love and loyalty to God ; others failed, and were cast out.

Moreover, it would seem to be a fact in God's government that every individual must pass through this personal testing and trial that he may have an opportunity of declaring *for* God, or *against* Him. There is a crisis in every man's history—a time when God says to us, "Choose ye this day whom ye will serve." Our answer to that challenge either makes or mars the life. It is the turning-point in our career. If we resolutely choose God and accept His will and His leading, that act of decision whereby we surrender all to God, is accepted by God as the evidence of our love and loyalty to Him ; and, by the direct influence of His Spirit, our hearts and wills will be confirmed, and we will be filled with such blessedness in the act, that temptation will thereafter lose its power upon us.

When the Lord Jesus was tempted in every department of His nature, and stood firm in love and loyalty to God, we read—" Then the devil leaveth Him, and angels came and ministered unto Him." And so will it be in our experience. And, having passed successfully through the testing and trial, we have the privilege of using this petition, " Lead us not into temptation."

It is worthy of note that Christ, in giving us authority to use this prayer, also gives us the assurance that it will be answered. However, in all cases our deliverance from temptation will depend upon our having already cheerfully surrendered our will and our way to God. We must always carry into these last petitions, that express our needs, the confidence and self-surrender of the first three. It is only when we have such perfect confidence in God that we can cheerfully and gladly surrender all to Him, that we are in a position to do without further trial. If God loves us He must try us, and even follow us with trials, until we become perfectly pliant to His hand, and perfectly submissive to His will—until we hold all things so lightly that we can cheerfully give up all for God. The moment we come into this state of perfect trust we do not require testing and trying any further; and instead of having to endure trials and temptations we shall enjoy perfect peace : " Thou wilt keep him in perfect peace whose mind is stayed on Thee, because he trusteth in Thee."

Clearly, then, the meaning of this petition is, that God in leading His people may see it to be necessary to bring them into circumstances of sore trial; but so soon as we cheerfully submit to His discipline, and gladly do His will, then we may confidently ask Him to lead us in a way where there are no temptations to vex and try us—and He will do it. But even in this happy state we must not forget that He is still our Leader; and we must, moment by moment, be willing to be led wherever He pleases.

It follows, therefore, that it is not such an easy thing after all to pray this familiar prayer, if we enter into its deep meaning. We have to ask ourselves the question, Am I ready to be spared from temptation ? Am I so thoroughly in sympathy with God in all things that I can do without further trial? Am I ready to trust His will in preference to my own will ? Am I willing to endure further trial, if God sees it to be best for me, and thus prove that I can trust His wisdom and His love? If we have come into this state of mind we may present this petition in the most perfect confidence that God will lead us in a plain path.

We have yet to note the influence this petition, intelligently presented, will have upon the life. It will prevent a man from deliberately placing himself in the way of temptation. I cannot conceive of a man who has any real earnestness of purpose, deliberately going on dangerous ground where there is the slightest possibility of his falling, after having sincerely offered up this prayer. To do so would not only be a mockery of God, but a mockery of himself. To go deliberately in the way of temptation, after having asked God for protection, proves that the prayer was not sincere.

One of the beneficial results of prayer is that it

pledges us to ourselves and to God to follow the aspirations and desires of our best and highest moments. There are sublime moments in our lives when we have higher and holier longings than at other times—when the tide of life reaches its highest point; and, if we are wise, we will take advantage of those moments, and resolve in the presence of God to live up to the ideal thus presented to us. In prayer we commit ourselves to such a course. And when temptation comes our pledge to God will strengthen us to endure and help us to overcome. The fact that we have already pleaded with God to keep us in the hour of danger will constrain us to seek His help more earnestly in the presence of temptation. Prayer steadies us and helps to make life consistent. The lives of many Christians are like the tide, constantly ebbing and flowing; and, like the tide, their highest and lowest points come in quick succession. When the flow of the tide is highest the ebb is lowest. And so it is with emotional Christians, whose lives are not regulated and steadied by earnest purpose and prayer. They are largely the creatures of circumstances. In a warm religious atmosphere they mount up to the highest heights of feeling. Then again under adverse circumstances they go down to the lowest depths. Hence we see the need of the unchanging God to keep and guide us in our feelings, as well as in our way.

But, further, this petition, "Lead us not into temptation," if intelligently and sincerely presented, will not only steady and support us in the presence of temptation, but will also send us to God's Word that we may learn His will, and thus know what to avoid.

We are there taught that if we would be safe against the grosser forms of evil we must banish every evil thought and desire from our hearts. If we would be pure and holy in life, we must be pure in heart: " Blessed are the pure in heart, for they shall see God." We are to " bring into captivity every thought unto the obedience of Christ." The all-wise and ever-loving God thus teaches us that if we would be strong in the presence of outward temptation we must keep the heart pure. "My son, keep thy heart with all diligence; for out of it are the issues of life."

Now it is a fact that prayer helps to keep the heart pure. When alone with God, and when conscious of His presence with us, as we may be if we walk in the light, the thought of evil is necessarily excluded. And if the thought of sin is thrust upon us by the Evil One, we struggle against it and cast it out. A person who lives continually in an atmosphere of prayer will find that the fiery darts of the Wicked One will fall powerless and harmless upon the heavenly armour with which he is clad.

In order to stand in the day of temptation, we are not only to have our loins girt about with truth, and have on the breastplate of righteousness, and have the shield of faith, and the helmet of salvation, and the sword of the Spirit, which is the Word of God—the precious promises; but we are to " pray always with all prayer and supplication in the Spirit, watching thereunto with all perseverance." Without prayer no one can be strong to fight in the battle of life.

To prove the value and power of prayer we need no further argument than the fact that the Lord

Jesus prayed, retiring frequently to spend whole nights in prayer in the stillness and seclusion of the mountain side. His human nature required to be steadied and supported by communion with God. See, too, the heroes of the olden time! Enoch walked with God in holy communion. His life was a life of prayer and fellowship with God; and nothing else could have preserved him from the flood of wickedness that destroyed the old world. There was the flood of wickedness as well as the flood of waters. Behold Abraham interceding for Sodom! God does not cease to grant until Abraham ceases to ask. Behold Moses staying the wrath of God against Israel, when He was about to cut them off for the hardness of their hearts! God could not destroy the people while Moses interceded for them. These holy men obtained power by living in an atmosphere of prayer, and they were preserved from the abounding wickedness of their time. In prayer, therefore, there is power and safety.

The Church of Christ has yet to learn the mighty power of prayer. What a sad thing it is to have so many professed Christians in the world, and yet multitudes in doubt whether there is any real value in prayer! If Christian men and women only lived such holy, consecrated lives as to make it evident that temptation had no power over them, then the world would see and know that God, in answer to prayer, does keep His people from every snare and from every evil way. Thus their very lives would be preaching Christ; and men would flock to them inquiring the secret of their marvellous power over sin, and their freedom from anxiety in the midst of trial and privation.

XXVIII.

THE MODEL MAN; OR, TRUE MANLINESS.

"Behold the Man."—JOHN xix. 5.

THESE three little words, "Behold the Man," are big with meaning. They may be used to express both the MANHOOD and the MANLINESS of JESUS. While the Lord Jesus claimed to be the Son of God and one with the Father, and abundantly proved His claim by the wisdom of His teaching and His mighty works, He was also careful to impress upon the minds of His followers that He was a true Man, exposed to human temptations, and having real human sympathies. During His earthly life He continually spoke of Himself as the Son of Man. And after His resurrection we find Him appealing to His disciples to satisfy themselves as to His true humanity: "Handle Me and see; for a spirit hath not flesh and bones as ye see Me have." Therefore, while He was very God, possessing Divine power and wisdom, He was also the pattern-Man—the perfect model of true manhood and true manliness.

It is a most striking fact that all thoughtful students of the life of Jesus unite in proclaiming Him to be, not only a good Man, not only the best of men, but a perfect Man. Even those who are not willing to proclaim that He is Divine, are compelled to admit that there was no flaw in His character, and no fault in His life.

It is not my purpose at present to prove that Jesus was Divine. If it were, His divinity might easily be established from the fact that He was sinless. He could challenge His bitterest enemies to point out any flaw, or fault, or failure in His life: "Which of you convinceth Me of sin?" Now, no other man who ever came into the world was wholly free from sin. Therefore, if He were not more than man, His sinless life would have been the greatest of all miracles. You cannot account for the sinlessness of Jesus in any other way than that He was Divine.

My purpose, however, is to draw some lessons from the human life of the God-Man, Christ Jesus, that may help to guide us in the practical duties of life.

And, first, I observe that the life of Christ on earth exhibits to us the true ideal of manliness—what man ought to be in order to fulfil the end of his being; what man must be if he would enjoy perfect happiness, and become good and great and Godlike. The true ideal of manliness is not attained until our manhood has reached the highest point of which it is capable. But only in the life of Christ has manhood ever touched its highest point. Therefore, the life of Christ must be our model and our standard of manliness.

Take all the higher and nobler qualities of the soul— all that makes life noble and true and blessed; all that makes us happy and peaceful and restful within, and strong and sympathetic and helpful to those around us; and we shall find that in the life of the Lord Jesus all these qualities are seen in their highest perfection. We study the lives of good and great men, and we seek inspiration from them; and there is no doubt but we get it. Their noble deeds of self-denial and perseverance, their triumphs over difficulties and discouragements, encourage us and strengthen us for the battle of life. However, if we would enjoy the highest inspiration within our reach we must get it from the highest life; and that is the life of Jesus. We must study this model until we are able to copy it, until we have a clear idea of the secret of His marvellous life; how it was that He never yielded to temptation; how it was that He was never tainted with selfishness, nor pride, nor self-seeking; how it was that He had no worry, nor anxiety, nor impatience; how it was that He never murmured nor repined at the meagre success which attended His ministry.

Now, what was the secret power that was able to produce such a unique and marvellous life? I think I find the secret in His constant fellowship with the Father, and the perfect surrender of His will to the will of the Father. At the early age of twelve we find that the one over-mastering desire of His heart was to do the will of God, and to enter upon His life's work. When His parents are returning from the Passover at Jerusalem they miss Him, and, after three days' searching, they find Him discussing with the doctors in the Temple. To the question of His mother, "Son, why hast Thou thus dealt with us? behold Thy father and I have sought Thee sorrowing," He quietly replies, "How is it that ye sought Me? Wist ye not that I must be about My Father's business?" God had entered into His life. He lived Godward. He adopted no human standard of manliness and duty. "My Father's business"—that was the controlling motive of His life. He did not think it unmanly to bind Himself to do the will of God ; but considered this to be the first step necessary to have power over men.

If we would truly comprehend the life of Jesus we must start with the view of Him presented to us by the Apostle John : " In the beginning was the Word ; and the Word was with God ; and the Word was GOD." In these plain and emphatic words we have clearly set forth, not only His fellowship with God, but also His true divinity. The Word was with God—fellowship. The Word was GOD—His divinity. He not only lived in fellowship with God ; He *was* God. In the beginning He was God. He was not made ; He " *was* "— that is, He eternally existed. And, being the Eternal God, He necessarily taught eternal truth, and founded an eternal religion, and wrought out an eternal redemption, and was qualified to bestow eternal life. It follows also that the revelation which He gave of the Father must be the complete and final revelation of God. We need expect no further or fuller revelation of God ; nor do we need it.

In that life which was to be the true pattern of manly life there was the mysterious union of the human and Divine. We cannot tell what effect this mysterious union had upon His divinity,—whether the garment of humanity, that helped to reveal His divinity and make visible the invisible God, did any more than *veil* His Divine glory for the time,—but we are certain that His divinity had a wonderful influence upon His human life. It gave Him power over men, power over self, power over the devil, and over every form of evil. But it did not make Him something else than man. He was a true man, capable of being tempted and tried—"tempted in all points, like as we are, yet without sin." He was the perfect man; and, therefore, the perfect type of true manliness. His divinity brought out the glory and beauty that originally belonged to human nature, before it was eclipsed by sin; just as the light of the sun brings out the sparkling radiance and beauty of the diamond. The sunlight does not change the diamond into something else. It simply enables it fully to utter itself—to show all its richness and beauty. If there were no light to shine upon the diamond, it would appear to be only a dull stone. The light opens up its hidden depths of beauty, but does not change its nature. The diamond is necessary to the light, and the light is necessary to the diamond. In the same manner it can be shown that our God-given human nature has hidden depths of glory and beauty and perfection, which can be brought to light only by the power of divinity. Therefore, the union of the human and the Divine in Christ gives us the perfect model of highest manhood.

The incarnation and life of Christ were not only a revelation of God, but also a revelation of all that is highest and noblest in man. In Him we see that human nature can rise to its highest and best only by union to the Divine nature. Hence it follows that if we, as individuals, wish to rise to our highest and best we must become partakers of the Divine nature. And this is just what the gospel promises to bestow. By faith we are united to Christ. In the new birth we receive a new nature. We are begotten of God by the power of the Divine Spirit; and thus we become "partakers of a Divine nature" (2 Peter i. 4).

The new birth is just as real an experience as our natural birth; and it is just as necessary an experience, if we would attain to our highest and best. Hence Jesus, the Model Teacher, said to Nicodemus, "Ye must be born again." The Apostle John speaks of "God dwelling in us," and we in God; and such are declared to be "born of God"—"not of blood, nor of the will of the flesh, nor of the will of man, but of God." Paul gives prominence to the same great truth when he glories in persecutions, and distresses, and infirmities, in order that "the power of Christ may rest upon him" (2 Cor. xii. 9).

This union of the human and divine in us must be abiding, if we would secure and preserve the highest type of life. It is not completed in the single experience of the new birth. Hence Jesus says, "Abide in Me, and I in you. As the branch cannot bear fruit of itself, except it abide in the vine; so no more can ye, except ye abide in Me." The highest life of which we are capable is possible only by continuous abiding in Christ by an ever-living faith, and having Christ abiding in us by His Spirit.

This, then, is the first step towards a truly noble and manly life—the union of the Divine and human in us, after the pattern of the life of Christ on earth. The Man Christ Jesus was the manliest of men. You cannot find a single unmanly act in His life. Every word that fell from His lips and every act of His life are worthy, not only of the best of men, but of God. And if we wish to become truly noble and manly we must study His life and mould our lives according to His life and teaching. If to be manly is to possess the best qualities to be found in man in their highest perfection, then the nearer we attain to the life of Christ the nearer will we have come to the true ideal of manliness. To become manly, therefore, we must " BEHOLD THE MAN;" we must look upon the life of Jesus as our model, and copy it.

One of the great evils of our time is that most young people have a false idea of manliness. If they are taught to be gentle, and courteous, and patient, and forgiving, and obedient to parents and teachers, they have an idea that such traits of character would indicate weakness. But such is not the case. It is not the strong man, strong in the consciousness of power, that flies into a passion, and resents an insult, and heaps abuse upon his antagonist, and refuses to be gentle and forgiving. Strong men are able to control themselves, to control temper, and passion, and appetite. If they are strong in intellect they can use argument instead of force. It is worthy of note that Jesus never lost His temper. While He dealt severely with the white-washed Pharisees, and administered most faithful warnings and most scathing rebukes to those who persisted in their wrong courses, He never uttered words in haste which He could have wished had never been uttered. He showed His great strength and force of character by maintaining under all circumstances the most perfect self-control. Therefore, it may be laid down as an axiom, that no man has attained to the true idea of manliness who has not perfect control over his temper, and appetite, and passions.

Self-control is an essential element in true manliness. The example of Jesus, the manliest of men, must ever be the standard of perfect manliness. What He would do under any given circumstances must always be the manliest thing that can possibly be done under similar circumstances. If He would not resent an injury, but forgive it, then to forgive is more manly than to resent an injury. If He could say, "Father, not My will, but Thine be done," then to do the will of God in preference to our own will is to be manly. If He could sacrifice ease and personal comfort for the wellbeing and happiness of others, then to make personal sacrifices for the good of others is noble and manly. Such a line of thought is needed to correct the false ideas of manliness that are abroad in the world. There are many who seem to think that they cannot follow Christ and be manly. But, if you take all the highest traits of character that enter into the true ideal of manliness, you will find that Christ lived them all out in His life.

Many young men think that to be manly they must be independent of control, and self-reliant. Well, these very qualities are found pre-eminently in Christ. While He lived in constant dependence upon the Father, yet He was never swayed by the opinions of men. The people said of Him, "He speaks as one having authority, and not as the Scribes." Again, we find the Pharisees addressing Him in such wonderful words as these: "Master, we know that Thou art true, neither carest Thou for any man; for Thou regardest not the person of man." What a testimony to His independence and steadfastness! He could not be made to swerve from the path of duty either by fear or by favour. And yet amid all this strength and steadfastness we hear Him say, "Of mine own Self I can do nothing." Absolute and constant dependence upon God does not interfere with our personal independence, but tends rather to lift us up above the opinions and criticism of those who may differ from us. If you wish to be strong, and free, and self-reliant, you must lean upon God. Strong in His strength, you will not fear the face or the frown of man.

The Lord Jesus, in courage and in confidence, was worthy of the imitation of every man aspiring to be heroic. See Him addressing the crowds on themes too profound for their comprehension; and when they answer Him with stones instead of arguments, with what marvellous coolness He replies to them, "Many good works have I showed you from My Father; for which of these do ye stone Me?" See how calmly and courageously He rebukes the raving maniac among the tombs and casts out the evil spirit! See Him calmly sleeping on the tempest-tossed boat, while the terror-stricken disciples are crying out, "Master, Master, we perish!" "Lord, save us, we perish!" Then see Him rise with conscious power to rebuke and still the wind and the waves! How sublimely calm and courageous He was!

Then, again, when they come to take Him to put Him to death, instead of retiring in the grey dawn to conceal Himself, He calmly goes out to meet them, saying, "Whom seek ye?" And when they say,

"Jesus of Nazareth," He answers without the slightest sign of trepidation, "I am He." It seems to me that that is the sublimest scene ever witnessed by mortal eye, and the sublimest act in the entire record of heroic deeds. In courage and heroism He was the highest type of true manliness. And in this respect His life is worthy of the admiration and imitation of all.

Or, if we take another essential element in our conception of true manliness, we see it exhibited in His life in a most marked degree—a readiness to forgive a wrong, and to overlook a fault—a condescension that welcomes the confidence of the humblest of men : "If any man shall speak a word against the Son of Man it shall be forgiven him." Less manly teachers, possessing His unlimited power, would have been tempted to do what certain hasty disciples suggested on one occasion, and would have commanded fire to come down from heaven to consume those who so bitterly and persistently persecuted Him. But Christ was never tempted to do anything so weak and cowardly and unmanly. He frankly acknowledged men's right to think for themselves; and He wished to win men to Himself by His personal love and power and teaching, and not to set up a religion of force.

Then in the great and culminating act of His life we have the highest possible exhibition of true greatness. How unselfishly He stands in the breach to save a sinning world ! "He endured the cross, despising the shame, for the joy set before Him"—namely, of bringing many sons to glory. The joy of His life was to make others happier and brighter and better ; and that must ever be the essence of true manliness.

Now, what have we found in the life and character of the model Man that will be helpful to us in our efforts to attain to true manliness? First, we have this fact—that the highest human life is possible only when the human is allied to the Divine. Therefore, if we would attain to our highest and best we must become partakers of the Divine nature by being united to Christ by a living, ever-acting faith, working by love, and by the indwelling of the Holy Spirit. Secondly, we must take the life of Christ as our example. His was the model life. In Him humanity touched its highest point. We must not rest satisfied with any lower standard of manliness. Thirdly, we see that in Him the highest life was lived in constant dependence upon God, and that it was a life of gentleness blended with courage and confidence—a life of perfect self-control, with all the lower passions and appetites kept perfectly in check. And, fourthly, we must be ready at all times to open our hearts to the touch of the Divine Spirit that He may mould and fashion us after the perfect pattern of the model Man, Christ Jesus. We need the illuminating power of the Holy Spirit to enable us to see the perfections of Christ, as well as His helping power to enable us to copy them and translate them into life. Therefore, if we would be manly, we must be Christlike. We must behold the Man, and walk daily in His footsteps.

XXIX.

THE UNPARDONABLE SIN.

" Whosoever speaketh a word against the Son of Man, it shall be forgiven him ; but whosoever speaketh a word against the Holy Spirit, it shall not be forgiven him, neither in this world, nor in that which is to come."—MATT. xii. 32.

THE Lord Jesus in this passage clearly teaches that there is a sin which hath never forgiveness. The Apostle John re-echoes the same startling truth : " There is a sin unto death ; I do not say that ye shall pray for it" (1 John v. 16). In dealing with this subject I do not wish merely to discuss a few difficult texts of Scripture, but rather to comfort and assure those who suffer anguish of spirit from fear of having committed this sin. Earnest, anxious souls, who have been long seeking peace without finding it, are peculiarly subject to this distressing state of mind. It is important, therefore, to understand clearly what is the teaching of Scripture on this subject.

To a superficial reader the language of the text might seem to teach that a single sin, committed in an instant of time, may be so heinous in the sight of God that He will never forgive it. This, I suspect, is a very common impression respecting the sin against the Holy Ghost.

To get at the true meaning of our Saviour's words here we must study the special circumstance that gave

Him occasion to use them. He was maliciously set upon by the Scribes and Pharisees. They found fault with Him for permitting His disciples to pluck and eat the corn as they passed through the corn-field on the Sabbath day. The law of Moses permitted a traveller to pluck and eat the corn: "When thou comest into the standing corn of thy neighbour, then thou mayest pluck the ears with thine hand; but thou shalt not move thy sickle unto thy neighbour's standing corn" (Deut. xxiii. 25). Therefore, the charge was that it was done on the Sabbath day. Then on the Sabbath day He healed a man with a withered hand and taught them that it was lawful to do well on the Sabbath day. They could find no fault with the miracle; so they accused Him of violating the Sabbath. Instead of gratefully acknowledging the mercy and kindness, and being thankful for the presence of a Divine Healer among them, they were filled with jealousy and envy, and took counsel to kill Him. The Scribes and Pharisees were selfish and ambitious, and when they found out that Jesus would not serve their selfish ends, they refused to acknowledge His Divine mission. All others were convinced by His miracles that He was Divine; but they so set themselves against Christ that His display of Divine power made no impression upon them. They openly denied His Divine power in the face of the most indubitable evidence. And when He healed a man possessed with a devil, they declared that He was in league with the devil: "This fellow casteth out devils by Beelzebub, the prince of the devils."

Nothing could be more absurd and self-contradictory;

and Jesus at once exposes the absurdity of their plea: "If Satan cast out Satan, he is divided against himself; how, then, shall his kingdom stand?" Their moral sense was so perverted that they "put darkness for light, and light for darkness;" "they called evil good, and good evil." They deliberately attributed to the power of the devil what was manifestly done by the power of God. It was this state of heart—this moral perversity—that Christ had in His mind when He uttered the warning words contained in the text. This I take to be the sin against the Holy Ghost—the sin that hath never forgiveness.

A man has committed the sin unto death when, by repeated acts of sin, he has become so degraded morally, that sin and falsehood cease to appear wrong to him. He has entirely lost the sense of moral perception; so that he rejects God's truth, as if it were the devil's lie. When a man has arrived at this state, he is given over to hardness of heart. In Scripture language he is "past feeling;" his "conscience is seared;" he has "no more conscience of sin"—that is, he has become so perverted morally that sin no longer appears to him to be sin. Of such it is said "it is impossible to renew them again to repentance."

The sin against the Holy Ghost, therefore, is the deliberate and persistent rejection of Christ and Divine truth, until the moral sense becomes so perverted, and the voice of conscience so stifled, that the person loses not only all regard for truth and right, but also all ability to perceive their goodness. Such a man has his doom within himself, and there is no possible way of escape. He has become utterly hardened, having given himself over to a reprobate mind.

There is no fact more clearly established in human experience than that by repeated acts of sin men become confirmed in evil habits. There are men whom we speak of as "confirmed liars." By habit it has become more natural to them to tell a lie than to speak the truth; and they do not seem able to see the sinfulness of such conduct. So it is of other sins—drunkenness, immorality, and vice of all kinds. By repeated acts of sin the nature is perverted and the voice of conscience is silenced. "This is the condemnation, that light is come into the world, and men loved darkness rather than light, because their deeds were evil." By which the Great Teacher evidently meant that by a life of sin the moral sense had become so perverted that they saw evil to be good and good evil.

It is clear, therefore, that what is usually called the unpardonable sin is not so much any single sin as a condition of heart that refuses to recognize goodness, or truth, or the power of the Holy Spirit. In the case of those to whom these words were originally addressed it is certain that their sin consisted in attributing to the power of the devil what was manifestly done by the power of God. Blinded by prejudice and a partisan spirit, they would not allow themselves to see goodness in a good act.

Those who for a time had refused to accept Jesus as the Messiah, and even those who had openly opposed Him, such as Saul of Tarsus, found forgiveness. All such sin may be forgiven unto men. But when the Holy Spirit shines into a man's heart, and he sees the beauty of goodness and refuses to acknowledge it, and beholds the power of the Holy Ghost resting upon another and attributes the power to other causes, such a person, if he has not committed the sin unto death, surely stands upon the very brink of doom. Hence Jesus declared that he who spoke against the Son—that is, the Son in His humiliation, going about as a man among men, opposing Him, not knowing Him to be the Messiah—may be forgiven ; but that no man can oppose the Holy Spirit, whose voice is heard in the voice of conscience, thereby going against his own moral convictions, and be forgiven.

The sin against the Holy Ghost, therefore, is not a sin that one can commit as it were by accident without knowing it. It is always a wilful, deliberate, and persistent rejection of Christ and Divine truth—rejecting Christ and His salvation, knowing that He is the only Saviour by the power of the Holy Ghost.

A man who has deliberately violated any or all of the commandments may find mercy, if he penitently and sincerely seeks the Lord. An idolater, a Sabbath-breaker, a thief, a drunkard, a backslider, if he turns from the error of his ways and accepts Christ as Saviour, is assured of forgiveness ; for our God will abundantly pardon.

Troubled souls, anxious and fearful lest they should have committed this sin, may know for their comfort that the fear of having committed it is positive proof that they have not yet reached the stage of final doom ; for those who have committed the sin against the Holy Ghost are given over to hardness of heart and cease to care for God or salvation. Conscience has been quenched and ceases to strive with them. They have become so hardened by opposition to God and all good that it is "impossible to renew them again to repentance." Their doom is in themselves, not in the unwillingness of God to receive and forgive them. But so long as Conscience is alive and tender; so long as you earnestly seek God's favour; so long as you yearn for forgiveness and peace, you may rest assured that God is tenderly leading you, and that in His own time, and by the way which is best for you, He will bring you into the full light and liberty and joy of the gospel. While your whole nature is yearning after God and longing for His favour and friendship, and you are filled with anxiety and sorrow because you cannot find Him, it is utterly impossible that you should have sinned away the day of grace, or have committed the sin that hath never forgiveness. For if you had come into this sad condition you would have been given over to a reprobate mind, and would have no more consciousness of sin, and, therefore, no anxiety to be forgiven, and no desire to secure the favour of God. Only those who are so perverted in the very root of their nature as to put darkness for light, and can call good evil, and evil good, can possibly have sinned away the day of grace. The warning words of our Lord were never intended to distract or discourage earnest tender souls longing for peace and reconciliation with God. They were addressed to those who persistently shut their eyes to the light of Divine truth, and deliberately closed their hearts against the strivings of the Holy Spirit.

However, Christ and the Scriptures make it clear

that there is a state of heart possible to man, in which his conscience becomes so perverted, and his evil habits so strong, that truth entirely loses its power upon him. " Can the Ethiopian change his skin, or the leopard his spots ? then may ye also do good who are accustomed to do evil" (Jer. xiii. 23). " There is a sin unto death ; I do not say that ye shall pray for it " (1 John v. 16).

This hardening of the heart against Divine truth and the power of the Holy Spirit is a gradual process; hence the danger is not apparent in the early stages of sin. However, there is nothing more certain in human experience than that good and evil habits have a tendency to become fixed and permanent. After a man has successfully struggled for years against temptation, and lived a life of intimate communion with God, he becomes so confirmed in the good that temptation loses its power over him. This is a wise and benevolent provision of our nature. As the twig is bent the tree is inclined. Human nature, like the tender twig, is easily bent; and may be turned downward quite as easily as upward and Godward. But whatever way it is turned, it has a growing tendency to remain and become permanent. Hence the Lord Jesus said, " He that shall blaspheme against the Holy Ghost hath never forgiveness, but is in danger of eternal sin " (Mark iii. 29). His sinful habits become to him a second nature, and he goes on sinning eternally.

This principle is true in every department of our nature—body, mind, heart, and the moral and spiritual nature. The stomach is made to digest food, and thereby nourish the body. But, if abused, it not only fails in its functions, but actually poisons the system. The eye is so made that the light is pleasant ; but when it is so abused as to become diseased, it loves darkness, and light, its native element, is painful. The mind, too, that is fed on sensational and impure literature, soon becomes so depraved that sober truth fails to interest, and the stern realities of the eternal world become repulsive. So also of the heart. If you set your affections on low and grovelling things you lose all ability to love the true, the lovely, and the good. And the same law holds good of the conscience, or moral sense. If you tamper with it, doing that which it forbids, after a time it becomes depraved and ceases to check you in your evil courses. Your sense of right and goodness is irrevocably lost. In like manner the strivings of the Holy Spirit may be quenched : " My Spirit shall not always strive with man." This state once reached, is eternal death.

XXX.

RESURRECTION AND THE RESURRECTION-BODY.

"How are the dead raised up? And with what body do they come?"—1 COR. xv. 35.

THE Resurrection of the Lord Jesus has been dear to the Christian Church in all ages. And as the revolving years bring round the Easter morning, our thoughts naturally turn to the events that have made the first Easter day memorable in the annals of the Church. To the early disciples it was a day of wonderment and great joy. Their hopes and expectations had suffered a terrible eclipse by the tragic death of their Lord. Notwithstanding all the intimations that He had given them, they would not allow themselves to believe that He would leave them through the avenue of death. And when the day of trial came they were not prepared for it, and were filled with dread and dire dismay. The women seem to have borne the trial better than the men; and they made all the necessary preparations for anointing and embalming the body. Their very activity helped to sustain them and to buoy them up amid the waves of sorrow. On the night of the Crucifixion they prepared spices and ointments, and "rested the Sabbath day according to the commandment."

On the first day of the week, very early in the morning, they came to the sepulchre, bringing the spices which they had prepared. They were prepared to embalm the body of their Lord; but they were not prepared for the sight that awaited them. Their great anxiety seemed to be about the stone, placed by authority against the door of the sepulchre: "Who shall roll us away the stone from the door of the sepulchre?" They imagined they would have to get to the body. They had no expectation that the body would come to them.

It is easier to imagine than to describe the feelings of the disciples on that resurrection morning. To all of them that Sabbath had been one of unutterable grief, and agony, and despair. All their hopes lay buried in that stone sepulchre. Their enemies had triumphed. Their Master had been taken away and slain by wicked hands. Helpless and heart-broken, they never dreamt of resurrection.

They knew something of trouble and sorrow before. They had stood by the open grave, they had buried loves and hopes before; but never had they such a burial as this before. Their love, their life, their all lay buried with their Lord. They had left all to follow Him; and now that He was taken away, they had nothing left. How their grief affected them! Their memory even seemed to have suffered a temporary eclipse; for no one thought of suggesting for their comfort, "He said He would rise again: He said, 'I have power to lay down My life, and I have power to take it again.'" The dark shadow of despair rested upon them, and they seemed utterly helpless. Theirs was a terrible grief. Jesus was more to them than all else besides; hence their bereavement meant utter desolation.

Those who love deeply know that to lose the one specially beloved is more than to lose all else besides. If their homes had been desolated, and the temple burned, and Jerusalem destroyed, and all their kindred carried away captive, it would have been as nothing, if Jesus had only been left to them.

With heavy hearts they spend the Sabbath in retirement, and with heavy hearts in the early morn the loving women, weary with waiting, wend their way to the sepulchre in the garden. Woman's love is deeper than man's, and so is woman's grief. The agony of bereavement will always be in proportion to the love. But love is stronger than death, and sorrow cannot drown it. When duty demands it, love can rise superior to grief. And such was love in the hearts of these women.

On the arrival at the sepulchre they find the stone, which troubled them so much, rolled away. By a kind of intuition, that proved better than reason, they proceed to anoint and embalm a body, which reason said could not be got at. This may account for the absence of the male disciples. They would allow themselves to be governed by reason, and would say: "It is useless to go, for we cannot get at the body. It is secured by the stone and the government seal." But the women gave themselves up to the impulse of love, and they were rightly guided. To their surprise and delight they find the stone rolled away. And, behold an angel waiting to announce His Resurrection:

"Why seek ye the living among the dead? He is not here: He is risen; remember how He spake unto you when He was yet in Galilee, saying, The Son of Man must be delivered into the hands of sinful men, and be crucified, and the third day rise again." Peter and John now hasten to the garden, and, having seen the empty sepulchre, return to their homes. But Mary lingers, weeping; for her heart is full. There is a surging tide of longing anxiety to see her risen Lord; and she is not disappointed. Jesus Himself draws near: "Woman, why weepest thou?" Her eyes are blinded with tears, and she takes Him to be the gardener: "Sir, if thou hast borne Him hence, tell me where thou hast laid Him, and I will take Him away." Jesus saith unto her, "Mary!" And now she recognizes the familiar tones of the voice, and falls at His feet, and worships Him. But Jesus said, "Touch Me not, for I am not yet ascended to My Father."

That there might be no doubt in the minds of the disciples with regard to the fact of the Resurrection, Jesus appeared repeatedly to them. First to Mary Magdalene. Then to the other women. Then to Peter. After that to the two disciples on their way to Emmaus. Then again, on the evening of the Resurrection, He appeared to the assembled disciples, Thomas being absent. After eight days—that is, on the first day of the next week—He appeared to the eleven, Thomas being now present. At this interview the risen Lord gave the clearest possible proof of the reality and identity of the resurrection-body. Thomas had said, "Except I shall see in His hands the print of the nails, and thrust my hand into His side, I will not believe." The Church of Christ owes much to the determination of Thomas to see for himself convincing proofs of the Resurrection of his Lord. And no doubt there was a merciful providence in it. It gave Jesus the opportunity of satisfying the legitimate desire of all the disciples to know—not simply to believe—that the Resurrection was real. We should never rest satisfied with a blind faith where positive knowledge is possible. So Jesus, without any tone of reproof, says to the earnest seeker after truth, "Thomas, reach hither thy finger, and behold My hands; and reach hither thy hand and thrust it into My side, and be not faithless but believing."

On another occasion also He urged them to satisfy themselves of His identity. They took Him for a spirit—a ghost—and were troubled. He said to them, "Why are ye troubled? And why do thoughts arise in your hearts? Behold My hands and My feet, that it is I Myself. Handle Me and see; for a spirit hath not flesh and bones, as ye see Me have."

It is a great thing to have the Resurrection of Christ so clearly established as an indubitable historical fact attested by so many credible witnesses; for it is the corner-stone of the Christian religion. The Apostles in their preaching gave as great prominence to Christ risen as to Christ crucified. In fact, Christ crucified could have been nothing to the Church apart from Christ risen. The Christian Church was founded by the preaching of the Resurrection. The Apostles everywhere bore witness to the fact that Christ had risen. "This Jesus hath God raised up, whereof we are all witnesses" (Acts ii. 32). "Ye denied the Holy One and the Just, and killed the Prince of Life, whom God hath raised from the dead; whereof we are witnesses" (Acts iii. 14). The Apostle Paul also declares that "He was seen by Peter, then by the twelve; after that, He was seen of above five hundred brethren at once, of whom the greater part remain until this present" (1 Cor. xv. 5, 6). They could not all be deceived; and they must have known that what Paul declared was an actual historical fact.

The importance of the Resurrection is seen in the declaration of the Apostle, "If Christ be not risen, your faith is vain; ye are yet in your sins." The teaching is clear that Christ crucified would avail nothing apart from Christ risen. It was not enough for Christ to die; He must also rise triumphant over death. The atoning work of Christ was not complete until He rose triumphant and ascended to the Father. There could have been no salvation for man if the Saviour had not risen. "But now is Christ risen from the dead, and become the firstfruits of them that slept" (1 Cor. xv. 20).

It is a most comforting truth that Christ in rising from the dead proved His power to resurrect us. This is the Christian's glorious hope. Death is not the end of life. Life goes on in death, and not only passes through the wondrous transformation unharmed, but becomes enriched and ennobled and glorified. To man in his natural state there is nothing more terrible than death. But Christ, by His death and resurrection, triumphed over death and the grave; and the moment we become united to Christ by a living faith, we know that He has power to triumph over death for us, and we no longer look upon the king of terrors with dread and dismay. The believer who has become one with Christ is one with Him in His risen life.

What a fragmentary thing human life would be if there were no continuance of life beyond the grave! And nothing but the existence of an Ever-living One, in whom human life is merged, can give completeness to our fragmentary lives. The greatest of all mysteries is not Resurrection, but Death. That the Ever-living One should die, that is the mystery of mysteries. " I am He that liveth and was dead, and behold I am alive for evermore." Into that life of lives death came, and He lived through death and came out unharmed. And so shall all those who are united to Him by an ever-living faith. Over them death has no power: "He that liveth and believeth in Me shall never die."

There is yet another interesting and instructive fact connected with the Resurrection of Christ. We see in His Resurrection-Body the pattern of what we shall be in our resurrected state. Our "vile body" is to be changed and "fashioned like unto His glorious body" (Phil. iii. 21). His glorified body was real and visible, and yet so completely under the control of the spirit as to be capable of being conveyed away at pleasure. Here then we have the answer to the question, "How are the dead raised up? and with what body do they come?" The body is to be similar to Christ's body after the Resurrection. "It is sown a natural body; it is raised a spiritual body."

The spiritual body is wholly distinct from pure spirit. It is material, visible, tangible; but it is not bound by the ordinary laws of gravitation. Moses and Elijah could come down to earth, and again ascend to heaven. Their bodies had been transformed and glorified at the time of their translation. Hence they appeared in the glorified body—a body so refined that it was no encumbrance to the spirit, but subject to it. It was the vehicle of the spirit without limiting its freedom to pass from one world to another.

At the dissolution of the natural body the spirit is not unclothed, but "clothed upon with our house which is from heaven" (2 Cor. v. 2). It is robed in the spiritual body. Possibly the spiritual body is a part of our present organisation—an inner body, and more intimately allied to the spirit than the natural body, and hence not thrown off in the article of death. In this spiritual body departed friends might be dimly visible to those still in the flesh whose eyes were opened to see them. It would seem that the angel-guard that attends the dying children of the kingdom to bear their ransomed spirits home, have some such visible body; for it is a well authenticated fact that dying saints, and children even, have their eyes so opened, as they draw near to the close of the earthly life, that they distinctly see and welcome the heaven-sent messengers.

This spiritual body would seem to be so refined that it does not come under the ordinary laws of the material universe, but is subject only to the laws of the spiritual kingdom. That Moses and Elijah should appear on the Mount with Christ at His Transfiguration in their material, though glorified, bodies, and then be able to ascend to heaven again, may seem to be contrary to the laws of gravitation and of the material universe. The Ascension of Christ in His material, glorified body may present a similar difficulty. However, these are only illustrations of the fact that the higher law of life is superior to the law of gravitation. Moreover, the spiritual body, being more refined than the natural body, is not so powerfully affected by the law of gravitation which binds material objects to the earth's surface. Probably it acquires a new affinity; and, while it loses its hold of the attractive power of matter on earth, it is attracted heavenwards by the forces of the spiritual world. If such be the case the ascension of glorified bodies is not a violating of natural law, but the operation of a larger law by which spiritual forces in the heavenly kingdom attract spiritual bodies. However, apart altogether from speculation, the true definition of a spiritual body is such as to remove all difficulty as to its passage from one world to another. A spiritual body is a body under the perfect control of the spirit, so that it can be borne at pleasure wherever the spirit wills.

In reference to the manner of the Resurrection, the Apostle makes it clear that the identical particles which composed the natural body at death will not enter into the composition of the glorified body. The seed-corn dies and decays as to its outward body, and the living germ takes to itself a new body, formed from the elements around it. The particles of the grain of wheat that was planted do not enter into the new grains. The Apostle's explanation is, "God giveth it a body even as it pleased Him, and to each seed a body of its own."

Now, a seed-germ may remain dormant for centuries.

The seed of a plant will not germinate except under certain conditions of warmth and moisture. So the inner germ that eventually takes to itself the glorified body may remain dormant until under the new conditions in a renovated world it puts forth its new and strange life and power, and clothes itself in a body appropriate to the new order of things. This life-germ may be located in the spiritual body, which becomes the vehicle of the spirit when it throws off the natural body.

Although the identical particles of the old body will not necessarily enter into the new body, still, all that constitutes identity will be there, and all that is necessary to identification. So long as Will, Memory, and Conscience live we retain our identity. The particles of matter that compose our bodies are continually changing, yet our identity remains intact. And when in the article of death we lay aside the entire earthly body our identity is not thereby affected. We still remain the same personality.

The new and glorified body will retain all that is necessary to identification and recognition. The form and features and lineaments of the face will be such that there will be no difficulty in recognizing each other. The disciples had no difficulty in recognizing Jesus after the Resurrection. His body still bore the marks of the nails and the spear. And seeing that "as we have borne the image of Christ's earthly body, we shall also bear the image of His heavenly body," it follows that in the glorified body we shall be easily recognized, and be able to hold familiar intercourse with those we loved on earth.

Nothing, therefore, can be more comforting than to have clear views of the Resurrection of Christ. It is our one grand proof of Immortality. Christ rose from the dead; therefore, death is not the end of life. Christ was glorified through death; therefore, physical death is but the gateway to a more glorious life.

XXXI.

LIFE IN HEAVEN: THE BLESSED DEAD.

"I heard a voice from heaven saying unto me, Write, Blessed are the dead which die in the Lord : yea, saith the Spirit, from henceforth, that they may rest from their labours, and their works do follow them."—REV. xiv. 13.

THIS is one of the precious texts of Scripture that draws aside the veil of the future, and gives us a glimpse of THE STATE OF THE BLESSED DEAD. This theme can never lose its interest so long as beloved friends are liable to be called away from us— called by God Himself to "Come up higher"—called to exchange the happy homes of earth for the happier home in heaven. And there is no consideration better calculated to sustain those who are bereaved, and those also who feel that they may be bereaved at any moment, than clear Scriptural views of the state into which beloved friends pass when called away from earth.

God alone can reveal to us the condition of the dead. It is a subject on which no living man can speak from experience; for none of us has yet entered upon that state. Nor can we collect the testimony of others; for of all who have gone on before no one has returned. Science and philosophy are necessarily silent on the matter; for they can build only on observed and established facts, and these facts are beyond the region of observation. A knowledge of the principle of life in us does indeed teach that life is not dependent on "the earthly house of this tabernacle." But *under what conditions* life goes on after the dissolution of the body, is a question which neither Reason nor Science can solve. The conditions and mode of life in the future state can be known only by Revelation. We are, therefore, highly favoured by God in His giving us such a clear and unmistakable utterance on the subject as this: "Blessed"—*i.e.*, Blessed by God and happy in themselves—" Blessed and happy are the dead which die in the Lord."

Of death as an object of terror we are not going to speak ; nor of death from a mere moralist's point of view, as the termination of human hopes and schemes and plans and ambitions. As Christians we believe that in these senses Christ has abolished death. Nor are we to speak of the condition of *the wicked dead*, but of THE BLESSED DEAD—" The dead who die in the Lord."

We observe, first, that *those who die in the Lord are blessed, because they go immediately to be with Jesus.* The word of comfort which our Lord left with His sorrowing disciples in order to reconcile them to His departure was, " I go to prepare a place for you ; and if I go to prepare a place for you, I will come again and receive you unto myself, that where I am there ye may be also " (John xiv. 2, 3). Christ has prepared a place for those that love Him, and shall they not occupy it ? Think of it : a place prepared, and no one to occupy it ! A vacant chair in heaven ! Some of us know well its sad import in the family circle on earth, as the pale messenger has laid his icy hand on one and another of those we held most dear. But in heaven! Impossible! "I will not leave you orphans," says the tender, sympathetic Jesus; "I will come to you." "Father, I will that those whom Thou gavest Me may be with Me where I am, that they may behold My glory." Note, therefore, how certain it is that our beloved ones who die in the Lord go to be with Jesus. It is the will of the Father; it is the will of the Son; it is the prayer of Jesus, whom the Father heareth always. Hear this other assuring word of comfort: " Eye hath not seen, nor ear heard, neither have entered into the heart of man, the things that God hath prepared for them that love Him." Eye hath seen blissful homes on earth with love and joy abounding and harmony unbroken. Ear hath heard of friendships and fellowships, with brief separations and happy reunions. It hath entered into the heart—imagination has conceived of a home-gathering, and a glory and felicity far transcending anything realized on earth; yet all these joys and delights are as nothing to the things that God has prepared for them that love Him.

We have said the blessed dead go *immediately* to be with Jesus. To the penitent thief on the cross Jesus said,. "To-day shalt thou be with Me in paradise." There was to be no long period of unconscious slumber —no weary waiting of the unencumbered spirit for the body that was laid aside—" To-day shalt thou be with Me." The language of our Lord was evidently intended to remove a misconception—namely, that the reunion which was prayed for must necessarily be in the distant future: "Lord, remember me when Thou comest into Thy kingdom"; as if he had said, "When Thou comest with power and great glory to destroy Thine enemies and set up Thy visible kingdom, remember me, and number me not with Thine enemies, but pass me by in the day of slaughter." I shall do more than you ask, is the reply. *Thou shalt be with Me*, as a friend most dear, for you have passed through a moral transformation during these brief hours, and this trickling blood atones for your guilt, *and it shall be to-day.*

The Apostle Paul never speaks of going down into the cold, cheerless grave to wait for the resurrection morn. To him death is but a departure—a leaving one country to go to another—a better, that is, a heavenly: "I desire to depart, and to be with Christ." He believed that when his spirit left the body, he would be present with the Lord. At death we get nearer to Jesus; for "while we are at home in the body we are absent from the Lord." Death, therefore, is not the end of life, but rather a grand event in life.

"Beloved," says the Apostle John, "now are we the sons of God; and it never hath been manifested *what we shall be*, but we know that when it shall be manifested *we shall be like Him, for we shall see Him as He is.*" That is wonderful language—*we shall be like Him!* Not only shall we be with Him, but we shall see Him as He is; and in a real and true sense—though it perhaps surpasses our finite comprehension now—*we shall be like Him*—like Him, in being in perfect sympathy with the Father in all things—like Him, in dwelling in the Father's love—like Him, in possessing a spiritual body under the complete control of the spirit, and fitted to be " ministering spirits sent forth to minister to those who shall be heirs of salvation." Herein, therefore, consists the blessedness of those who die in the Lord: they have gone to be with Jesus—they see Him as He is—they are, in some real and true sense, like Him.

The greatest blessedness of which we are capable in our present state is experienced when in the immediate presence of those we most dearly love. Now, if Jesus is to us " the chief among ten thousand and altogether lovely"—if we can truly say, and delight to say it, " I am my Beloved's, and my Beloved is mine"—then there can be no joy like being with Jesus, and the messenger that comes to hasten us into the immediate presence of the King ought to be welcomed. Death ought not to be terrible to the believer. Death, to the Christian, is, in reality, an angel with a golden key to open the gates of glory, and to usher him into his eternal and blissful home.

Erroneous theories, held respecting the state of the spirit on its separation from the body, have had a tendency to make death gloomy, and to fill life with fearful forebodings. The teaching of Scripture, however, is cheerful and joyous. *Heaven is a home—a real, abiding home—a place of reunion and recognition, where friend holds fellowship with friend.* Lazarus, in the parable, is taken to Abraham's bosom. The rich man, though separated by a great gulf, recognizes both Abraham and Lazarus. Abraham, too, recognizes Lazarus, and speaks to him by name. Again, Christ speaks of the blessed " coming from the east, and from the west, and from the north, and from the south, and sitting down with Abraham, and Isaac, and Jacob in the Kingdom of God." This implies intimate friendship and fellowship. David said of his departed child, "I shall go to him, but he shall not return to me." We have also the oft-recurring expression in the Old Testament on the death of patriarchs and kings, "He was gathered to his fathers"—an expression very different from either death or burial, referring not to the body, but to the spirit. The disciples recognized Moses and Elijah on the mount with Jesus. Paul believed he would recognize his Thessalonian converts: "For what is our hope, our joy, our crown of rejoicing? Are not even ye in the presence of our Lord Jesus at His coming?" Heaven, then, is a home, with a large, loving, happy family in it; and we shall know and love each other there. We need such an eternal home to give completeness to life; for, if this earthly life was all of life, what a fragmentary thing life would be! *Where* heaven is, is beyond our ken at present. It is, no doubt, the grand centre of the universe, just as the sun is the centre of the solar system; but more than this we cannot say. But *what* heaven is we know. It is a real locality—a place prepared, into which Jesus has gone, where God has His throne, and where saints and angels dwell together in love. Such a heaven is perhaps but dimly realized even by well-informed Christians, and yet it is clearly revealed in Scripture by types and word-pictures and incidents. Eden and Canaan were types of heaven. Eden was the *home* of our first parents. Life there was real; intercourse with each other and with God was real. Canaan was the *home* of the Israelites after their weary wilderness wanderings. But Canaan was real, not ideal. Heaven, then, is an Eden of delight and beauty, a Canaan of rest, and plenty, and homely joys.

Heaven, moreover, is material, as well as local. Enoch and Elijah (and, let me add, Moses) went there in body —a body transformed indeed, but yet a real, material body. Jesus took His resurrection-body with Him when He ascended into heaven—a body described by Himself as having flesh and bones. Paul, while in the body, was caught up into the third heavens. Heaven, therefore, is not simply an ideal abode for disembodied spirits; but a real habitable home, where loved ones gone before enjoy a real family life of loving ministry and blissful communion.

Another element of blessedness for those who die in the Lord is that *they shall rest from their labours and receive their reward.* There will be no toil, nor trial, nor temptation there—no sorrow and no sickness—no cares nor fears; but all will be rest and joy and blissful companionship. The toil is over, and the reward is given. The race is run, and the crown is bestowed— a crown that cannot fade. *What, then, is death?* An angel with a golden key, did I say? Nay, more. Death is the voice of Jesus saying, "Well done, good and faithful servant, enter thou into the joy of thy Lord."

Now, as true Christians, *we would see the hand of God in death, as in all other events.* In His love He has given us many comforting promises to strengthen and sustain us under such trials: "Whom the Lord loveth He chasteneth" (Heb. xii. 6); "We know that all things work together for good to them that love God" (Rom. viii. 28); "Our light afflictions which are but for a moment work for us"—*for* us, not *against* us—"work for us a far more exceeding and eternal weight of glory" (2 Cor. iv. 17); "Blessed are they that mourn, for they shall be comforted" (Matt. v. 4); "He knoweth the way that I take ; when He hath tried me, I shall come forth as gold" (Job xxiii. 10); "Cast thy burden upon the Lord, and He will sustain thee" (Psalm lv. 22); "Thou wilt keep him in perfect peace whose mind is stayed on Thee"—leans lovingly on thee —"because he trusteth in Thee" (Isa. xxvi. 3); "He doth not afflict willingly"—He has no pleasure in seeing His people suffer, except it be for good to them ; "Who is there among you that feareth the Lord, that obeyeth the voice of His servant, that walketh in darkness and hath no light, let him trust in the name of the Lord and stay (lean lovingly) upon his God" (Isa. l. 10). Jesus, too, proved His sympathy with human sorrow when He wept with Mary and Martha, when their brother was taken from them. His were sympathetic tears. He shared their sorrows. "Lord," they said, "if Thou hadst been here, my brother had not died." Their grief was intensified by the fear that Jesus had ceased to regard them. We are all apt to fall into the same error—to think that affliction is an evidence, not of our Father's love, but of His displeasure. But see how Jesus takes them aside, and draws them to Himself: "Said I not unto thee, if thou wouldst believe thou shouldst see the glory of God ?" Thus He comforts Martha. Heart meets heart ; and the murmuring mood melts away before sympathy, like autumn snow before the morning sun. But another sorrowing heart is in need of sympathy; so the loving Saviour tenderly asks, "*Where is Mary?*" Martha bears the message : " The Master is come and calleth for thee." He has come to cheer, to comfort, to console. He will do it personally, privately. How well He knows the human heart. In deepest sorrow it cannot bear publicity. The great congregation is not the place for it now. It must be alone—alone with Jesus. Even the two loving sisters, with common love and a common sorrow, had better be apart when Jesus comes to comfort. So Jesus calls for Mary to give her a nearer view of Himself, and a further proof of His unfailing regard. Mary is telling the story of her brother's death, and the silent tear trickles down her pale cheek. Mary weeps, and Jesus weeps with her— not *for* her, not for her brother, for He knows it is well with them both. He weeps *with* her, sharing her tears and her sorrows. " Where have ye laid him?" " Lord, come and see." It is a melancholy pleasure to conduct our friends to the city of the dead, where the dust of our dear departed friends is deposited. Ah, Mary, was it not much to have had the Master's tears ? Yes ; more than oceans of human tears. But giving does not impoverish Him. "*Lazarus, come forth!*" " Mary, take your brother." Which is the greater gift and proof of love—to give *healing* simply, or to give *life?* " I loved you, Mary, all the time. I did not rob you, did I, Mary?" What a lesson of love and hope and trust and heaven was learned that day by the grave of Lazarus! Afflictions are not sent to try our patience, nor to rob us of our joys ; but to teach us precious lessons of love and trust and submission which could not be learned in the school of prosperity. If we wish to see the stars in the daytime we must descend into the dark pit. So, too, the pit of sorrow enables us to see Jesus, when the sun of prosperity might otherwise have obscured Him from our view. Then welcome trials and bereavements that bring our Lord so near!

We are apt to think that the greatest possible blessing is to be saved from sorrow and suffering. But this is not the law of being. If we were living for this life alone such a theory of life might do. Those who are living for eternity must, like their Saviour, *be made perfect through sufferings.* Thus only is likeness to Jesus and nearness to Jesus secured. He never says to us, "Go through the waters of affliction," but "Come with Me": "When thou passest through the waters *I will be with thee.*" The law of being is suffering, self-sacrifice, self-denial, until perfection, or perfect submission to God's will, is attained.

This suffering may not be entirely for our own sakes, but to qualify us to benefit and bless others. Thus the Saviour suffered for sinners. Thus the mother suffers for her child. The law of the higher life is vicarious suffering.

We must all meet sorrow. We cannot be saved from suffering. We cannot be blessed with exemption from trial and bereavement; and it is not desirable that we should. May we be saved and blessed *by* them? Yes: sorrow is God's minister of mercy sent to strengthen faith and fit us for service. Our tears are not lost. God treasures them up: "Thou hast put my tears in Thy bottle. Are they not in Thy book?" God keeps a record of our submissive suffering and patient endurance, and we shall surely receive our reward. There is a time in the experience of all true believers when the Christian character is matured more rapidly, and the disposition is mellowed more surely, *by sorrow and suffering* than by any other agency. And if full compensation is not received in this life in greater Christlikeness, and peace and rest, and power in service, it will surely be received when we are called to come up higher. Those nearest the throne are those who have come out of great tribulation.

Let us, then, bear in mind this grand truth in the government of God in all His providential dealings with His people—*that He has always a wise purpose of love in leading us through the waters of affliction.* He always leads His loved ones by the right way; and, although at the moment we are bewildered and cannot understand His methods, yet in the end He will give us to see that we are richer for eternity by having passed under the cloud of sorrow and through the waves of trial. The time of reunion and recognition will soon come; and the loves of earth, though brief and early interrupted, will soon be resumed in the land that knows no shadow.

We may all thank God that we are permitted to love —that strong affections are not sinful—that earthly ties are Christlike—that human love need never die, if it be only in the Lord—that we all may do as Jesus and John and the Marys did—love in parting, love on in death, love those gone on before, love as those who shall meet again, where hearts are never broken, where love is never wounded, and where tears are never shed. Therefore let us look hopefully forward to the time when we, too, shall be borne over the river on angel-wing, and be ushered into our Father's house, and enjoy the rest that remaineth, and hold sweet fellowship with the good and the noble and the loved who have gone before. Here we know but in part; there we shall know even as we are known. Here we see but as through a glass darkly; there we shall see face to face—we shall see Jesus as He is, and, in some real and true sense, be like Him. Here the felt sense of Jesus near, though precious and comforting, is often but feebly realized, through infirmities and doubts and fears; but *there*, there shall be no storm-cloud to hide His radiant face, no fading hopes nor transient joys, no sorrows and no sickness, no sighs and no tears, no partings and no deaths—no dear ones suddenly snatched away—no family circles broken—no vacant chair at the table—no absent voice in the music—no tones of discord in the anthem of praise; but all voices blended in one glad song.

Such are the privileges, and joys, and fellowships that await those that die in the Lord. And may it be ours now to take Jesus to our hearts and our homes, that this glorious end may be ours! May it be ours now to live a life of humble trust, a life of holy obedience, a life of glad and willing self-surrender, a life of hearty earnest toil for God, a life of perfect purity and love; so that at life's close we may be able to say, "I am now ready to be offered, and the time of my departure is at hand. I have fought a good fight, I have finished my course, I have kept the faith; henceforth there is laid up for me a crown of righteousness, which the Lord, the righteous Judge, shall give to me at that day; and not to me only, but unto all them also who love His appearing."

XXXII.

EXCURSUS ON SHEOL, HADES, AND HELL.

"Drought and heat *snatch away* the snow waters; so doth *Sheol* those which have sinned."—JOB xxiv. 19.

IN the Hebrew word *Sheol* the Revisers of the Bible met perhaps their greatest difficulty. There is no difficulty in regard to the meaning of the word; for it is correctly defined in the preface as "the abode of departed spirits." The real difficulty was to find a single word by which it could be translated. There is no such word in the English language. Formerly the word *hell* was its nearest equivalent; but that term is now universally applied to the final abode of the wicked. The former translators had the same difficulty; and not being able to find an exact equivalent for it, they used three different words to translate it—"grave" thirty-one times, "hell" thirty-one times, and "pit" three times. In the historical portions the general rule observed by the former translators was to send a good man at death to the *grave*, and a wicked man to *hell*, although the Hebrew Bible sent both to *Sheol*. The Revisers have retained the former terms, "grave," "hell," "pit," in several passages, but in many instances the word *Sheol* is untranslated; so that now we have four different expressions for the one Hebrew word. However, in all cases where *Sheol* does not appear in the text, it is given in the margin; so that now the English reader need have no difficulty.

It would perhaps have been better if the Revisers had adopted the Greek word *Hades*, already used in the Revised New Testament, as it is the exact equivalent of the Hebrew *Sheol*. As they have not done so, English readers will do well to bear in mind that *Sheol* in the Old Testament and *Hades* in the New Testament correspond to each other.

That the former translation was misleading is evident from the fact that there are other terms for *grave*, as the place of sepulture for the body, and for *hell*, as the place of final punishment. *Kĕbhĕr* is the Hebrew word for grave, or sepulchre, as in Exod. xiv. 11: "Because there were no graves in Egypt hast thou taken us away to die in the wilderness?" It may be marked by a monument (Gen. xxxv. 20, l. 13). It may be opened, and the body removed (2 Kings xxiii. 16; Gen. xlvii. 30). Such is never affirmed of *Sheol*. It is clear, therefore, that *Sheol* does not mean "the grave," although it is thus translated thirty-one times in the Authorised Version. It is even contrasted with the grave. Jacob says, "I will go down to *Sheol* to my son mourning" (Gen. xxxvii. 35). But from verse 33 we learn that Jacob was under the impression that Joseph could not possibly have a grave, as he supposed that he had been devoured by wild beasts. Then again, it is declared, in Isa. xiv. 15, that Lucifer "shall be brought down to *Sheol*," although, in verse 19, he is represented as "being cast out of his grave," or sepulchre (*Kĕbhĕr*).

Secondly, *Sheol* is not *Hell*, as the final abode of the

lost. It is represented as the dwelling-place of all the dead, righteous as well as wicked, who departed from earth by the dissolution of the body. We learn from Gen. xxxvii. 35 that the patriarch Jacob expected to go to *Sheol*, and there meet with his son Joseph. So also Job (Job xvii. 13), and David (Psalm xvi. 10), and Hezekiah (Isa. xxxviii. 10)—" In the noontide of my days I shall go into the gates of *Sheol.*"

Thirdly, *Sheol* is not the *Pit*. The term *Pit*, signifying "the bottomless pit," or "the abyss" (Heb. *Bōr*), is frequently used in the same passage as *Sheol* to convey a further idea. "Pit" is properly used to denote the final *Hell*, and is therefore closely associated with that part of *Sheol* occupied by the departed spirits of the wicked. "Thou shalt be brought down to *Sheol*, to the uttermost parts of the pit" (Isa. xiv. 15). "O Lord, Thou hast brought up my soul from *Sheol*; Thou hast kept me alive that I should not go down to the pit" (Psalm xxx. 3). "Let us swallow them up alive as *Sheol*, and whole, as those that go down to the pit" (Prov. i. 12).

But, further, the *Sheol* of the good is not the final Heaven. *Sheol*, or *Hades*, is always spoken of as beneath, as in "the lower parts of the earth"; but Heaven is always upward. Jacob and Job speak of *going down* to *Sheol*; Elijah *went up* to Heaven (*Shamâyim*).

Finally, *Sheol* is not a general term for *the unseen world*, including heaven and hell. Beyond *Sheol* are the final heaven and the final hell. Heaven is *Shamâyim*, the abode of the righteous, when body and spirit are united. Enoch and Moses and Elijah were taken to heaven; yet their bodies did not undergo dissolution and decay, but were transformed into the heavenly or spiritual body. Jesus was to be "the firstfruits of them that slept"; so that none of those who slept in the grave could enter heaven until after His resurrection. The wicked, like the fallen angels, are finally consigned to *Tartaros* (2 Peter ii. 4), or "the hell of fire" (Matt. v. 22), or "the pit of the abyss" (Rev. xx. 3), or "the lake of fire" (Rev. xx. 15), or "the pit"—*Abaddon* (Rev. ix. 11). All these expressions are distinct from *Sheol* and *Hades*, and beyond them; for "death and Hades" are said to be "cast into the lake of fire" (Rev. xx. 14). The Revisers, therefore, have done well in omitting the term "hell" in most passages as a translation of *Sheol*. It must not be supposed, however, that in so doing the proofs of a place of suffering for the finally impenitent have been weakened. They have, in fact, been greatly strengthened. To rest the argument for the eternity of punishment upon the passages where *Sheol* was translated "hell" in the Authorised Version, was only to court defeat; for it could easily be shown that *Sheol* did not necessarily last eternally. Being merely the abode for spirits, it naturally ceases at the date of the final resurrection at the farthest; and so far as it concerned the righteous dead they were delivered from *Sheol*, or *Hades*, at the resurrection of Christ. Christ's own words point to a union of soul and body in hell— *Gehenna*—after death, and no further argument ought to be needed : " Fear not them that kill the body, but are not able to kill the soul ; but rather fear Him who is able to destroy both soul and body in hell " (Matt. x. 28).

See also Matt. xviii. 8, 9 ; Mark ix. 43, 45, 47, 49 ; iii. 29 ; Jude vi. 7 ; 2 Peter 4.

From the teaching of Christ respecting the death of the rich man and Lazarus (Luke xxiii.), it is evident that in *Sheol* there were two divisions, separated by a great gulf. In the one Lazarus was comforted; in the other Dives was tormented. While, therefore, the spirits of both the righteous and the wicked went down to *Sheol*, and, therefore, might be said "to go to one place" (Eccles. iii. 20), yet they were in separate divisions of the spirit-world, and in very different conditions.

It follows, therefore, that *Sheol*, or *Hades*, is a place in the unseen world, distinct from heaven and hell, having two divisions, into which the souls of all the deceased went prior to the Ascension of Christ, and since that event the souls of all the wicked,—the souls of the righteous going immediately to be with Jesus.

The department of *Hades* into which the righteous went was called *Paradise* until the Resurrection of Christ. From that time the term "Paradise" seems to have been transferred to Heaven. To the dying thief on the cross Jesus said, "To-day shalt thou be with Me in Paradise," viz., Paradise in *Hades*. But Paul was *taken up* to Paradise, viz., Paradise in heaven (2 Cor. xii. 4). So also the tree of life "is in the midst of the Paradise of God" (Rev. ii. 7). Paul desired "to depart and to be with Christ" (Phil. i. 23). From such passages it is evident that, under the gospel dispensation, believers at death go immediately to Christ in glory. But under the old dispensation they went

EXCURSUS ON SHEOL, HADES, AND HELL. 351

down to *Sheol*; and only those who, like Enoch and Elijah, did not taste death, went direct to heaven.

Christ Himself, between His death and resurrection, descended into *Hades*, and made proclamation to the righteous dead that He had now completed the work of redemption : " Being put to death in the flesh, but remaining alive in the spirit, in which also He went, and made proclamation to the spirits in prison" (1 Peter iii. 18, 19). "The spirits in prison," or the spirits *kept in waiting*, as in a guardroom, are the Old Testament saints, including those who "for a time were disobedient in the days of Noah," but nevertheless repented before the flood carried them away, although too late to enter the ark. To all those who died, looking forward to the finished work of the Redeemer of man, the crucified Saviour now declares that " He has suffered for sin, the Just for the unjust, that He might bring them to God." This view is borne out by the teaching of the Apostle (Heb. xi. 40) : " They received not the promise, God having provided some better thing concerning us, that apart from us they should not be made perfect." They did not enter upon the bliss of heaven until the new dispensation was ushered in.

This would seem to be the only admissible interpretation of this difficult passage. The Roman Catholic interpretation, which places purgatory in the spirit-world, and which represents Christ in this passage as offering salvation to those who died in an impenitent state in the time of Noah, finds no countenance from this text correctly interpreted. Neither does the commonly received Protestant interpretation—namely, that

Christ by the Spirit went and preached the gospel to these antediluvians through Noah, "the preacher of righteousness." If the Apostle meant to convey that idea he would certainly have used different language. The key to the true interpretation is in the Greek word translated "preached." It means literally "to cry as a herald"—to make proclamation. This, and this only, did Christ do among the spirits in prison.

XXXIII.

THE ORIGIN OF HUMAN EVIL.

(AN ESSAY.)

THERE is scarcely a serious man in the world to-day who denies the fact of sin and its universal sway among men. A greater variety of opinion, however, prevails as to *how* sin entered into the world; and many thoughtful men have very serious difficulties as to *why* sin was permitted at all.

Man at his creation, like all the works of God, was pronounced "very good." Hence the origin of human evil has usually been regarded as a great mystery, to be looked upon with wonder and awe, and as altogether incapable of solution. It has been the study of great minds in all ages of the world; but, apart from the Biblical record, no satisfactory light has been thrown upon it.

Origen tried to meet the difficulty by the conjecture that *man's spirit existed in a previous state*, and had voluntarily sinned; and that on his appearance on earth his spirit was already tainted with sin. This conjecture does not meet the difficulty, but only removes it a step further back.

The Manicheans held that evil was inherent in matter.

They taught that *sin was a substance*—that *all matter was essentially evil*—that spirit only was good. It is a sufficient refutation of this theory to note that it would make either *the sinlessness of Jesus impossible*, or *His assumption of a human body impossible*. If evil is inherent in matter, He ceased to be sinless the moment He took to Himself a material body. But He did take to Himself a material body, and yet was without sin.

And as it regards man, if evil is inherent in matter, man, being created with a material body, must of necessity manifest evil, and he could not, therefore, be held responsible for it. It would not be sin to him. This theory, therefore, is wholly untenable.

In all ages there have been superficial thinkers who would make God the author of evil. But God, who is goodness itself, cannot be the originator of evil. The first sin was disobedience to God; God cannot be the author of disobedience to Himself. The statement is self-contradictory. God's command, " Thou shalt not eat of the fruit of the tree," is an expression of His will, and He could not, without self-contradiction, *will* that man should disobey that command. To authorise disobedience to His own law would be to contradict Himself. It would be not only fickle, but frivolous in man, and is impossible in God. Evil is not a substance—a thing. It is not a creation of God. Evil is the perversion of good,—the wrong action of powers and faculties good in themselves.

But it may be asked, *If God possesses all power, could He not have prevented the first sin, and, therefore, all sin?* And, possessing the power to prevent sin, if He declined to exercise that power, may He not justly be regarded as the author of evil? In other words, Is not God's permission of evil, when He could have prevented it, equal to authorship?

This form of argument seems plausible and difficult to meet. Intentionally we have put it in the strongest light possible, that we may answer it in its most difficult form. Now, we not only admit, but affirm, that an all-wise God, possessing unlimited power, could have prevented sin. God could have so constituted man that sin would have been impossible. Then, why did He not do it? Because He did what was better. He permitted sin for wise purposes; and, as we hope to be able to show, for benevolent and gracious purposes.

God could not *wisely* have prevented sin, else Supreme Wisdom would not have permitted it. (We are assuming the perfections of God—perfection in wisdom, power, love, benevolence.) God could have given to man a moral constitution in which sin would have been impossible. But God Himself could not have prevented sin in man, constituted as he is, with a free will and power to choose; for the will that cannot choose the wrong is not free.

Now, if we can show that man was made on the best possible model, and was endowed with the best possible moral constitution, and yet was liable to sin, then it is clear that God could not wisely have prevented sin.

We have a threefold argument to prove that the moral constitution given to man is the best possible. The first proof is from the perfections of God. An all-perfect God must do the best possible every time. If He fail to do this, He fails in wisdom or in power, and thereby becomes less than perfect—less than God. Another proof is from Scripture. At his creation man was pronounced "very good." The expression is superlative—"good exceedingly," equal to BEST. God gave to man the best possible nature and endowments.

A third proof is found in Reason and Experience. To this argument we give special prominence, because it is conclusive even to those who may have difficulty in accepting the teachings of the Bible on the subject. Human experience, and human reason when intelligently exercised, both affirm that man is made on the best possible model.

What are man's characteristic endowments that elevate him above the brute creation? Take these— Intelligence, Conscience, Free Will, and the capability of holding fellowship with God. These are good gifts. They make man great and Godlike. So much so that man is said to be made "in the image of God." Deny to man—ideal man—any or all of these, and he would be inferior to man as at present constituted.

Intelligence, an originating, designing mind, makes man superior to the brute creation, and gives him authority over them. Deny to man intelligence,—the power to understand God's command,—and failure to comply with it would not be sin. God, therefore, could have prevented sin by denying to man intelligence.

The knowledge of right and wrong is stamped on man's constitution. Call it Conscience, or what you will, man possesses the power of distinguishing good from evil, right from wrong. If a man wilfully injures or wounds his fellow-man, he is conscious of wrong-doing; and *it is sin to him.* One dog bites and abuses

THE ORIGIN OF HUMAN EVIL. 357

another. He does not know that it is wrong. It is not sin to him. Had man no faculty for discerning right and wrong in motives and in actions, he would not be responsible. Like the dumb animals, no act of his would be a sin. God, therefore, could have prevented sin by denying to man the power of distinguishing right from wrong.

But again, God has endowed man with a Free Will. This is a good gift. If man were not free to choose he would be low in the scale of creation. He would be a slave to a superior will—a mere machine impelled by a power extraneous to himself, able to move only as he was moved. Without freedom of choice there would be no responsibility for his acts, *and no sin*. God could have prevented sin by denying to man freedom of choice. But then man would not be capable of holding fellowship and intercourse with God, just as a slave cannot hold fellowship with his master. Without freedom of choice there could be neither love nor obedience. Love that is compelled is not love. Obedience, without the possibility of disobedience, would not be pleasing to God; and instead of virtue and holiness there could be at most but simple innocence. We do not love our watches because they point out the time for us. They have no choice in the matter. They cannot go backwards if they would. Only intelligent, voluntary obedience and love, with the possibility of disobedience, can be well-pleasing to God. *Without free will, therefore, sin would have been impossible.* But it is better that man should be free and fall and be restored than be denied the noblest of all gifts, which makes him fit for companionship with his

Maker. But a free will carries with it the *possibility of sinning*,—not the *necessity*, but the *possibility;* for if the will cannot choose the wrong, then certainly it is not free. God, therefore, having chosen to endow man with a free will, could not have prevented sin. In the best possible moral constitution given to man sin was possible.

All will admit that it was good in God to endow man with *Intelligence* and *the power of discerning right and wrong;* otherwise he would be on a level with the dumb animals. It will also be admitted that *Free Will* is a good gift, making man capable of becoming noble and Godlike. But, having granted to man these gifts to be freely exercised, God Himself could not have prevented sin, except on the supposition that *man should not be under law to God*. God could have prevented sin in a free agent by allowing him perfect license to do as he pleased, to assert his independence of God, and to injure his fellows, if he chose, without restraint; for where there is no law there is no transgression. But here again it must be admitted that it is better for man to live under a good law than in a state of lawlessness. If men were allowed to injure their fellow-men without restraint, society would be totally disorganized, and life would not be worth living.

So much as it regards man himself. But, as it regards man in his relation to God, *law was necessary*. It was absolutely necessary that man should be asked to obey, and thereby acknowledge his dependence on God. Harmony could not be preserved in a universe with more than one free will, except there was subordination of all others to one Supreme Will. This subordination may be effected either by the power of love, or by authority; but it cannot be dispensed with without disaster. And this is God's method of dealing with man. He reveals Himself as Father and Friend, and invites man to yield himself up in loving submission. But if, in the exercise of his free will, man refuses to yield from motives of love and gratitude, then God, to preserve harmony, must compel submission by the power of authority. If man were not asked to obey God, God would be no longer God. He would not be supreme. Man would be His rival and equal. It was necessary, therefore, that man should be under law to God.

Now, the very essence of the first sin of the first pair consisted in the assertion of their independence of God, and in claiming at least equal wisdom. God said, "Thou shalt surely die"—you will lose fellowship with Me. Man replies by his act, "I do not believe I shall die; and, even if I should lose God's favour and fellowship, I can do without God; I am independent of Him." In the exercise of his free will, with a full knowledge of God's command and the consequences of disobedience, man deliberately disobeys God, and dies in the act; for death, in its deepest sense, means separation and alienation from God. Self-will, self-seeking, and the desire for self-indulgence, are the primal causes of all sin. God in His law, or in Conscience, says, "Do not touch it!" Self-will says, "I will!" and runs the risk. God says, "If you eat of this tree it will inflame the lower passions of your nature, so that the body will no longer be in complete subjection to the spirit; it will fill you with shame, so that you cannot abide in My presence without dread and discomfort." Self-indulgence says, "It seems good for food. It is not possible that such beautiful fruit should injure any one." And then, to crown all, Ambition says, "It is desirable to make one wise. We shall be as God Himself (*Elohim*), knowing good and evil."

But it may be objected, *Why did God deny them the fruit? Was it not an arbitrary and unnecessary prohibition?* No: neither arbitrary nor unnecessary. There must be some prohibition as a test of obedience and subordination to the Supreme Will; else, as we have already shown, God would cease to be God. And God made the prohibition as light as possible. The fruit of only one tree was prohibited, and that not necessary to their happiness.

But further: Every free will requires *a confirming choice*. If the creature, whether man or angel, deliberately chooses to love what God loves, and to hate what God hates, and lovingly and cheerfully determines to accept God's will as a Rule of Life, *that distinct act of free choice confirms the will* in predominant loyalty to God; and gives such inward blessedness in the very act that ever after the will of the creature will cheerfully surrender itself to the will of God. It was necessary, therefore, and well, that man's will should be tested and proved, in order that it might be confirmed. The angels in heaven were tested; some fell, and others were confirmed in loyalty to God. That some stood firm proves that free will carries with it, not the necessity, but only the possibility of sinning. The sinless life of Christ proves the same. He, too, in His bitter agony had to yield up His will to the

Father's—"Not My will, but Thine be done." Thus it would appear that every free will requires to be tested, and is confirmed only by deliberate free choice. Man, too, was free to choose the path of obedience, or, under temptation, the path of disobedience. Having the power to obey, or to disobey, an opportunity must be given to man to declare *for* or *against* God. Hence temptation was necessary.

A will that is perfectly free is nicely balanced. And that the will should be fairly tested there must be a balancing of motives. Already there is a strong motive to incline man to obey—namely, the favour of God and fellowship with Him. Therefore, a counter motive must be presented as a test and trial. Thus we are naturally brought to the Tempter and the Tree; both of which we take to be real and objective.

Nothing is revealed respecting the tree, except that it bore fruit that was pleasing to the eye. Probably the fruit possessed poisonous or stimulating qualities, which inflamed the passions and the sensuous nature, destroying the proper balance between the spirit and the flesh. Originally the flesh was in complete subjection to the spirit. Ever since the Fall there would seem to be a continual striving for the mastery between them, "the flesh striving against the spirit and the spirit against the flesh." The effect of partaking of the fruit was, no doubt, more moral than physical, and yet the record would seem to point to a physical effect as well. The discovery of nakedness, and the feeling of shame accompanying the discovery, as well as the inability to look upon God, might all be accounted for by supposing that the physical effect produced was the awaking of inordinate sexual passion. Some ancient writers have represented the first pair, before the Fall, as enveloped by a halo, or radiance, which served them for a covering—such a radiance from the whole body as was seen in the face of Moses when he came down from the Mount. Moses' face shone so that he had to put on a veil in the presence of the people. They could not look upon him. His spirit shone through the body, making it luminous. According to Paul, man originally had not only the image but the glory (*doxa*) of God. At the very instant of disobedience the glory of the spirit would be quenched, and man would need a covering; for the flesh had obtained the mastery over the spirit. That fact is clear, whether the immediate effect of partaking of the fruit was moral or physical, or, as is most probable, *both moral and physical*.

The essence of the first sin consisted, no doubt, in harbouring a suspicion of God's love—that envy and jealousy in God, and not love, were the grounds of prohibition. God is love; and His laws are but the limits imposed by His love. It was for the good of His creatures, and not merely to deprive them of a harmless luxury, that God issued the prohibitory command. This Eve doubted, and by her act denied. Thus, while we find the essence of the first sin in the heart and will, there may also have been the physical effect of eating actual fruit. It is clear, therefore, that God is not the author of evil. The first sin was brought about by the wrong action of a will perfectly free to choose just as it pleased. Adam and Eve, like the holy angels, and like "the man Christ Jesus," might have resisted temptation, and by that act have been confirmed in love and loyalty to God. Sin was not owing to any defect in man's nature and organization; and there was no necessity in the nature of things why he should disbelieve and disobey God; and therefore sin must be brought home to man as his own free voluntary act; just as every sin of men to-day has its origin in the wrong action of powers and faculties good in themselves.

Looking at the matter, therefore, from every possible point of view, we see that God has given to man the best possible moral constitution; and yet "sin entered into the world." Sin, therefore, could not wisely have been prevented. Man must have the gift of Intelligence, or be denied it. Man must be endowed with a faculty by which he can distinguish right from wrong, or be denied it. Man must be endowed with Free Will, or be denied it. Man must be under law to God, or live in a state of lawlessness. There are no other possible alternatives; and we have seen that the positive alternatives are infinitely better than their opposites. But man, as at present constituted, possesses these, Intelligence, Conscience, Free Will, and a good law to be observed. It follows, therefore, that God could not have prevented sin, except by making man inferior to what he now is; and we have already shown that God is not the author of sin,—that sin is the result of the wrong action, by man's free choice, of powers and faculties good in themselves,—powers, too, intended by God to make man noble and Godlike, and without which he would not be capable of holding fellowship with God.

And further, let it never be forgotten that God had something more in His mind when He created man, than simply the happiness of the creature. He wished to reveal His own perfections,—not only His wisdom, and power, and holiness, but also His marvellous love, His power to forgive, to redeem, to new-create, and His power to console. These glorious attributes, which may be said to represent the tender side of God's nature, could never have been revealed, except for man's sin, and the need of redemption and pardon and consolation consequent upon it.

Thus, when we take in God's entire plan in regard to man, we see that man was made upon the best possible model, and that God out of seeming evil can bring good. And if our frail finite minds should fail to see the wisdom and perfection of God's great universe-plan, . let us not blame Him who is all goodness and love; but let us reverently bow before His perfect wisdom and perfect love, and acknowledge that God is greater than we know. Let us, moreover, never think of sin, and the misery and sorrow consequent upon it, without also thinking of the glorious plan of redemption, which God had purposed and planned before He gave to man that moral constitution which made sin possible,— salvation through the precious blood of Christ, "the Lamb slain from the foundation of the world."

XXXIV.

GENESIS AND GEOLOGY.

THE first chapter of Genesis has been for years a kind of standing battle-ground between secular Science and revealed Religion. A few years ago the war was waged with energy and earnestness. The Bible and Science seemed to be in conflict. Discoveries in Geology seemed to throw discredit on Genesis. We say, *seemed*, because the discrepancies were only apparent and not real. Enthusiastic scientists began to imagine that they had got in advance of Moses. The destructive critics, who gloried in pulling down the bulwarks of the Christian faith, were jubilant. Ill-informed theologians, who were wedded to traditional beliefs and traditional interpretations of Scripture, were alarmed; and, with undue haste, denounced scientific research as dangerous. The clouds overhead were dark and lowering, and timid Christians began to be anxious about the future of the Christian faith. A ray of consolation, however, was soon found in the fact that every new theory differed more from every other theory than any of them differed from Revelation. It was also found that whatever was settled in Science did not differ so much from the Biblical record as from human interpretation of that record. And now that geological science and theological science are sufficiently advanced that the one can be studied in the light of the other, it is found that there is no contradiction whatever between the two. And not only so, but the first chapter of Genesis is found to be a most admirable and concise summary of the latest results of scientific research.

Scientific inquiry, like all honest inquiry, has been of immense service to Theology. It has demolished many crude notions that were formerly held about the work of creation. Such, for example, as the creation of the earth and all living creatures out of nothing in the space of six literal days, about the year 4000 B.C. It was assumed that because the whole record of creation was given in one short chapter the events there recorded must also have taken place within a very short period. But there is no such hint given in the record. The first verse rather points to a period a very long way back : *"In the beginning* God created the heavens and the earth." The second verse points to the fact that the earth had not assumed its present form when the matter now composing it was at first created. It is distinctly stated that the earth originally was without form. The elements were in a state of chaos for a time ; and, by successive stages, it was brought into its present order and symmetry and beauty. This is the Biblical record ; and it agrees in every particular with the teaching of Science.

The ascertained facts of Science point to the conclusion that other systems of worlds were formed before the system of which this earth forms a part. Genesis is in harmony with this truth: "God created the heavens and the earth"—the heavens before the earth.

Science suggests a period during which the earth was surrounded by mists and vapour, so that the light of the sun would appear merely as a dim, diffused light; and not until these mists had disappeared could the sun be seen as at present. This, too, is in harmony with the record in Genesis: "God said, Let there be light." This fiat was distinct from the fiat on the fourth day, "Let there be lights,"—luminaries, light-giving bodies —as distinguished from the dim, diffused light of the first day. And so we might go through each successive creative event in this chapter, and show that every one of them is proved by the latest results of Science to be literally accurate; and, what is even more striking, they are all in the exact scientific order, so that this first chapter of Genesis might have been written to-day from the records of Geology.

Science teaches that, while the earth gradually cooled, certain gases were eliminated—oxygen and nitrogen combining to form atmospheric air, and oxygen and hydrogen combining to form water. This is in exact accord with verses 6 and 7, "Let there be a firmament in the midst of the waters, and let it divide the waters from the waters"—the water on the earth from the water in the clouds.

Science points to great convulsions, and mighty upheavals of the earth's surface forming mountain ranges, islands, and continents. This is in perfect harmony with verse 9, "Let the dry land appear."

Science teaches that flowerless plants, such as lichens, fungi, ferns, etc., propagated by spores and not by seeds, were the earliest forms of vegetable life. In verse 11 we read, "Let the earth bring forth grass."—

literally, *young herbage*, referring to flowerless plants not propagated by seeds.

Science next finds flowering plants, such as conifers, etc., having naked seeds, and therefore distinct from fruit-bearing trees, corresponding exactly with "the herb yielding seed." Then appeared a higher class of flowering plants, yielding an inferior kind of fruit, correctly described as "the fruit tree yielding fruit." These low forms of vegetable life do not require the direct rays of the Sun ; and Science teaches that the sun's rays were obscured by dense vapours during these early periods. Fruit fit for human food cannot be matured without abundance of sunlight. Hence, before man and cattle appear, how appropriate that the dense vapours that surrounded the earth should be cleared away, so that the sun's rays might shine forth in all their fructifying and life-sustaining power ! Hence we read, verse 16, "And God *appointed*" (not made) "two great *luminaries*"—*Meōroth*—not *ōr*, *light*, as in the third verse. The Sun and the Moon were already in existence ; now they are appointed to a specific work--namely, "to be for signs, and for seasons, and for days, and for years."

Science teaches that the appearance of the Sun introduced a new order of animal and vegetable life, both in the sea and on the land; and the birds of the air appeared. In the New Red Sandstone footprints of birds are found for the first time. "And God said, Let the waters bring forth abundantly the moving creature that hath life, and let there be fowl that may fly above the earth."

Science next finds great sea-monsters, the Ichthyosaurus and Plesiosaurus, corresponding to verse 21, "God created great sea-monsters"—*tannīnīm*—water-animals, but not "whales."

Science demonstrates the fact that huge beasts, such as the Megalosaurus, found in Hastings and in Cuckfield, Sussex, being nearly fifty feet in length, appeared on the earth immediately before the advent of cattle. This order is observed in verse 25, "And God made the beast of the earth after his species, and cattle after their species." Sheep, according to Science, preceded by a very short time the advent of man. Here, again, we have perfect harmony between the book of Nature and the book of God; for the Scriptural narrative introduces man immediately after the cattle and creeping things—" Let us make man in our own image, after our likeness."

Man was the last to appear upon the scene, and since his appearance no new species either of plants or animals are known to have been created. Here again Science is in harmony with Scripture; for after the creation of man it is said, "God ended His work which He had created and made."

What, then, is the inference to be drawn from this marvellous coincidence between geological science and the Mosaic record? Surely this. The record in Genesis must have been given by inspiration of God. Here are at least fifteen distinct creative acts; and, not only are the descriptions accurately given in every instance, but they are also every one in the exact geological order. The chances are more than *a billion to one*, according to the law of permutations, that some one event should have been misplaced in the enumeration, if we suppose Moses to have written them without infallible guidance. That would have been the greatest of all miracles, and a thousandfold more difficult to accept than that he received his information by direct inspiration of God.

Another point of special interest is the *time* occupied in the work of creation. Can Genesis and Geology be reconciled on this point? Very many have great difficulty in reconciling the record in Genesis with the record in Geology, if the six days are to be taken as six literal days of twenty-four hours each, and not as long periods of time. The Hebrew term (*yōm*) is often used in Scripture to denote periods of time much longer than a single day. In the narrative of the Creation it is used to cover the whole creative period of six days (Gen. ii. 4). In Psalm xcv. 8 "day" is equal to forty years. In Daniel xii. a day stands for a year; and in 2 Peter iii. 8 it stands for a thousand years. It is clear, therefore, that if we adopt the usage of Scripture, we cannot affirm that the term "day" is necessarily limited to a period of twenty-four hours.

We are accustomed to measure the day by the appearance of the sun, and hence our day in this latitude is limited to twenty-four hours. But at the poles, if the day be measured by the rising and the setting sun, the day would be lengthened out to a year; for the sun rises on the 16th of March and does not set until the 25th of September, rising again in March. That is, the sun rises and sets once a year.

However, the teaching of Scripture on the subject is not limited to a single term, or a single text, and the difficulty is not wholly removed by making each and all of the creative days long periods of time. We do not recognize any force in the extreme view enunciated by some writers, that, if "the literal day theory" be rejected, the obligation to observe a seventh-day Sabbath of rest falls with it; for God's positive command to observe a holy Sabbath of rest at the end of six days' labour is binding, as a command, even if it could be shown that the command is not supplemented and supported by God's own example.

But there is another difficulty to be met. God, in giving the Ten Commandments to Moses, expressly grounds the institution of the Sabbath on His own example; and this must be taken as a plain statement of fact: "Six days shalt thou labour and do all thy work; for in six days the Lord made heaven and earth. . . . The seventh day is the Sabbath of the Lord thy God; in it thou shalt not do any work, for the Lord rested the seventh day." It seems clear, therefore, that the seventh day was a literal day of twenty-four hours; for it was observed as such by Moses and the children of Israel.

From the record in the first chapter of Genesis it is also evident that after the fourth day, on which the two great lights were made, the days were literal and successive; for, after the appearance of the Sun, the day must have been measured by *it*, as it is expressly stated that the greater light "ruled the day." But since Geology demands Genesis may grant long periods of time for each of the days before the fourth. The "light" which appeared on the first day is altogether different and distinct from the great luminary created on the fourth day ; and, apart altogether from Geology, it seems certain that the appearance of the Sun introduced a new order of things. The Sun already existed, but on the fourth day it was appointed (*àsâh*) "to divide the day from the night," and "to be for signs, and for seasons, and for days, and for years." This language implies that previous to the fourth day the seasons, and days, and years were different from what they were after that day. Scripture clearly demands a radical change at this point in the creative period. Science makes the same demand ; and thus harmony is established between them.

The first three "days," therefore, may have been millions of years, if Geology requires it ; for there was no means of measuring the days so as to limit them to a fixed and definite period ; but from the fourth day to the end of the week the days must be taken as literal and successive. We thus can cordially accept the discoveries of Science, and grant its demands, without in the least detracting from the accuracy and authority of God's Word.

XXXV.

JOSHUA AND THE SUN.

"Then spake Joshua to the Lord in the day when the Lord delivered up the Amorites before the children of Israel, and he said in the sight of Israel, Sun, stand thou still upon Gibeon; and thou, Moon, in the valley of Ajalon."—JOSHUA x. 12.

GREAT difficulty has been found in the statement that "the sun stood still, and the moon stayed." Does it not imply a reversal or interruption of a law of Nature that, from all experience, is proved to be constant? As the text reads there is a real difficulty. The Book of God seems to contradict the book of Nature. This, however, we hold to be impossible, for the author of both is one, and He the all-wise God. What, then, is the true solution of the difficulty? Clearly the day was lengthened. This could be effected, however, without any interruption or violation of natural law—namely, by the refraction and reflection of the rays of the sun. By a careful study of the Hebrew terms translated *Sun* and *Moon* we find that they refer more exactly to the *light* of these bodies than to the bodies themselves. *Shemesh* is often translated *Sun*, and *Yareah, Moon;* but in such instances it is really the *sunlight* and the *moonlight* that are referred to. Just as we say in common parlance, "The sun is in the room," or "Come out of the sun into the shade," meaning of course the rays of the sun, and not the sun itself. It is only in this free sense that the original words can be translated *Sun* and *Moon*. In Isaiah xxiv. 23, Job xxx. 28, Canticles vi. 10, Isaiah xxx. 26, and many other passages, the Hebrew terms for Sun and Moon are not *Shemesh* and *Yareah*, as in the text, but *Hhamah* and *Levanah*. In Isaiah xxx. 20 we have a clear case in point, "The light of the moon (*Levanah*) shall be as the light of the sun" (*Hhamah*). Here the Moon and the Sun are spoken of as distinct from their light, and hence the terms found in Joshua are not used, but the terms that properly designate the body of the sun and the moon. This is proof positive that " sun " and " moon " in the text refer to the rays of the sun and moon, and not to these orbs themselves. The miracle, therefore, dealt, not with the sun itself, but with its light, and the lengthened day is easily accounted for by refraction, and therefore quite in accordance with natural law. This law of refraction operates most largely in a very cold atmosphere, and in a very dense or moist atmosphere. In Arctic regions the sun continues during intense cold to appear above the horizon for many hours when it is actually below it. Now the record tells us that these two conditions were present at the time. There was the dense cloud, and there was intense cold producing great hailstones. Hence we conclude that there was no interruption of natural law on this occasion ; and the miracle—for it was a miracle—consisted in the timing of the event so that the phenomenon corresponded in time with the battle and the victory. This interpretation we hold to be much more worthy of God's Word than that which makes the record a mere poetic exaggeration.

XXXVI.

JONAH AND THE WHALE.

"The Lord prepared a great fish to swallow up Jonah."—JONAH i. 17.

THE whale, which has been such a stumbling-block to infidels and sceptics, finds no place in the narrative. In the New Testament the word "whale" occurs, but it is a mistranslation. The Revised Version gives "sea-monster" in the margin. Either of these terms, "a great fish" (Jonah i. 17), or "a sea-monster" (Matt. xii. 40), removes the twofold objection that whales are not found in the Mediterranean Sea, and that they have too small a swallow to admit a man. There are other great fish found in the Mediterranean Sea which can swallow a man with perfect ease, and without injury to his body.

It is also alleged that suffocation would inevitably have taken place. But these large fish themselves require air, and often come to the surface for fresh supplies. Moreover, under certain conditions of the body, as in a trance, human life is preserved even when the body has been buried in the earth. Therefore the argument from suffocation is groundless. The body of Jonah being alive would not be affected by the gastric fluid, for it has no power to digest living tissue. Every objection, therefore, breaks down; and the wonderful story, like all Biblical truth, stands the most rigid test of criticism. There is miracle. The hand of God is in it; but it is in timing the event. The Lord prepared the fish to receive Jonah, and again directed the fish to part with its precious freight.

XXXVII.

THE DEATH AND BURIAL OF MOSES.

"So Moses, the servant of the Lord, died there in the land of Moab, according to the word of the Lord. And he buried him in a valley in the land of Moab, over against Beth-peor; but no man knoweth of his sepulchre unto this day."—DEUT. xxxiv. 5, 6.

THIS is a subject of some difficulty to thoughtful students of Scripture. The commonly received opinion that Moses died a natural death, and received a literal burial, requires some modification in order to harmonize the several Biblical allusions to the death and the subsequent appearance of this distinguished servant of God. At the transfiguration of Christ Moses appeared in visible human form to the disciples. "There appeared unto them Elijah, with Moses; and they were talking with Jesus" (Mark ix. 4). "There appeared unto them Moses and Elijah, talking with Him" (Matt. xvii. 3). Moses, as well as Elijah, was visible to the disciples; and they saw and heard him talk with Jesus "of His decease which He should accomplish at Jerusalem" (Luke ix. 31). It is certain, therefore, that Moses did not come to earth as pure spirit. He was visible to the three disciples, and so manifestly human that Peter suggested to have a tent provided for him, as well as for Jesus and Elijah. Being "in the body" at this time, it necessarily follows that he did not die a natural death in such a sense that the body was separated from the spirit and received literal burial, in the modern sense of the word, by being deposited in the earth. There could have been no resurrection of the body of Moses prior to this event. Jesus was "the firstfruits of them that slept" (1 Cor. xv. 20); "the firstborn from the dead" (Col. i. 18); the first to rise of all who died a natural death by the complete separation of the body from the spirit. This view is incidentally confirmed by the Epistle of Jude, verse 9: "Michael, the archangel, when contending with the devil—he disputed about the body of Moses—durst not bring against him a railing accusation." There seems to be here a reference to the prevailing Jewish belief in ancient times that the devil had a claim for a time to the bodies of men, as a kind of right of conquest, seeing that by his subtlety and power he had been able to withdraw man from his allegiance to God. The expression, "disputing about the body of Moses," would seem to imply that the devil considered that he was wronged because the body of Moses had *not* come under the power of death and dissolution. It is not necessary to suppose that Jude adopts this fanciful theory; but it seems clear that, speaking by the inspiring Spirit, he believed the body of Moses did not come under the power of death.

The only consistent theory, therefore, is that Moses did not die a natural death; but, like Elijah, was caught up to heaven, his body being transformed at the time into a "spiritual body," similar to the resurrection-body of Jesus. There is a "spiritual body" distinct both from pure spirit and from the natural body. This spiritual body is a real material body, but so refined as to be under the perfect control of the spirit, and that can be borne away by the spirit at pleasure. In such a body Jesus ascended. In such a body Moses and Elijah appeared on the Mount of Transfiguration.

It still remains for us to reconcile this view with the record of the death of Moses in the last chapter of Deuteronomy. It is not necessary to hold, with some critics, that this chapter is not genuine, although manifestly it could not have been penned by Moses. No man can write the account of his own burial. The Hebrew words translated "died" and "buried" do not necessarily mean death and burial in the strictly literal modern sense. The Hebrew word *Muth* sometimes is used in the sense of "disappear," as in Job xii. 2; so that the removal of Moses from the earth fulfils the requirements of the original word. The expression " was buried"—Hebrew *Kābhar*—is satisfied by any proper disposal of the body, either in a grave, or in an open sepulchre, or in any other way, without reference to any particular mode of burial.

That the body of Moses did not undergo a natural dissolution receives further confirmation from the fact that at the moment of death it is said that "his eye was not dim, nor his natural force abated." There is, therefore, a clear and cumulative argument in favour of the translation of Moses.

One advantage of this view is that it not only harmonizes the various statements of Scripture to which we·have referred, but also softens down what otherwise would seem to be very harsh treatment of

Moses. That Moses should die with his foot upon the very borders of the promised land, and be buried in an alien country where no friendly hand could do honour to his bones, seems harsh and almost cruel, when his fidelity to God is remembered. But if we regard Moses as being translated to the Canaan above, of which the earthly Canaan was but the type, we see a tenderness of treatment worthy of our God.

That the symbolism of the Old Testament should be carried out, it was necessary that Moses should now disappear from the scene. As the representative of the Law he could lead the people out of Egyptian bondage and through the wilderness. But Joshua, who is Jesus, must lead the people into the beauty, and rest, and plenty of the promised land. The Law can bring men out of the bondage of sin; but the Gospel only can give permanent rest, and peace, and joy. Moses received more than he asked, if taken direct to heaven—not less, as would appear by making him die on Pisgah. By being permitted to appear with Elijah at the Transfiguration his prayer was literally answered. He now literally sets his foot upon "the good land that is beyond Jordan."

BY THE SAME AUTHOR.

Recently Published. Crown 8vo, 3s. 6d.

THE GOSPEL IN GREAT BRITAIN,

From St. Patrick to John Knox and John Wesley.

OPINIONS OF EMINENT THEOLOGIANS.

"'The Gospel in Great Britain' is an excellent production, and fitted to be at once popular and useful. The estimate it gives of the great standard-bearers referred to seems to be most just. And the whole work, which must have cost a great deal of labour, does the author very great credit."—*Principal Chalmers, D.D.*

"The theme is a noble one, and it puts the history of the time in a somewhat new light. The Gospel unites all the periods with an important and interesting thread of continuity. . . . The narrative is clear and luminous, nervous and instinct with energy. It carries convincing power with it. . . . The book must do a great deal of good."—*Rev. Prof. Lyall, LL.D.*

"Contending earnestly for the faith pervades every chapter."—*Rev. And. A. Bonar, D.D.*

"A valuable compendium, and admirably suited for circulation among those who have not time, or opportunity, or perhaps inclination, for much historical reading. I hope for it a great success."—*Rev. Donald Fraser, D.D., London.*

"The theme is interesting and timely. . . . The work will get, I am persuaded, a warm welcome from many readers."—*Rev. John Edmond, D.D., London.*

"The idea of the book is a very excellent, and, so far as I know, a fresh one; it has been carried out in a way that makes it deeply interesting. It is fitted to be useful to all classes of readers, and is especially fitted for the family and the minister's class. I hope it will find extensive circulation."—*Rev. Prof. John Ker, D.D., Edinburgh.*

"I have read 'The Gospel in Great Britain' with very deep interest. It is a capital book—thoroughly Protestant, thoroughly Evangelical—and has a pith and point, a freshness and freedom, that are sure to make it both popular and useful in our times."—*Rev. Wm. McCaw, D.D.*

OPINIONS OF THE PRESS.

"This is a really valuable contribution to religious literature. Though delivered as separate lectures, there is a logical connection between them which gives unity to the whole. The style is popular, yet the lectures give enough details for all practical purposes. The author disclaims any attempt at beauty of style, and yet we think his simplicity is in itself beautiful."—*Christian Commonwealth.*

"Admirable lectures, terse and telling. Rich in history, and as rich in instruction and warning. We very heartily commend the book."—*Evangelical Magazine.*

"'The Gospel in Great Britain' is a brief and most interesting record of the Church History of England and Scotland for the long period described. It shows clearly that England did not receive her Christian light through Rome, but that the direct mission from Rome tended to obscure the light she had obtained previously. There is an interesting sketch of the early period, with its pure Christianity, extending in Scotland up to the thirteenth and fourteenth centuries; then of the Reformation in both countries, and finally of the last revival of Evangelical life. The history of the English Reformation is well and truthfully told. We warmly commend the book. It is written in a clear and attractive method, with marvellous power of condensation, while still preserving the interest of details. It is also important as a safeguard against the misrepresentations of Romish and Ritualistic writers."—*Christian Church.*

"It was a happy thought on the part of Mr. MacNaughton to give a series of lectures on the progress of Evangelical thought and life in England. We would heartily commend this method of illustrating historically great Biblical texts and themes, and would ask our clerical readers to procure and study this volume for the purpose of imitation. Mr. MacNaughton's work is well done, and no Methodist could have better traced the plan of our Church in the Evangelical succession. We personally thank the author both for his book as a whole, and for his genuine and cordial appreciation of Methodist work."—*Methodist Recorder.*

"The author of this volume is the Minister of the Presbyterian Church of England, Preston, and is already favourably known in the world of letters. In these pages he presents us with a most useful outline of the Church history of this country, which we strongly recommend to all who have not access to larger works, or who cannot spare the time to study them. Mr. MacNaughton has evidently made every effort to have his facts accurate; and, although he does not pretend to be a professor of Church History, or assume the position of a judge from whose decision there must be no dissent, he has given us some graphic and picturesque sketches of Christianity in Great Britain from the days of St. Patrick in Ireland to those of John Knox in Scotland and John Wesley in England. His book might with great propriety be introduced into ministers' Bible classes, teachers' training classes, and the like; while even students of theology might find a bird's-eye view of historical points which might prove of real advantage. One thing is very evident—namely, that the author understands his subject, and has not only read largely, but is able to communicate his stores of information to others in a practical and handy form. This volume will certainly add to Mr. MacNaughton's reputation."—*Liverpool Mercury.*

"This is a good popular account of the rise and progress of Christianity in our land. The introduction and early triumphs of our religion are briefly recorded, but the more detailed narrative may be said to commence with the age of Wycliffe. A true Protestant fervour characterises the volume; which is, moreover, written in so lucid a form as to make it an attractive history, such as young people would read with pleasure as well as profit."—*Baptist.*

"One of the most readable and instructive books which the Quincentenary of our first great Reformer has called forth. . . . It is just the kind of book we would like to see in every Sunday School and Church library, and within reach of young men and women who have been troubled by Anti-Protestant notions about Apostolical Succession." —*Leeds Mercury.*

"The fruit of much serious independent thought by a Christian lawyer."—*The Christian Leader.*

"This interesting and able volume covers the period from St. Patrick to John Knox and John Wesley, and deals with the most important and interesting events in the ecclesiastical history of the country. The author writes in a broad and Catholic spirit, and has the ability which enables him to set the facts before his readers in an attractive manner. . . . On the whole it is a volume of more than ordinary value in these times. It is full of instructive information and well-narrated facts. The author's style is perspicuous, and his arrangement lucid. It should be placed in Church libraries, and have a place on the shelf of the Christian family. It has our warmest commendation as a book fitted to do good and to give pleasure."—*The Christian News.*

"A very readable book on a vast theme, and one of immense importance. The author, in working out his design, had to deal with the men and the incidents connected with the gospel in this country for more than fifteen centuries. How he has managed to perform his self-allotted task within moderate compass is to us a marvel. In one post octavo volume of 308 pages he has managed to pack stores of information which might, without any inordinate verbosity, have been made to occupy double the space. Mr. MacNaughton is a writer of experience; and by long practice, we fancy, he has acquired the rare art of being able to say, and to say well, in a few comprehensive sentences what less laconic authors would spread over a big page or more. ... Mr. MacNaughton has made his book all the more honest-looking, earnest, and emphatic, by allowing his own individuality to be impressed upon its pages. He had two special objects in view. He wished to show that Britain was not indebted for the Gospel to the Church of Rome, but that long before its missionaries reached our country a pure Evangel was preached to, and embraced by, its people. He also sought, by sketches of the civil history of the nation, to illustrate the varying phases and features of its spiritual life. Both objects, and others scarcely less important, have been fully realized. The sketches of themselves, apart from their special purpose, are extremely graphic, and add much to the value of the volume."— *Dumfries Standard.*

"Here we have twenty-four lectures on the History of Christianity in Great Britain from St. Patrick's day down to the time of the great Methodist revival. Mr. MacNaughton's style is clear, fluent, and picturesque. For his facts he has drawn upon the best authorities. His purpose is admirable; his plan is good; and the manner in which he carries out his plan is highly creditable to his industry and skill. He renders good service in popularizing the results of the most recent historical investigations. We recommend this volume as a comprehensive survey of British Christianity from the standpoint of an Evangelical Presbyterian."—*Presbyterian Witness.*

"If consultation with plentiful authorities of the highest rank and with critics of admitted power could afford an absolute guarantee of the reliability of the historical facts adduced, the readers of Mr. MacNaughton's new volume should be able to receive with perfect trust all the data and incidents he chronicles for the purpose of his argument; for it is evident that he has omitted no means of qualifying himself for his task by research among Protestant sources of information. . . . Whatever differences of faith may separate us, we can all alike follow Mr. MacNaughton with pleasure and with pride, while he shows that the principles which lie at the root of Protestantism to-day were taught by St. Patrick in Ireland, and by St. Columba in Scotland, centuries before a Papal missionary had ever set foot in England; and that all down the ages the pure light of the Evangelical gospel was preached and practised in these realms alongside of Roman corruption, and often in defiance of it. . . . The author has such a happy knack of saying what he wants to say without the use of confusing verbiage, that the reader puts down the book after reading any one chapter with a peculiar sense of knowledge acquired and firmly fixed in the mind. The story of Wycliffe and the Lollards, and Tyndale and his contemporaries, of the Marian Martyrs, the Puritans, the Independent Supremacy, and the Wesleyan Revival, are sketched one and all with a strong, clear hand. . . . The matter is full and well-digested; the heroes of the piece are sketched with a loving and powerful hand; the criticisms are manly and fair; and the interest of the story is fully sustained from St. Patrick to John Wesley."— *Preston Herald.*

"The author traces the history of Evangelical truth as to its introduction and development in our own land and the sister isle. Beginning with the work of Succat, known as St. Patrick, he continues his researches through the centuries up to the time of Wesley and Whitfield, and proves the fallacy of the popular belief that England owes its possession of Christianity to Roman Catholic zeal. Soundly Protestant in its bias, the book all through holds up the fundamental doctrines of the Gospel, and the pre-eminent value of spiritual truth as opposed to all mere clericalism and ceremonial observance. It is a most useful and reliable compendium of valuable information, such as most people are but too little acquainted with."—*Christian.*

" An interesting book. . . . The author has done good service by showing that this country was not indebted to the Church of Rome for the Gospel, but that a pure Evangel was preached long before the arrival of the first Roman Catholic missionaries. He traces the Evangelical succession, outside of Rome, and opposed to it, all adown the centuries, and notes, with some degree of fulness, the prominent Evangelical agencies, ending with the rise of Methodism. A great deal of valuable information is condensed in these lectures."—*Christian Age.*

" A book full of information."—*Christian World.*

. . . " No small pains have been taken to lucidly set forth the author's exposition of the several dealings of Henry VIII. and Wolsey with the Vatican. . . . The conversion of Latimer is cleverly treated, and with great perspicuity. . . . The summaries of arguments are particularly good. . . . The lectures embrace some fine passages, and the author has been prudent in always using quotations aptly."—*Preston Guardian.*

" An admirably succinct account of the early phases of Christianity in this country. The author is fair on controversial matters, and, so far as we have observed, he is accurate as regards facts."—*Literary World.*

" This is a book which deserves a cordial welcome at the hands of Protestant readers."—*Northern Whig.*

" The author rightly holds to the belief in an Evangelical succession outside of Rome, and opposed to it all down the ages ; and notes, with some degree of fulness, the prominent Evangelical agencies that brought blessings to the nation at different times. The Civil history of the people is also given, so far as it illustrates the history of the Gospel. The volume is highly interesting, and will prove helpful to anyone who wishes to engage in like work with evening classes."—*Freeman.*

" Mr. MacNaughton writes in a clear strong style. . . . He has succeeded well in a very difficult task, and has packed into his book a broad mass of information, which, we hope, will be widely diffused."—*Presbyterian Messenger.*

Post free from the Author,

ROSE BANK, ADDISON ROAD, PRESTON.

By the same Author. Tenth Thousand. With Portrait. Bevelled Boards, 1s. 6d.; Morocco Gilt, 4s. 6d.

JOY IN JESUS:

Memorials of Bella Darling.

OPINIONS OF THE PRESS.

"This is an admirable memoir of a very admirable young Christian. Bella Darling, comely of countenance—as shown by the life-like photograph prefixed to the memoir—was beautified by grace. She was known to many, and was warmly loved by all who knew her, because of her gentle, winning words and ways, and because of her unwearied kindly deeds. We are sure the volume will be gladly welcomed by the many who were co-workers with her in labours of love; and we hope it will have a very wide circulation, to the profiting of multitudes."
Times of Blessing.

"A touching record of a beautiful life, which, though brief in years, was singularly full of blessed deeds. Joy in the Lord and thorough consecration to His service were the distinguishing characteristics of the subject of this memoir. The study of her radiant and useful life is admirably fitted to commend religion to our youth, and to induce them to begin and pursue the same Christian course."—*League Journal.*

"To all, and especially young people, it is fitted to be greatly blessed. Both old and young may learn what it is to be a happy because a useful Christian. . . . No fictions, not even the best and purest, approach such true pictures as these of what the highest of all motives does in bringing about the highest of all lives."—*Daily Review.*

"It was our privilege to know the sunny character who forms the subject of these brief memorials. We are sure they will be cherished by many who remember the devotion and enthusiasm of a fellow-worker whose young life was literally a living sacrifice to Christ."—*The Christian.*

"This interesting biography of a charming young lady has lately been published with a beautiful photograph of her, and is an admirable book to give to any young ladies to lead them to Christ."—*The Christian Herald.*

"These brief memorials bring before the reader one who was naturally lovely, and who, early coming under the influence of Divine grace, richly displayed the beauty of holiness. . . . As a sweet singer and earnest Christian worker, she won all hearts by the amiability of her character, the ardour of her zeal, and the elevation of her piety. The book will be read with much interest by those who were associated with her in Christian work, and is well fitted at once to stimulate and guide young disciples to works of faith and labours of love."—*United Presbyterian Magazine.*

By the same Author, 100 *pp.*, *cloth*, 9d. *Second Edition.*

OUR CHILDREN FOR CHRIST:

A Plea for Infant Church Membership: with a full Discussion on the Mode of Baptism.

OPINIONS OF THE PRESS.

" Free from all controversial bitterness."—*Edinburgh Daily Review.*

" This neat little book of 100 pages consists of two parts. In the first are presented, in succinct form, the usual arguments for Infant Church Membership, while the second part discusses briefly, but most satisfactorily, the question of the Mode of Baptism. The author evidently takes a deep interest in his subject, his views are thoroughly Scriptural, and he writes in a simple, lively, unctional style, so that all may understand and be edified. . . . To all who may desire a small but comprehensive and easily-understood book on this interesting subject, we can sincerely recommend this one."—*Original Secession Magazine.*

OPINIONS OF EMINENT THEOLOGIANS.

" I thank you very heartily for your little book—' Our Children for Christ.' It possesses what many of the best similar treatises lack generally—viz., brevity and simplicity. It is most conclusive and forcible, both in argument and scholarship. I have often desired such a brief treatise for circulation, and I am glad that you have given it."— *Rev. Horatius Bonar, D.D., Edinburgh.*

" Your book on Baptism is an excellent manual, which might be circulated with advantage to our principles in many parts of Nova Scotia."—*Rev. P. G. Macgregor, D.D., Halifax, N.S.*

" I am much pleased with your work on Baptism. You place the right of infants to this ordinance on a sure and enduring basis, which cannot be overthrown. On the Mode of Baptism, or rather on the meaning of the word *Baptizo*, you have done good service. Please accept of my thanks for your work."—*Rev. Isaac Murray, D.D., P. E. Island, Canada.*

. . . " Our youthful author had previously given evidence of his literary tastes and talents in an eloquently-written Prize Essay on ' The Duty of the Christian Church in Relation to the Temperance Reform,' and we can honestly say that he fully sustains his reputation—we should rather say, adds new lustre to it—by this recent production. He has evidently studied the subject very extensively and candidly. . . . As a needful contribution to our native literature, and on the ground of its own intrinsic excellence, we cordially bespeak for this instructive little volume extensive circulation and careful perusal."—*Extracts from Review in the " Eastern Chronicle."—Rev. Thomas Cumming, Stellarton, Nova Scotia.*

By the same Author. Revised edition. Fourth Thousand. Price 9d. Sewed, 4d. Reduced rates for circulation. To be had from the author.

THE WINES OF SCRIPTURE;

Or, 𝔗otal 𝔄bstinence the 𝔗rue 𝔗emperance.

OPINIONS OF THEOLOGIANS AND THE PRESS.

" I have read your admirable pages on the WINE question with great delight. Most heartily I give your pamphlet my strongest recommendation."—*Rev. Professor Kirk, D.D., Edinburgh.*

"Many thanks for an early copy of your 'Wines of Scripture.' I have read it with care, and think that it is vigorous, fresh, and lucid, and demonstrates the position taken by the Temperance party. It has my cordial commendation."—*Rev. William Adamson, D.D., Edinburgh.*

" Your 'Wines of Scripture' will do good service. I think it is immensely nearer to the truth than the Belfast Professor and his host have attained. . . . You have fought the battle well."—*Rev. P. G. Macgregor, D.D., Canada.*

"A singularly clear, terse, telling little treatise."—*The Outlook.*

"This is a capital contribution to the literature on the Wine question."—*The Social Reformer.*

" The two kinds of wine mentioned in Scripture are learnedly commented on. . . . *Tirosh,* which is shown to be unintoxicating, means 'Wine in the Cluster,' or 'Wine in the Vat' (grapes, or grape-juice). Mr. M'Naughton's little treatise will be very useful to Temperance Reformers."—*The People's Journal.*

" It discusses, in a somewhat elaborate and scholarly style, the vexed question of 'The Wines of Scripture,' and seems to us, by abundant proof, to make good the position that these wines are clearly distinguishable into two grand classes, namely, fermented and unfermented—*intoxicating* wines or other drinks being always spoken of with warning and woe, while wine, when spoken of with approval, is invariably *unfermented* and *unintoxicating.* We cordially commend a careful perusal of this pamphlet."—*Brechin Advertiser.*

" We have read this pamphlet with much interest and not a little profit. . . . Nowhere have we met with what is called the Wine question presented in smaller compass, or in clearer language. The author is peculiarly effective in his dealing with Dr. Watts."—*League Journal.*

" We know of no work which is more satisfactory as a brief, easily understood, and popular exposition of the Wine question. We trust it will have a large circulation."—*The Christian News.*

www.ingramcontent.com/pod-product-compliance
Lightning Source LLC
Chambersburg PA
CBHW030427300426
44112CB00009B/887